Vibrattuning

Kiki Quest

VIBRATTUNING

12 Step-by-Step Protocols
Using Weighted Tuning Forks
On the Body
for SuperCharged Wellness

Boost Your Body's Voltage

&

Raise Your Everyday Resilience

©2018 Kiki Quest.

All rights reserved.

ISBN: 978-179-299-0489

vibrattuning.com

This book is dedicated to Joe.

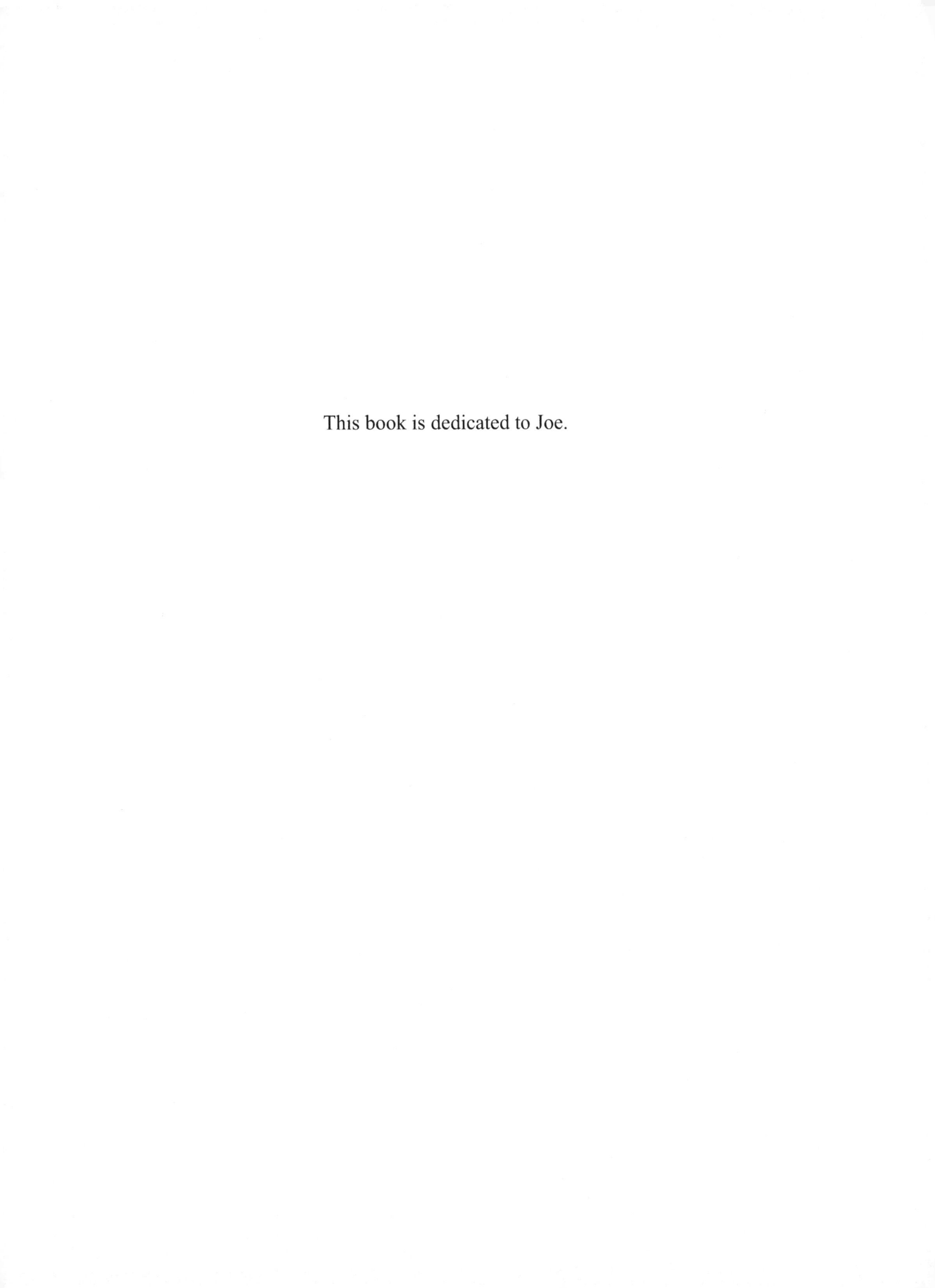

CONTENTS

Introduction	ix
What is Vibrattuning?	1
Vibrattuning Enhances	2
Benefits	3
Nitric Oxide Production	4
Contraindications	5
What is Vibration?	6
What is Sound?	6
Resonance and Entrainment	7
Beat Frequency and Binaural Beat	7
Your Electric Body	8
The Vagus Nerve	10
The Crystalline Structure of the Body and Fascia	11
Stress	13
Hypothalmic-Pituitary-Adrenal Axis	14
Inflammation	15
The Healer and Healing	16
Intention	17
Preparing for a Session	18
The Treatment Room	19
Body Mechanics and Movement	19
Anatomy of a Tuning Fork	21
Tools	22
How to Hold a Weighted Tuning Fork	23
How to Activate a Weighted Tuning Fork	23
How to Perceive with a Weighted Tuning Fork	24
Application of the Weighted Tuning Fork	24
Pace, Rhythm and Pressure	25

Care of Weighted Tuning Forks	27
Storage of Weighted Tuning Forks	27
Practitioner Self-Care	28
After-Care Reminders	29
Method	31
The 12 Introductory Protocols	33
Protocol 1: Head and Face (supine)	34
Protocol 2: Head/Neck (prone)	55
Protocol 3: Neck (supine)	66
Protocol 4: Neck (prone)	77
Protocol 5: Shoulders/Chest (supine)	87
Protocol 6: Shoulders (prone)	95
Protocol 7: Shoulders/Arms/Wrists/Hands (supine)	108
Protocol 8: Spinal Toning (prone)	122
Protocol 9: Hips/Legs (supine)	130
Protocol 10: Hips/Legs (prone)	139
Protocol 11: Diaphragm/Abdominals (supine)	152
Protocol 12: Head/Neck/Shoulders/Back (seated, no pictures)	158
Further Study	159
Reference List	160
About the Author	162

Introduction

Thank you for choosing this book, picking up some tuning forks and delving into exploring the therapeutic effects of vibration and sound on yourself and others. Quite possibly you, like many of us, are experiencing a remembering of, and re-awakening to, various remedial sound applications.

This first Vibrattuning guide introduces participants to twelve suggested on-the-body protocols, beginning with fundamental skills that can lead to advanced and intermediate levels of proficiency. Practicing these sessions will help you to develop a feel for the sense of flow and timing integral to using weighted tuning forks on the body.

When in a state of physical, emotional, mental or spiritual stress, both our voltage and our resilience are lowered. It's all about how we bounce back and if we don't have enough energy to rebound on any level we are somehow compromised. It's been well-documented that stress is the number one killer, precipitating inflammation which can become chronic and lead to a weakened immune system and impaired health. To address this, Vibrattuning uses weighted tuning forks directly on the body to de-stress the nervous system, boost the body's voltage and raise its resilience. In this recharged state, our bodies can optimally unwind, repair and restore.

And just as we all have specific physical, emotional, spiritual, environmental, occupational, and intellectual needs, we also sometimes require particular vibrational nourishment. There are plenty of frequencies that we have found to resonate well with everyone we've used them with, for example, the 128Hz and the 136.1Hz weighted tuning forks, which we employ often. Though, in Vibrattuning, we don't assume that one frequency, or combination of frequencies, is necessarily a "one size fits all." What resonates with, and soothes, one person may have the opposite effect on another. If something doesn't feel correct to you, then it's most likely not.

Unfortunately, we seem to be losing that discernment as we disconnect from our bodies by adopting a "no pain, no gain" programming where limited mobility and pain are no longer signals that something is askew—they are now an expected, and accepted, part of modern living. Constantly bombarded with blatant, shaming messages that we are not enough as we currently are and must be "fixed," we spend time and money buying useless potions, lotions, notions and tools of all sorts, lining the pockets of exploitative charlatans who convince us that we are not rich enough, skinny enough or young enough. Deep down, we all really know that there is no one "formula" or program that will bring us unlimited happiness, abundant income, radiant health or spiritual fulfillment.

In *Small is Beautiful: Economics as if People Mattered* (2010), economist E.F. Schumacher warns us of some of the "filters of materialism," scarcity, fear, greed, rage, and revenge; all the enemies of wholeness and the antithesis of connection. We could easily add competition to that list. This monster gets busy as soon as we squint open our eyes each morning.

Reaching for our cell phones, we begin voraciously scrolling through social media, comparing and contrasting our sleepy, limited lives to the self-styled illusions of what a perfect woman, mother, athlete, model, singer or (fill-in-the-blank) looks and acts like. She always seems to be throwing her head back, mouth parted just enough so you know that she is in the middle of a deeply ecstatic, though candidly private, moment--at a beach house that you couldn't even afford to rent for the weekend. Talk about starting the day off with a megadose of self-loathing and isolation, knowing full well that you and your world will never look anything like their deluded ones on social media. May I suggest replacing the morning cell phone ritual with a simple meditation? Or, if you don't have time for that, you could always try tilting your head to one side and laughing out loud as you bounce out of bed each morning.

Soul searching since the early 1980s, seeking to be free from generations-old, painfully abusive, destructive speech, behaviors and patterns--I delivered obscene amounts of money to countless facilitators, shamans, teachers, healers, guides, gurus, coaches and technicians in the self-help, bodywork and subtle energy arenas to meet, observe and study with them. Some waved their hands and arms wildly over the demo body with a smug, superior air and nebulous results. Others have humbly walked the talk and shown me that when I listen and respond with my heart and gut, my mind is at rest and I am who I am. So far, the most enlightening teachers to me have been animals, showing me again and again that when I am present and aware, that is where the magic happens.

Though not a scientist in this lifetime, I am a careful, curious, perceptive, and experimental teacher, artist, writer and bodyworker with over three decades of clinical practice, and multiple thousands of hours sharing, discovering and learning with clients, students, friends, family and colleagues. This work is based on my own, and my clients', observations and results, and I do not make any claims to cure or heal any body of any thing. This is a book more about connection and flow than theory. It is a starting point, a guide (neither encyclopedic nor advanced), meant to allow you to start applying Vibrattuning right away into your own life and practice. To fully address the many topics mentioned in this book would take volumes as this work opens up so many avenues of discussion.

Finally, although Vibrattuning is geared towards professionals such as massage therapists, bodyworkers, hands-on therapists, estheticians, etc., it's also very suitable for anybody interested in using tuning forks as self-care or on friends and family. No experience with bodywork or energy work is necessary to begin learning Vibrattuning, just a willingness to be present with another human being and a desire to be of service. Flexibility and creativity are paramount as well; as mentioned, what works for one, may not work for another. Our approach is to create a collaborative, non-judgmental space allowing participants to step into their own style of working using weighted tuning forks on the body. Journaling can also be helpful to observe your development and to jot down and expand on any questions or discoveries that emerge.

Profuse gratitude for all who have contributed to this project and fueled me along the way, particularly, Babatunde Olatunji and Florence + the Machine. Thank you to Andrea, Daniel, and especially Nicole, for all the assistance with the photos.

Disclaimer:

When using Vibrattuning the practitioner is not diagnosing or treating the physical body which is the domain of the medical field and other allied health care professionals. Instead it is inviting a shift in the body from stress to ease allowing the possibility for change or transformation which can be experienced by the client. As such, it is understood that there is a distinction between "shifting" using Vibrattuning and "healing" via the practice of medicine or any other licensed health care practice.

While Kiki Quest has extensive experience as a Licensed Massage Therapist and knowledge of many therapeutic modalities, she is not a psychologist, psychotherapist, physician, or other licensed health care professional.

What is Vibrattuning?

Coherence, as illustrated by Itzhak Bentov in *Stalking the Wild Pendulum* (1977), is like a well-ordered marching band: in-step, in-phase and in-tune. If one member of the band trips or somehow throws off the rhythm, it creates a ripple effect, and disruption, disorder and chaos ensue. Incoherence, within and around the body, creates stress which can lead to lowered energy levels in the body, low-grade, chronic inflammation and slower healing.

Vibrattuning is a non-diagnostic, resonant, energy-based, therapeutic bodywork method that uses weighted tuning forks directly on the body to de-stress the nervous system, boost the body's voltage and raise its resilience. Vibration from the tuning forks penetrates the fascia, bones, joints, musculature, nervous system and organs, allowing them to recharge and regenerate. In this optimized state, our bodies can unwind, repair and restore. And by using waveforms as therapeutic agents to tune the flow of information between and among different energy fields, communication within and around the body improves. Lynne McTaggart writes that "one of the most important aspects of waves is that they are encoders and carriers of information...and have a virtually infinite capacity for storage" *The Field: The Quest for the Secret Force of the Universe* (2008). Pain reduction, higher energy, headache relief, increased immune response and greater blood flow to the brain and muscles are a few benefits that can occur, shifting the body from a state of stress to one of ease.

In today's world, it seems as though the body is continuously affected by trauma and stress, while rarely getting the opportunity to relax, recharge, repair and replenish. And though every creature is a powerful, self-healing organism, sometimes we need some assistance moving towards the next level of well-being. The techniques and protocols set out in this book invite connection and communication, with ourselves and each other.

As more and more studies are being conducted showing that the repair and regeneration of cells and tissues, via the energy of particular frequencies and applications, is possible--the excitement is real. I invite any body-minded professional (or any body, in general), who is curious about integrating weighted tuning forks into an already-established practice, supercharging wellness and self-care targets or simply upgrading your toolkit, to practice the suggested step-by-step protocols. Join us in person for a 2-day, hands-on-intensive class if you'd like to go deeper and learn more. Please visit vibrattuning.com for more information.

Vibrattuning Enhances and Combines Well with:

- Massage Therapy
- Shiatsu
- Esthetics and skin care
- Cranial Sacral
- Structural Integration
- Polarity Therapy
- Reiki
- Chiropractic
- Physical Therapy
- Sports Therapy
- Myofascial Release
- Trigger Point Therapy
- Emotional Freedom Technique
- Any soft tissue or energy work
- Self-care

Benefits can include:

- Releasing stress
- Boosting your body's voltage or energy
- Raising your everyday resilience
- Reducing inflammation
- Relieving headaches
- Improving sleep
- Easing pain
- Relaxing overworked muscles
- Increasing blood and lymph flow
- Releasing anxiety
- Clearing emotional debris
- Shifting patterns that impede growth
- Contributing to a lighter, brighter sense of being
- Releasing drama/trauma
- Stimulating the body's healing process
- Activating rest-and-digest (parasympathetic nervous system) mode
- Allowing for more awareness of your body
- Creating more freedom of movement as the body physically adjusts
- Making space for new thoughts or attitudes
- Assisting in releasing habits and patterns that are no longer of service to us
- Increasing Nitric Oxide production (see Nitric Oxide Production below)

Nitric Oxide Production

Comprised of one nitrogen and one oxygen atom, nitric oxide (NO), a soluble gas produced where and when it is needed in the body, then "puffed" into the surrounding tissues, is a much-researched health topic lately. Mostly recognized as a vasodilator, it's also a free-radical. Dr. Jerry Tennant considers it to be the "master hormone" of the body as it controls many body functions, the most-mentioned being circulation--getting oxygen and nutrients to our cells. Our ability to make NO does fall off with age and pharmaceuticals, aspirin, naproxen, ibuprofen and antiseptic mouthwash all inhibit the production of it. *Healing is Voltage* (2014)

When weighted tuning forks are activated and placed on the body, NO is released and a deep feeling of well-being takes place. John Beaulieu has shown through his research that the 128Hz, 136.1Hz, the C256Hz and the G384Hz tuning forks "have the ability to release nitric oxide well above baseline pulsatile levels." *Human Tuning* (2010). These peaks in NO when applying the above mentioned tuning forks can lead to deep relaxation and myriad benefits as well. Some more benefits of Nitric Oxide can include:

- Helping regulate heartbeat
- Enhancing cell vitality (protects cell's mitochondria)
- Reducing inflammation
- Reducing depression
- Improving digestion
- Providing pain relief
- Enhancing the immune system
- Sharpening mental clarity and assisting memory

Contraindications

- Pacemakers or other implanted electronic devices, such as defibrillators, vagus nerve stimulators or insulin pumps: Avoid working on the client as we don't want to disturb devices.

- Pregnancy: If mother is experiencing a healthy pregnancy, then it's ok to proceed gently and carefully, avoiding the abdominal area. If you have any questions, concerns or gut feelings about whether or not to do the session, please err on the side of caution.

- Cancer or any advanced disease (body systems are most likely compromised and can't manage the energy shifts and possible detox). That said, if the client is in remission post-3 months, it's ok to tune the body. Go easy on the whole body, particularly the liver and kidneys, if the client had received a lot of chemotherapy, radiation and medications during the last 6-12 months.

- Recent concussions: Wait at least 6 months before doing any head or face work.

- Recently broken bones: Avoid for 6 months.

- Fractured bones: Avoid.

- Open wounds, cuts, burns and rashes: Avoid working directly on these areas. It's ok to work around them.

- Recent scars: Avoid for at least 2 months.

- Varicose veins: Avoid working directly on and around them.

- Non-malignant tumors or other growths: Avoid working directly on them.

Please remember that Vibrattuning is not intended to replace the advice, diagnosis, and/or treatment of any disease or condition. Please consult your primary care physician before receiving Vibrattuning.

What is Vibration?

Vibration is movement, first one way and then back again in the opposite direction, faster or slower. Everything in existence is vibrating, even if it looks completely still, because even on a sub-atomic level there are still moving particles. And since everything is vibration, everything we sense and perceive is in some state of movement; atoms, cells, tissues, organs, bones and muscles are all constantly vibrating. These vibrations produce sound and light, whether perceptible by us or not. Sensed by nerves in the skin, vibration can be felt viscerally and on a cellular level. It also travels well along bones; when a tuning fork end glides down a shin bone it feels surprisingly exquisite. Physical destruction (dynamiting through mountains of rock to create roads) or other fantastic shape changes can occur through vibration too. For astonishing examples of how matter responds to vibration, just look at the work of Hans Jenny and Cymatics. Jenny was a Swiss physician and natural scientist who, along with many other cultures on record, considered sound to be the creative principle. Bringing that concept to fruition, he subjected various substances to different frequencies and observed the resulting shapes: visual geometry brought to life.

According to Bruce Lipton, our bones, muscles, fluids and all the cells in our body read, and respond to, vibration via antenna-like structures on cell membranes. He writes that "these receptor antennas stimulate cellular responses by certain vibrational frequencies." *The Biology of Belief: Unleashing the Power of Consciousness, Matter & Miracles* (2015).

What is Sound? (Super Short and Simple Version)

All sound is a form of energy caused by vibration that travels through air, water, bone, muscle, or other media as sound waves radiating out from their source. Naturally, both we and the world around us are affected as these waves move atoms, molecules and particles. Made up of about 70ish percent water, the human body is an excellent conductor of sound and electricity. And while we are only sometimes aware of sound through hearing, our bodies are continuously responding to an orchestra, created by every vibrating thing everywhere.

Sound waves are measured in cycles per second (cps). Frequency or pitch, is the number of vibrations or cps, measured in hertz (Hz). For example, 64Hz = 64cps. Slow waves create deep, bass sounds while fast waves create high, treble sounds.

Humans can only hear a small portion of the full sound spectrum, about 20Hz-20,000Hz, the highest range usually decreasing with age. Bats and dolphins use ultrasound, higher than humans can hear, to locate their prey while elephants and giraffes can communicate via infrasound, lower than we can hear. And the sonogram produced by bouncing infrasound waves off a developing fetus creates baby's first image.

Resonance and Entrainment

1. The Natural Resonance Frequency: The fundamental vibratory rate, along with the natural rhythms, patterns and tones of any object, bone, muscle, nervous system, tissue, organ, etc. Our personal vibratory rate is our sonic signature. And whether or not an object is within our audible range, if it is vibrating, it's putting out sound.

2. Sympathetic resonance: Occurs when harmonically related frequencies resonate with each other.

3. Entrainment: Occurs when one vibrating source changes the vibration of another object. A lock in resonance or phase lock occurs as one object becomes in synch with another.

By using weighted tuning forks on the body, resonance and entrainment create a rhythmic communication within and around the body. The steady, coherent input of vibration from the tuning forks allows the body to "auto-tune" and move into more harmonious states.

Beat Frequency and Binaural Beat

If two tuning forks of different frequencies are held on either side of the ears (binaural), a third tone is actually created by the brain. For example, hold a 136.1Hz and 128Hz fork on either side of the head and the brain perceives a third frequency, 8.1Hz (136.1-128 = 8.1). This 7-8Hz range brings the brain to a very relaxing alpha-theta cusp. A beat frequency also provides a way to deliver very low frequencies to the body as the two forks can also be placed on the body next to each other to create a pulse.

Your Electric Body

We now know that electricity is vital to life; not only do our bodies run on it, it's believed that we live in an electric universe. Electromagnetic light beings, we are a vibrational matrix of many different oscillating fields describing what ancient ayurvedics called an aura (containing the Akashic record—the complete past, present and future inventory of all human thoughts, experiences, emotions, memories and intent). Shaman Alberto Villoldo refers to it as the Luminous Energy Field--a holographic, doughnut-shaped energy flow from the base of our spine and out the top of the head that "stretches to infinity and...contains stars and galaxies within it." *One Spirit Medicine* (2015).

For a fascinating and informative examination of our bioelectric selves, *The Body Electric: Electromagnetism and the Foundation of Life* (1985) by Robert O. Becker is essential reading.

In *The Electric Universe* (2007), Wallace Thornhill and David Talbott offer the cosmology-shifting concept that electricity plays a very significant part in the universe, going against what modern science has determined.

Voltage

The voltage that runs through our bodies and powers us is also referred to as prana, energy, chi or life force. We are powered by the Earth and the Sun and electricity is also created in our bodies. Electrons are created when we move our muscles (see Piezoelectricity below), every time the craniosacral pump activates, and from the scalar energy in DNA. *Healing is Voltage (2014)*

Piezoelectricity

Piezoelectricity is "the electric charge that accumulates in certain solid materials (such as crystals, certain ceramics, and biological matter such as bone, DNA and various proteins) in response to applied mechanical stress. The word *piezoelectricity* means electricity resulting from pressure, derived from the Greek *piezein*, which means to squeeze or press, and *elektron*, which means amber, an ancient source of electric charge. French physicists Jacques and Pierre Curie discovered piezoelectricity in 1880." Interestingly, the piezoelectric effect is also a reversible process, as "materials exhibiting the piezoelectric effect also exhibit the reverse piezoelectric effect, the internal generation of a mechanical strain resulting from an applied electrical field. Piezoelectricity "finds everyday uses such as acting as the ignition source for cigarette lighters and push-start propane barbeques, as well as being used as the time reference source in quartz watches." *Wikipedia: Piezoelectricity*

The Brain

It's well known that the brain is an electrochemical organ and the electroencephalogram (EEG) measures the electrical activity of it. The resulting waveforms are subdivided into bandwidths with an unfixed, corresponding range of frequencies.

Four commonly measured brainwaves are:

- Delta .5Hz-4Hz: Deep sleep, dreaming
- Theta 4Hz-7Hz: Inward focus, transitions, drowsy, free-flowing, uncensored ideas
- Alpha 7Hz-13Hz: Dreaming and light meditation
- Beta 14Hz-30Hz: Alert, working, engaged. Possible anxiety at higher end

We can beneficially alter brainwave patterns using vibration. An example being the binaural beat produced by the brain when two tuning forks of differing frequencies are held on either side of the ears. A few of the effects we have experienced with this simple technique include relaxation, relief of anxiety and depression, headache relief, greater clarity and more focus.

To balance the left and right brain hemispheres--use two forks, one on either side of the:

1. Unicorn point (midline of front hairline) and just below occiput at the back of head.

2. Third eye and directly behind it at the back of head.

3. Sides of head (just above and in front of the ear).

4. Top of head and perineum (or not).

Repeat the above three or four times each or just choose one or two that feel correct and spend 3-7 minutes self-administering.

The Muscles

Movement is necessary to generate electrons which then recharge our muscles. They are rechargeable battery packs, stacked like batteries in a flashlight, creating a power pack for each organ of the body. The surrounding fascia is the body's semiconductor wiring system, transporting the voltage. *Healing is Voltage* (2014)

The Heart

The human heart generates a stronger voltage and electromagnetic field than the human body itself and the electrical activity from it can be measured by an electrocardiogram (EKG), providing a graphic representation of it in the form of waves; the higher the wave, the higher the voltage. The HeartMath Institute has popularized Heart Rate Variability (HRV) monitors which measure subtle changes in the heart rhythms, or the variable intervals between heartbeats. The more variability, the more adaptable and resilient we are. heartmath.org

Cardiologist Thomas Cowan reports that "90% of people who have a heart attack, have a decreased parasympathetic nervous system tone, followed by sympathetic nervous system activation. This is caused by a number of things, including chronic stress, poor sleep, high blood pressure, diabetes, a high-sugar, low-fat type of diet and smoking." *Human Heart, Cosmic Heart: A Doctor's Quest to Understand, Treat, and Prevent Cardiovascular Disease* (2016). Stimulating and raising the vagal tone will activate the parasympathetic nervous system. See The Vagus Nerve below.

The Vagus Nerve

Sometimes called the "second brain," this longest nerve of the autonomic nervous system "wanders" from the brain down to the digestive and cardiovascular systems, the vocal cords, and among many of the viscera. The autonomic nervous system controls the function of the internal organs, like blood pressure and breathing; it also contains the sympathetic (fight-or-flight) and the parasympathetic (rest-and-digest) nervous systems. If heart rate, respiration, and brain waves calm or agitate the nervous system, it would follow that when we reduce stress, the sympathetic nervous system can relax, allowing a higher vagal tone to activate the parasympathetic nervous system--letting the body do what it needs to do, from basic maintenance to serious repair. A few simple things for stimulating, regaining and maintaining high vagal tone are laughter, probiotics, cold showers, toning and humming. Luckily, there is an abundance of research and information available about the vagus nerve and how it affects our moods, stress levels and hormones.

The Crystalline Structure of The Body and Fascia

Crystals are unique and multi-faceted as they are extremely ordered arrays which can absorb, store, amplify, transmit and transduce vast amounts of energy and information throughout and around the body. And though we've long recognized bones as having a solid crystal structure, James L. Oschman, notes in *Energy Medicine in Therapeutics and Human Performance* (2003), that "crystalline arrangements are the rule, not the exception, in living systems" and "crystalline components of the living matrix act as a coherent molecular antenna, radiating and receiving signals." energyresearch.us

Gabriel Cousens, M.D., describes the human body as a "linkage of oscillating solid and liquid crystals that form an overall energy pattern for the total body." Furthermore, "each organ, gland, nerve system, cell and protein structure, even the tissue salts in the body, show a level of organization with some degree of crystalline function." *Spiritual Nutrition Book: Six Foundations for Spiritual Life and the Awakening of Kundalini* (2005). treeoflifecenterus.com

Fascia (mostly collagen with elastin and ground substance), is a connective tissue that permeates every part of our bodies and actually hold us all together. And it's the most expansive crystalline structure in the human body. This fascial network is one continuous, shapeshifting, crystalline spiderweb of connective tissue surrounding everything in our body. Christiane Northrup, M.D. calls it the "crystalline structure that literally holds all the information of your life!" DrNorthrup.com According to John F. Barnes, the creator of Myofascial Release, the fascial system functions as a "fiber optic network that bathes each cell with information, energy, light, sound, nutrition, oxygen, biochemicals, hormones and flushes out toxins...connecting every aspect of our mind/body at an enormous speed." Most intriguing is that he perceives the fascial system as a "complex series of fractals in multi-dimensions." *Myofascial Release Perspective: Therapeutic Insight—Fascia, A Liquid-Crystalline Matrix* (2009) myofascialrelease.com

In its healthy state fascia has a gel-like consistency which allows the body tissues to glide unrestricted. Unhealthy fascia is dehydrated, sluggish and hardened, making tissues stick to each other which is as painful as it sounds. When we sit for long periods of time then get up and feel stiff in the hips or lunge to catch the wine glass falling off the counter, restricted fascia can rip instead of gliding. It seems as though the longer we maintain questionable posture, hunched over our laptops or cell phones, the more our bodies, minds and self-expression atrophy and resist. As this progresses, both our internal and external communication, as well as our functioning in general, become less than flexible and fluid, resulting in not only physical pain but also emotional pain. Thomas Myers, author of *Anatomy Trains: Myofascial Meridians for Manual and Movement Therapists* (2014) says, "movement becomes habit, habit becomes posture, and posture becomes structure." anatomytrains.com

Fascial restriction can be due to prolonged sitting, repetitive cell phone or laptop use, and lack of stretching. Sustained yoga poses and rolling can be very helpful in beginning to take control of your health. Myofascial Release, Polarity Therapy, Structural Integration, Cranial-Sacral Therapy and Vibrattuning are a few very effective manual therapies that can bring more ease and freedom to the body. Basically, once the muscles are relaxed then the fascia can begin to release. As we have seen, fascia is a dynamic communication system capable of transporting staggering amounts of energy throughout and around our bodies so start slowly and with gratitude, if possible, for our bodies.

You may have heard the oft-repeated expression, "the issues are in the tissues," which points to the observation and belief that when the body is overloaded with stress, the resultant energy, trauma, is unresolved and stored in the body. The Fascia-Memory Project champions this theory, and presents documentation, that fascia "retains a physical record of stresses, strains and injuries to muscle fibers." chalicebridge.com/FasciaMemProject.html

Stress

Hans Selye, the visionary Hungarian-Canadian endocrinologist behind *Stress in Health and Disease* (1976), also known as the "Father of Stress," developed the General Adaptation Syndrome (GAS), which has also been referred to as "the stress syndrome" or "the syndrome of being sick." Selye defined stress as the "nonspecific response of the body to any demand" and considered arthritis, hypertension, and heart disease, among others, to be "diseases of adaptation." Stress can show up as general or local, and many diseases and conditions have now been shown to correlate with a prolonged imbalance of specific hormones, including the "stress hormone," cortisol. Secreted by the adrenal glands, it shifts the body into the sympathetic nervous system and a "fight or flight" response is stimulated. This creates what Itzhak Bentov calls "noise in the system," compromising communication signals and leading to inflammation in the body. Inflammation is considered an excessive reaction caused by a stressor though individual manifestations of disease vary depending on several different factors. Selye's belief that "it's not so much what happens to you but the way you take it" points to stress not being the only factor involved in disease. Previous illness or injury, genetics, mindset, and diet, among many other factors, contribute to how we manifest, and respond to, stress in our bodies and lives. Sounds like Dr. Selye was also an early player in the then-unnamed field of epigenetics, a branch of medicine that deals with the impact that the environment has on our genetics.

At the forefront of contemporary epigenetics is Bruce Lipton, who has shown us that the "brain" of the cell is its liquid crystal membrane, not its nucleus. He has also proven that stress has a direct impact on, and changes, the way our genes are activated, adding to or detracting from our health. Specifically, the internal environment of our bodies--the health and balance of our gut, organs, blood, etc.--directly affects the maintenance and repair of, or the breakdown of, the cells and their expression of health. He also concludes that our negative thoughts can create inflammation, our positive thoughts can reduce inflammation. *The Biology of Belief (2015)*. brucelipton.com

James L. Oschman notes in *Energy Medicine in Therapeutics and Human Performance* (2003), that "every thought you think is echoing through your connective tissue communication system, turning genes on and off, producing either stress responses or healing responses."

Fritz Albert Popp also examined the effects of stress and discovered that "in a stressed state, the rate of biophoton emission went up—a defense mechanism designed to try to return the patient to equilibrium." *The Field* (2008).

Selye described two types of stress effects: eustress (from the Greek eu- true or good: as in euphony, euphoria, eulogy) and distress (from the Latin dis- or bad: as in dissonance, disease, disgust) and noted that the same stress making one person ill is tonic for another.

Stressors can be physical, emotional or mental, social or cultural, self-limiting thoughts and beliefs, hunger, body temperature, lack of skin-on-skin touch, limited connection with the Earth, sleep deprivation, hormone levels, money, traffic, air and water quality, racial, political or religious conflict, aggression, violence, isolation and loneliness, lack of community, social media, medication, occupation, incarceration, age, home environment, relationship, family, myriad body products, cosmetics and household cleaners, life change, holidays, allergens or electromagnetic fields (EMFs), to name a few.

Hypothalmic-Pituitary-Adrenal Axis

The Hypothalmic-Pituitary-Adrenal (HPA) axis is a brilliant mechanism designed to protect us in times of external threat, though in *The Biology of Belief* (2015), Bruce Lipton writes, "the bad side of the coin is when our bodies become chronically stimulated by misperceptions (unfortunately our stress managing system cannot distinguish whether a brain-directed response is derived from a real or an imagined fear) and sadness that we can't let go of." In other words, whether the body senses impending physical danger, is thinking about the overdue rent, or is watching the nightly news, the hypothalamus signals the pituitary gland which triggers the adrenal glands to kick into gear, squirting out hormones that allow us to fight off, or escape from, danger. These "fight-or-flight" responses send blood to the limbs and restrict it to the forebrain (the conscious mind and center of reasoning and logic), among other things. Also happening is a suppression of the immune system, which would consume too much energy, and can interfere with our ability to stay healthy. Lipton says, "we are constantly besieged by multitudes of unresolvable worries about our personal lives, our jobs, and our war-torn global community. Such worries do not threaten our immediate survival, but they nevertheless can activate the HPA axis, resulting in chronically elevated stress hormones."

So if stress can cause inflammation, which can lead to ill health, then what can we do to reduce our levels of stress? An immediate start could be inviting new ways of de-stressing into your life including meditation, communion with nature, connecting to the electrical rhythms of the Earth (called earthing or grounding), creating a sense of place within a community, establishing a new connection with self, spending time with people who enjoy experiencing your unique expression of self, vocalizing (toning, singing, chanting, humming, just make sound!), using weighted tuning forks on yourself, drumming, dancing, laughing, waking up with gratitude BEFORE the litany of the usual thoughts cascade in, and possibly some qigong, yoga, or tai chi. No need for a regimen or commitment, just start with a few minutes of whatever is easiest and most fun. This is about de-stressing, boosting your body's voltage and raising your resilience so it's best to do smaller doses than none at all.

Inflammation

The swelling, redness, heat, tenderness and pain that occur when we stub our toe against the hard edge of a chair leg is called acute inflammation. It's a short-term protection of the body by the immune system as a first responder to an injurious stimuli, protecting the body and starting the healing process. This occurs in bodies that are relatively coherent and charged up with voltage. Chronic inflammation is a long-term, chaotic situation that impairs cellular function by creating an electron feeding-frenzy for free radicals. These positively charged molecules (missing one or more electrons), are constantly searching for, and gobbling up, electrons from our healthy cells. Jerry Tennant, in *Healing is Voltage* (2014), calls them "electron-stealers." This thievery creates a vicious cycle as the immune system sends in more troops to assist, creating more and more free radicals in the body.

Also, with a lot of inflammation starting in the gut, it's important to consider our diet and the human microbiome, as well. Either raw, fermented vegetables or a probiotic supplement is now generally regarded as important to maintain the balance of beneficial bacteria in the gut. Of course, there is a plethora of factors affecting gut health, thankfully, there is more than enough research and information on this subject to reference.

The Healer and Healing

Can you imagine paying someone to pray for you? Well, I did just that in an effort to purge trauma that I no longer wished to define me. And, if I remember correctly, this particular intervention involved my body being cocooned in plastic wrap while holy water was splashed over my head and face. Little did I know at the time, in my desperation to feel whole, that healing energy runs within us and emanates from us. And by using this energy to its best advantage for the purpose of self-healing, the body is an extraordinary auto-correcting mechanism as it contains all the information and abilities to heal itself. It's a very nurturing and frequently transformational choice to regain control of your own health and it took me decades to understand that healing, just like happiness, is not an end point. Fritz Albert Popp considers health to be "...a state of perfect subatomic communication, and ill health, a state where communication breaks down. We are ill when our waves are out of synch." *The Field* (2008). And as we develop communication among our own energy fields, those of the client, and the rest of the universe, are we are tapping into Oneness and experiencing being truly present? Ultimately, as practitioners, we are both the witness and participant through "the healer is on the table" perspective of Richard Gordon. *Your Healing Hands: The Polarity Experience* (2004).

And what about all of the sound baths and sound healings that are popping up everywhere these days? Just because someone has a few crystal bowls, a gong, some tuning forks or tingshas, and maybe a "certificate" of sorts, does that make them a sound healer? Lately, it seems like anyone who can get a few singing bowls together, wear flowing clothes and gaze mysteriously heavenward is offering up an overpriced sound bath or sound healing these days. They may be a very accomplished practitioner or they could just be a hipster hobbyist making some quick cash while they practice, clanging tuning forks together and haphazardly waving them over people. After most of these events, I've floated out on a magic carpet though on a few occasions I have been left feeling jangly and annoyed. Either way the results were short-lived.

Intention

If intention is putting our awareness on a desired outcome, would that would seem to have expectation, judgment and ultimately separation wrapped up in it? It seems least complicated to hand it over to the Universe (Source, Light, Creator, God, Higher Power, Nature, Directing Intelligence, or whatever you choose to call it) by intending for it to know exactly what the client is required to receive or even discharge during a session. That allows attention to be focused on the client and frees the mind from getting in the way. Basically, it has nothing to do with what we as a practitioner or client needs or wants. Be with yourself, be with your client, be with the moment and everything will unfold as it's supposed to. The body uses energy and intent in the way it sees fit, not always in the way we imagine or expect. If we are attached to the results, that attachment and expectation will interfere with the outcome. It seems like a constricted, limited way to work and cuts off flow. The opposite of that is detachment where there is no need to control and direct the results. This space of expanded awareness and observation allows us to be in deeper communication and process with the client.

<u>Preparing for a session:</u>

- Be well rested. The importance of an 8-hour sleep is well-documented.

- Breathe deeply, while centering and grounding.

- Clear your space by your method of choice (palo santo, sage, using a 4096Hz tuning fork, dowsing rods, etc.). A great book on clearing the energy of people and places is *Clear Home, Clear Heart* (2017) by Jean Hamer.

- Avoid having a full stomach prior to sessions (practitioner and client). It's more comfortable (especially if laying prone) and allows the body to fully relax and receive full benefit from the session instead of digesting a meal. A snack is fine but wait an hour after a light meal and at least 2-3 hours after a heavy meal.

- Comfortable, loose-fitting clothing is appropriate to both give and receive sessions. Remove belts and any bulky jewelry prior to the session.

- Have a blanket available in case your client gets chilly during the session.

- Go over intake and ask your client any questions necessary.

- Approach the session with curiosity and sensitivity.

- Begin the session with zero expectations; "I'm not making anything happen. I'm present only to facilitate energy flow and assist you and your body in clearing energetic blocks only when ready, willing and able."

The Treatment Room

Keep the treatment room as clean and uncluttered as possible. A massage table, draped with a neutral sheet, and a blanket readily available, is generally the most comfortable and professional for both the client and practitioner. Lamps or wall sconces are infinitely more pleasant and relaxing than overhead lighting. Fluorescent lighting seems to be the most distracting of all as it flickers rapidly and tends to agitate our nervous systems and drain people. The opposite of what the session is all about. No music or background sound is necessary either as this is a time to deeply tune in and listen. Also important to note are Volatile Organic Compounds (VOCs), gasses emitted from certain solids or liquids, some of which could have adverse health effects. Whether we smell them or not, we are all affected by the chemicals around us; many people are chemically sensitive and some people have environmental allergies. That said, it's best to play it safe and avoid using any sprays, essential oils, incense, air fresheners, perfumes, colognes, scented candles, scented flowers, dryer sheets or scented detergents.

Body Mechanics and Movement

Center, breathe, and ground to connect with the person on the table. Pay attention to how you are holding your body from your feet all the way up to your head. It's important to have both feet firmly on the ground, to be facing the client and to be as close to the client as comfortable for the least strain on your own body while working. Keep your wrists as straight as possible, with little to no angle so that you will remain as pain-free as possible, for as long as possible in your session and, ultimately, your career. That said, just stay aware of your body mechanics and adjust accordingly. Sometimes it will be necessary to have a bent wrist for a short time while working on an area. This is fine as long as you keep an eye on your body mechanics and readjust as needed. When beginning to handle the tuning forks, it is important to establish strength and flexibility of the fingers, wrists and forearms. Try placing a sheet of paper in the middle of your hand and crumple it up into a ball. Repeat this a few times using the same sheet of paper. Then position your hand flat on a table, palm down, fingers fully extended. Using the opposite hand, slowly lift each finger off the table one by one. Then stretch the forearms by standing at a table and placing both palms face down on the table, with fingers pointing behind you. Move into the stretch. Next, turn your hands over so the backs of the hands are on the table, with fingers pointing behind you. Again move into the stretch. Lastly, shake out your hands in a brisk manner for about 15-20 seconds. Repeat all of the above two or three times before and after your sessions to stay limber.

A few reminders to:

- Breathe fully, be centered and grounded.

- Stand in a relaxed position, as close to the client as is comfortable.

- Face the client, feet shoulder-width apart.

- Keep knees unlocked.

- Hold the tuning forks in a firm yet relaxed manner. Avoid a white-knuckled grip.

- Work in minimal foot wear, if possible.

Minimal footwear works best for me and thankfully there are more companies manufacturing it as the demand rises. Lucky for us, biomechanist Katy Bowman, author of *Whole Body Barefoot: Transitioning Well to Minimal Footwear* (2015) and *Move Your DNA: Restore Your Health Through Natural Movement* (2014), is prolific, innovative, articulate and the absolute definition of "walking the talk." A literal example being hiking the mile and a half from the airport, with her kids, to pick up a rental car, and stopping along the way to celebrate what nobody ever sees when whizzing by in a vehicle. Listening to some of her many podcasts and reading her books & blogs has really brought more awareness to my overall body mechanics and movement in general. nutritiousmovement.com

Another movement inspiration is Erwan Le Corre, the creator of MovNat, Natural Movement and author of *The Practice of Natural Movement: Reclaim Power, Health and Freedom* (2019). movnat.com

Teaching and empowering people to use their bodies for real-world physical competency through movement in nature rather than going to gyms or remaining sedentary seems more essential now than ever before.

Anatomy Of A Tuning Fork

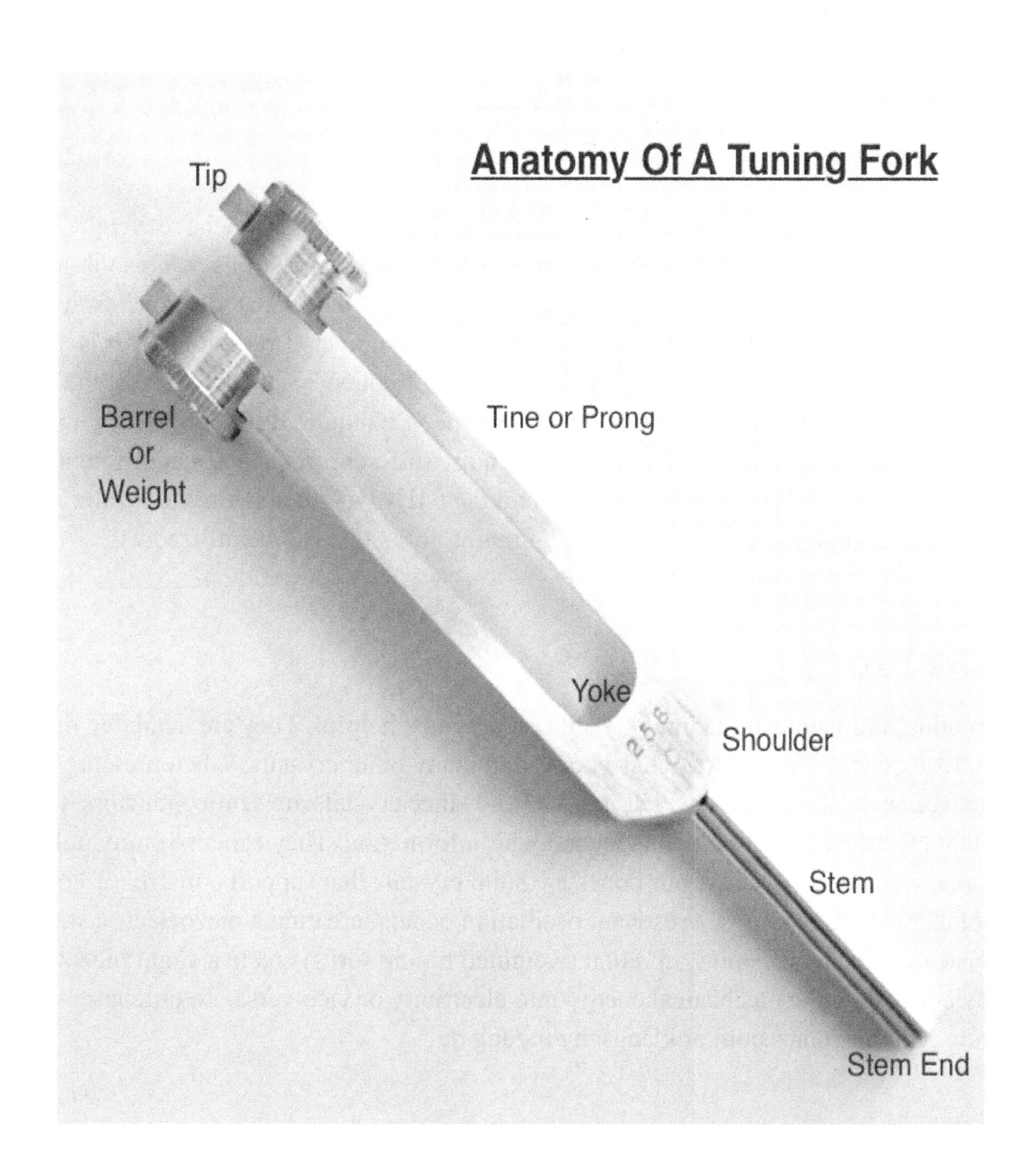

Tip

Barrel or Weight

Tine or Prong

Yoke

Shoulder

Stem

Stem End

Tools

Weighted Tuning Forks

Usually two weighted tuning forks are used together in Vibrattuning. They have weighted barrels on the ends of either tine allowing them to vibrate longer and stronger. This vibration travels down the handle and is perfect for using on the body, providing a coherent, steady and rhythmic input, boosting your body's voltage and raising your everyday resilience. It is important to note that there is not one frequency or set of frequencies that will affect the same change in any one person on any specific day. Just as people require different foods, nutrients, clothing, temperatures and movement, they also require different frequencies at different times. In Vibrattuning, the 136.1Hz, 128Hz, 68.05Hz and the 64Hz weighted tuning forks are commonly used though there are any number of tuning forks that can be utilized.

Crystal/Gem Feet

In Vibrattuning, the 15mm and 25mm crystal feet are most helpful. They are available in amethyst, rose quartz, clear quartz, chalcedony, and many other crystals. When pressure is applied to a crystal it generates an electric flow. And since crystals are semiconductors, they can conduct that electrical energy, which is loaded with information. They can also store, pulse, focus or amplify energy. Because our bones are solid crystals that support a matrix of liquid crystal connective tissue arrays, a resonant oscillation occurs, creating a piezoelectric streaming effect. Basically, the crystals plus vibration (weighted tuning forks) create a slight piezoelectric current by converting the mechanical energy into electricity or vice-versa. To purchase crystal/gem feet: biosonics.com or klangschwingung.de

Activators (Golf club weighted swing ring/Thigh straps/Hockey Pucks/Your Body)

After experimenting with many different activators, the preferred method is putting a golf club weighted swing ring in each front or side pants pocket, allowing a hands-free activation so that both hands can wield the tuning forks. A thigh strap is a much more expensive solution though it also allows hands-free activation. Least favorite and most cumbersome are hockey pucks; they stink of outgassing rubber, can lead to wrist problems and only allow for single tuning fork activations. The easiest, and always available, solution is using your own body: alternate strikes on either the shoulders, hips or knees. It takes some practice and can lead to bruising so proceed with care.

Quality of Tuning Forks

The quality of tuning forks varies greatly. Poured tuning forks are generally cheaper and of inferior quality, tone and lifespan. The poured tuning forks we've investigated have been laughable in their construction and tone, never mind that the barrels were of different sizes and inconsistently attached. Higher-quality tuning forks are made from a range of alloys and are cut from a solid piece of metal called a blank, then filed and hand-tuned. Quality, construction and tone in these tuning forks can also vary from company to company regarding size, raw materials (alloys), stem length, smoothness of the cuts and length of tone.

How to Hold the Weighted Tuning Fork

1. Hold the fork by the stem with a relaxed grip.
2. Be careful to keep the fingers no more than slightly above the yoke/U of the tuning fork.
3. Practice different hand and finger placements on the stem while feeling the length of vibration on your own body with each activation.
4. Remember to keep your wrist as straight as allowable.

How to Activate the Weighted Tuning Fork

An appropriate strike is:

- Keeping fingers, wrist, and shoulders relaxed, with a slightly bent elbow.
- Striking the tuning fork on the rough edge of the barrel. (*This action is the same as lighting a match*).
- Hitting the tuning fork hard enough to tone it, with no jolting sound.
- Activating the tuning fork away from the client's head.

An improper strike is:

- Clenching the tuning fork stem with a death grip.
- Activating the tuning fork at varying, inconsistent places.
- Applying force that allows the barrels to clang together.
- Activating the tuning fork near the client's head.

A Note on Re-Activating Weighted Tuning Forks

When working with two weighted tuning forks, it can be quite jarring if both of them are removed from the body at the same time in order to re-activate them. A more comfortable approach is leaving one tuning fork on the body while re-activating the other. When moving on to a different area, remove one tuning fork, then the other and continue on.

How to Perceive with the Weighted Tuning Fork:

- Activate the tuning fork. Position the stem end on your, or your practice, body on any area that calls you. Remember that if the weights or tines touch anything, it will dampen or stop the vibration.

- What do you notice vibrationally in your fingertips? A pulsing or sluggishness? Is it choppy or sporadic?

- Any there any bodily responses or sensations--from you or your client?

- Pay attention to your own breathing and the breathing of the client. Did the breath catch? Was there a relaxing exhale?

- Re-activate the tuning fork as needed. Don't overthink it. Move on to the next point and practice being in the moment with what you and your client notice.

- Tune in and practice this often, with deep listening, spontaneity and curiosity.

Application of Weighted Tuning Forks:

- Position: Place weighted tuning forks on the body, either individually or by placing two weighted tuning forks next to each other, or at different points, on the body.

- Walk: Just like it sounds—first, the lead tuning fork takes a step, then the other takes a step and lands just behind the lead tuning fork. Repeat until arriving at destination.

- Glide: The stem end, of one or both tuning forks, glides from one area of the body to another, maintaining contact with the body until re-activation of tuning fork is required.

- Pinch: The stem ends of both tuning forks straddle an area of soft tissue (ex: the trapezius muscle), and squeeze towards each other while the weighted ends move away from each other, creating a pinching motion. Start with larger "pinches" and less pressure while practicing. Either stay in one spot or release the pressure and move along to the next spot to be pinched.

Pace, Rhythm and Pressure

The adaptogenic qualities of the tuning forks can dispel excess energy such as fluid retention, sinus congestion or joint pain by allowing the tuning forks to run down and by working at a slower, more soothing pace. Conversely, by keeping the vibration on the tuning forks strong and working at a brisker, more energizing pace, they can penetrate deeply into the tissues and cells, invigorating sluggish spots and nourishing deficiencies. The pace, rhythm and pressure used during the session are guided by the client's needs and may change at any moment. It's important to reactivate the tuning forks as required and this can only come with practice; this includes remembering to leave one tuning fork on the body while re-activating the second one, if working with two. Also, if the pace allows, the beneficial qualities of both silence and of the space between sounds is mostly overlooked and I encourage you to experiment with this.

Inflammation or Excited Spots

Allowing the tuning fork to run down before re-activating has a soothing effect. Fluid retention, sinus congestion and joint pain can all be assisted by working with a slower, smoother rhythm. Anxiety seems to respond well when taking this approach as well.

Sluggish Spots

If the tuning fork dampens quickly, this could indicate a sluggish spot or even blocked energy. These are places on the body that require us to spend some time there providing a steady flow of coherent energy. Re-activate the tuning fork more frequently to keep the input steady. Don't allow the tuning forks to run down. The pace and input at these spots can be brisk and invigorating.

Flow Points

We are complex beings with many different operating systems and requirements. Sometimes there is a disconnected flow or lack of transmission between different areas of our bodies. With the weighted tuning forks, we can locate compromised flow points and re-establish a transfer of information through communication and relationship. The two points, when held together at the same time, create a conversation with, or flow between, them. All atoms, cells and systems (metabolic, immune, nervous, muscular, cardiovascular, lymphatic, etc.) are in communication with each other and a breakdown or lack of communication can lead to levels of stress and, possibly, diseases.

Pressure

The desired pressure for any area of the body can be different for many bodies. In general, bone requires less pressure than soft tissue. Larger musculature such as shoulders, back, buttocks and legs generally require a deeper, firmer pressure. Of course there can always be exceptions and getting feedback from your client is critical in determining the correct pressure. Bones and all crystalline structures (including muscles and fascia) are piezoelectric in nature which means they create a slight voltage or electrical charge when under pressure.

When positioning the weighted forks on the body:

- Press into the body with a lighter pressure at first.

- If there is initial pain or discomfort, work slowly into a deeper pressure, if appropriate. Build up pressure gradually to allow the body to unfold and receive.

- Time spent on the area being worked differs: sluggish or under active spots can use a quicker, more energetic application of forks (3-5 seconds). Work slower in areas of inflammation or over-activity (20 seconds or until the sound runs out).

- A steady, coherent input of vibration is desired.

Care of Weighted Tuning Forks:

- Wipe tuning forks and gem feet with non-chemical, anti-bacterial spray or wash with warm water and a mild soap. Rinse well and hand dry.

- <u>Avoid getting water in the barrels.</u> If it happens, just make sure to dry them completely.

- Keep tuning forks dry, especially when storing.

- Take care not to drop or nick the tuning forks as this can affect the frequency.

- Use a scotch-guard pad, lightly, on the tuning forks if they tarnish. It will not affect the performance of them.

- Handle your tuning forks with care, which includes activating only on appropriate surfaces (golf club weighted swing ring, thigh strap, hip, etc.) without undo force or clanging.

- Avoid extreme hot or cold temperatures as the frequency of the tuning forks can be affected.

- Put tuning forks in carry-on luggage when flying, to avoid extreme temperature changes.

- Allow tuning forks to come to room temperature, for accurate frequencies, before using them.

Storage of Weighted Tuning Forks

- Whether it's a soft roll-up wrap or a hard case, treat your tools of the trade with respect and put them in something protective.

- A proper case is necessary to transport your tuning forks and will extend the lifespan of them.

- Make one or re-purpose something into a suitable case for your tuning forks and gear.

- Look around at hardware or container stores for storage options. Be creative. Wrench cases have made great storage cases for tuning forks.

- Store tuning forks in a ziploc bag if they will be in a humid or moist environment, or in danger of coming into contact with water.

Practitioner Self-Care

Sometimes it seems as though we are great at assisting others in their self-care, yet we neglect our own. What would it look like if we started following our own advice? Adding some meditation, yin yoga, daily earthing sessions and sunshine, vocal toning, massage or an occasional drum circle into our lives can really make a huge difference in keeping us charged up and ready to be fully available to ourselves and our clients. Has anyone ever been to a practitioner whose light seemed a little dim, their attention and awareness tapped out? It's unpleasant as we end up energetically giving to them instead of filling ourselves up.

Impartiality

Maintaining an impartial stance is essential in any form of bodywork as it allows a natural flow. It's also easier on our bodies as we get out of our thinking minds and become more spontaneous. Let's check our egos at the door and proceed with curiosity and non-judgement. Step aside and allow the body's own knowing and organizing structure to guide the session.

Breathe

When we inhale more fully and exhale with awareness, our life and our practice become more centered. Deep, diaphragmatic breathing is a skill that requires practice and patience. When we pay attention to our breath and breathing, we cannot help but be present.

Earth/Ground

Earthing or grounding is thought to remedy an electron deficiency thus reducing inflammation. The easiest way to ground is to walk or stand barefoot in dewy grass. There are also many products sold under the Earthing name, such as grounding pads, sheets or blankets, that may be beneficial. *Earthing: The Most Important Health Discovery Ever!* (2014) is a great resource.

Get plenty of sunshine

The energy of the sun is vital to us. Go out and have some fun in the sun, charge up and maybe even get into the practice of sun gazing: standing barefoot on the earth, looking at the sun, either at sunrise or sunset, starting with just a few seconds. Add a few more seconds the next day, gradually introducing the light into your eyes.

Hydrate

Drink plenty of the best quality water which may require further investigation/investment by you. Eating fresh fruits and vegetables or drinking coconut water is a good source of structured water, which has the same molecular structure as in nature, is more readily utilized by the body and can hold and deliver energy, just like a battery. According to Gerald Pollack it's the same composition (H3O2), as the negatively charged water in our cells and blood. *The Fourth Phase of Water: Beyond Solid, Liquid and Vapor* (2013)

Receive bodywork

While we can utilize softballs, lacrosse balls, rollers and tools on our own bodies, alternate a hot and cold shower stream for nerve strength, sweat in an infrared sauna, or dry-brush, it's also important to be a client occasionally and receive work.

After-Care Reminders

- Drink extra water to flush out any toxins released by the cells.
- Plan on allowing the body to relax by not eating heavy meals or sugary snacks.
- Avoid social media and TV for as long as possible.
- Avoid going into stressful or chaotic situations such as major stores or malls.
- Enjoy a cup of herbal tea and avoid iced drinks.
- Rest. Take a nap.
- Earth/ground. Walk barefoot on the beach or in nature.
- Surround yourself with beauty. Buy or pick some fresh flowers.
- Engage is some light movement, according to your energy level.
- Be kind to yourself and choose for you.
- Spend time alone or with people who appreciate you exactly as you are.
- Express yourself. Pent up emotions are stagnant energy and can lead to all kinds of physical problems. Allow any emotions that come up to flow through.

- <u>Take a bath.</u> As the skin is a highly porous membrane, taking a bath with 1½ cups epsom salts (Magnesium sulfate) will create reverse osmosis and pull salt and harmful toxins OUT OF the body and allow magnesium and sulfates INTO the body. I've heard that adding a half cup of baking soda to the bath really bumps up the magnesium absorption. 40 minutes is ideal as we need about 20 minutes to remove toxins and 20 minutes to absorb minerals from the bath. Avoid using soap as it interferes with the reverse osmosis action. Just rinse in a cool shower after bathing and then rest. Do not use if you have open wounds or burns on your body. Dead Sea Salts are wonderful as well, though a more expensive option.

Sometimes results are immediate, and lead to lasting change; realistically, you'll need multiple sessions. Frequently a multi-modality approach is highly effective, depending on your starting point and targets.

Method:

1. <u>Breathe, center and ground.</u> An essential step for both the practitioner and the client in any energy work. Stand at the foot of the table and gently place your hands on top of the client's feet. Invite client to inhale deeply with you. Breathe out fully, guiding your client through a visualization of their feet being electrical plugs with two contact prongs on the bottom, plugging directly into the massive power outlet called Earth. Ground deeply into the middle of the Earth. Do it along with your client.

2. <u>Conduct a visual assessment.</u> As quick or as in depth as your training allows. Is one shoulder higher? Is the head tilted to the left? One leg longer?, etc.

3. <u>Say hello to the body.</u> Sweeping down both legs, then an ankle pull--one ankle at a time-- is a nice beginning. Also, a tactile assessment can sometimes help to identify areas to use the tuning forks.

4. <u>Angle of approach:</u> Establish a starting point, plan or protocol. Don't give it a lot of thought. We are looking to get out of our heads and allow our knowing to take over.

5. <u>Locate starting point.</u> Before activating the tuning fork, locate the starting point with the guide hand--the non-dominant hand that remains on the body or point while activating the tuning fork.

6. <u>Activate the tuning fork.</u> A golf club weighted swing ring, thigh strap activator or your body works best as it allows the use of both hands during the session. Activate a weighted tuning fork by striking the rough edge of the barrel against the activator. *(This action is the same as striking a match).* We are looking for a sustained vibration with minimal effort or force. A clanging sound is never desirable or necessary, and it can minimize the vibration.

7. <u>Position the tuning fork on the body.</u> Doing this with finesse takes some common sense and care on your part as well as plenty of feedback from your practice bodies. There are multiple considerations such as: Is the placement of the tuning fork on bone or soft tissue? Thicker muscle or fat can dampen the effect of the vibration and multiple passes and/or a deeper pressure may need to be applied. Is it on a larger area or a more delicate area like the head and face, which require more attention and precision? There are many considerations.

8. <u>Communicate with the client.</u> Check in with the client. What's the pressure feel like? What are you aware of?

9. <u>Let the energy guide you.</u> Turn off your mind and tune in to the energy.

10. <u>Be aware of client's breathing,</u> eye movements and body movements.

11. <u>Pay attention to your own breathing,</u> bodily sensations and transfer of information.

12. <u>Listen.</u> This is a receptive state, one of minimalism and non-attachment. We are simply a witness and no ego is necessary.

13. Everything is constantly changing. What works today or in this moment, may not work in the next. Just as what works for one body may not work for another.

14. Continue on to the next points until the session is complete.

15. Finish with 2 or 3 leg-sweeps and instruct the client to slowly roll to their side. Assist client in coming to a seated position on the table.

16. Offer your client a glass of water and after-care reminders.

The 12 Introductory Protocols

As protocols are largely for the left, logical brain, they are included here only as suggested starting points. We encourage you to experiment, play, explore and share. This is not symptom-based, diagnostic work, looking for the "wrongness." A diagnosis is a decision, a determination, an assumption, a judgement, and sometimes even a death sentence, which arises from the conscious mind. The less we are influenced by our conscious mind, the quicker we can get out of our own way and allow the body's healing intelligence to determine what it needs. For this reason, we prefer to step aside and allow our knowing to be in communion with the needs of the client. We are looking to create a space of connection to, and oneness with, the process and the client. It's a space of curiosity and spontaneity leading to flow and connection. Trust yourself. You will know where to place the tuning forks.

A few notes for the twelve Introductory Protocols:

- Where there are either no pictures or multiple pictures for any step in a particular protocol, it is noted.

- Where supine is noted, the client is face up on the massage table. Prone is face down.

- The angle of the forks in some of the demo pictures is being exaggerated in order to show where the fork is placed on the body. In practice, the forks are in more of an upright position unless applying the pinching technique.

- Each protocol, or portion thereof, can be repeated up to three times.

- The only seated protocol, number twelve, is unillustrated.

1. **Protocol for Head and Face (supine)**

1-1. Position one activated tuning fork on top of the head and the second activated tuning fork on the heart center.

1-2. Position the activated tuning forks on either side of the head (above and just forward of the ears). This creates a beat frequency. It brings awareness to vibration and flow in the body. And it's super relaxing. Repeat a few times.

1-3. Position both activated tuning forks at the back top of the ears. Glide down the back of the ears and hold at mastoid process on either side of the head. (*Two pictures: 1-3a and 1-3b*)

1-4. Position the activated tuning forks behind the sternocleidomastoid and gently glide down to the collarbone and pause for a beat or two. (*Two pictures: 1-4a and 1-4b*)

1-5. Position both activated tuning forks at the midline of the forehead, just at the hairline. Glide out to the temples and pause on both sides. (*Two pictures: 1-5a and 1-5b*)

1-6. Make gentle, clockwise circles on the temples with activated tuning forks. (*NO picture*)

1-7. Position both activated tuning forks at the midline of the forehead, 1½ inches below the hairline. Glide out to the temples and pause on both sides.

1-8. Make gentle, clockwise circles on the temples with activated tuning forks. (*NO picture*)

1-9. Position both activated tuning forks between the eyebrows and lightly glide over them. Pause at the ends of the eyebrows. (*Two pictures: 1-9a and 1-9b*)

1-10. Position both activated tuning forks on either side of the nose, just below the inside corners of the eyes. Glide down either side of the nose then just under the cheekbones and out to the temporal mandibular joint. Pause here, with activated tuning forks, for a beat or two. (*Three pictures: 1-10a, 1-10b, 1-10c*)

1-11. Position both activated tuning forks at the midline of the chin. Glide up either side of the jaw to the temporal mandibular joint. Pause here for a beat or two. (*Two pictures: 1-11a and 1-11b*)

1-12. Position both activated tuning fork ends next to each other above the upper lip and just below the nose (specifically, the philtrum). Glide around the upper lip out towards ears. Pause at the corners of the mouth on either side. (*Two pictures: 1-12a and 1-12b*)

1-13. Position both activated tuning fork ends next to each other below the lower lip. Glide around the lower lip out towards the ears. Pause at, or before, the corners of the mouth on either side. (*Two pictures: 1-13a and 1-13b*)

1-1. Position one activated tuning fork on top of the head and the second activated tuning fork on the heart center.

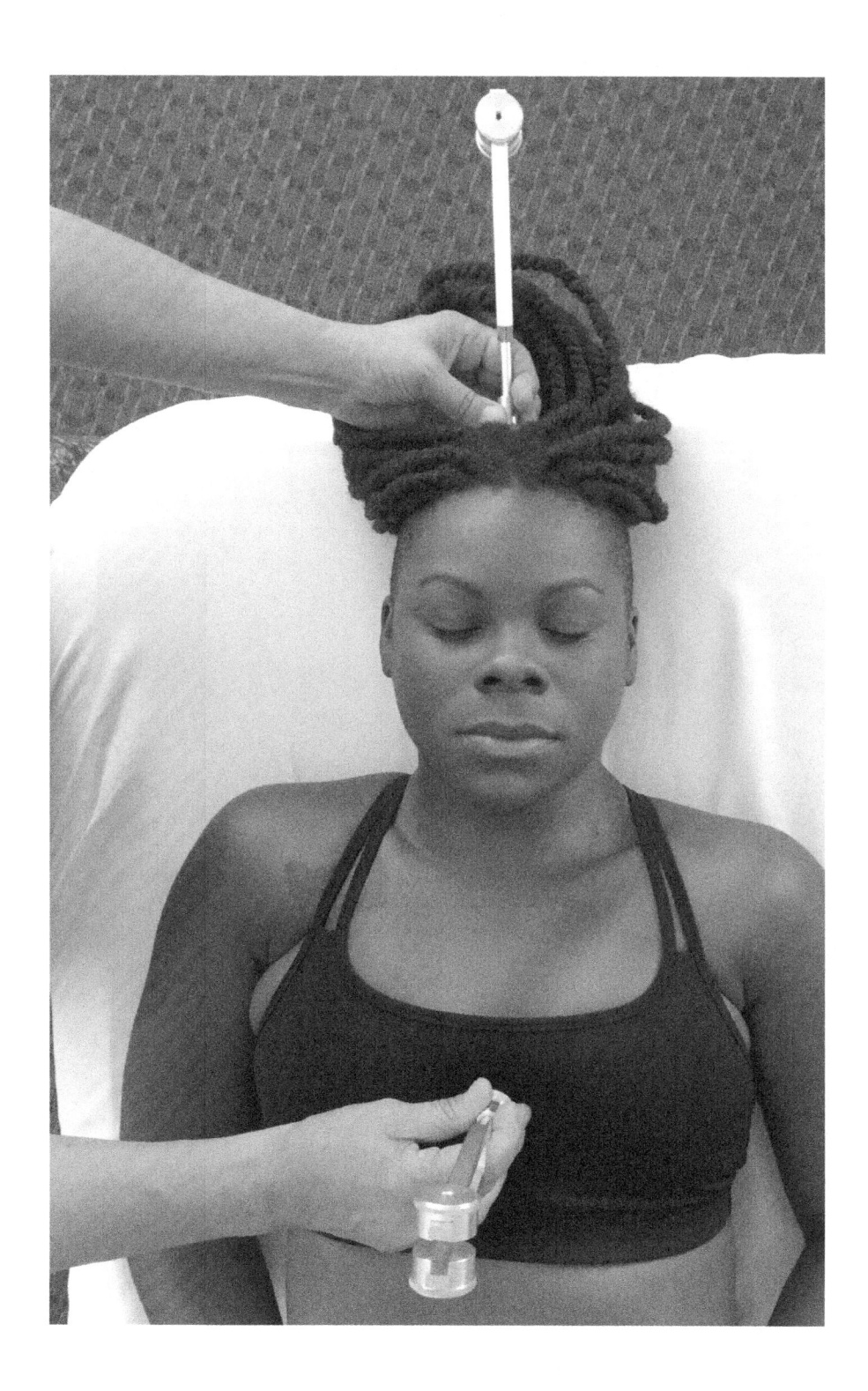

35

1-2. Position the activated tuning forks on either side of the head (above and just forward of the ears). This creates a beat frequency. It brings awareness to vibration and flow in the body. And it's super relaxing. Repeat this a few times.

1-3a. Position both activated tuning forks at the back top of the ears. Glide down the back of the ears and hold at mastoid process on either side of the head. (*Two pictures: 1-3a and 1-3b*)

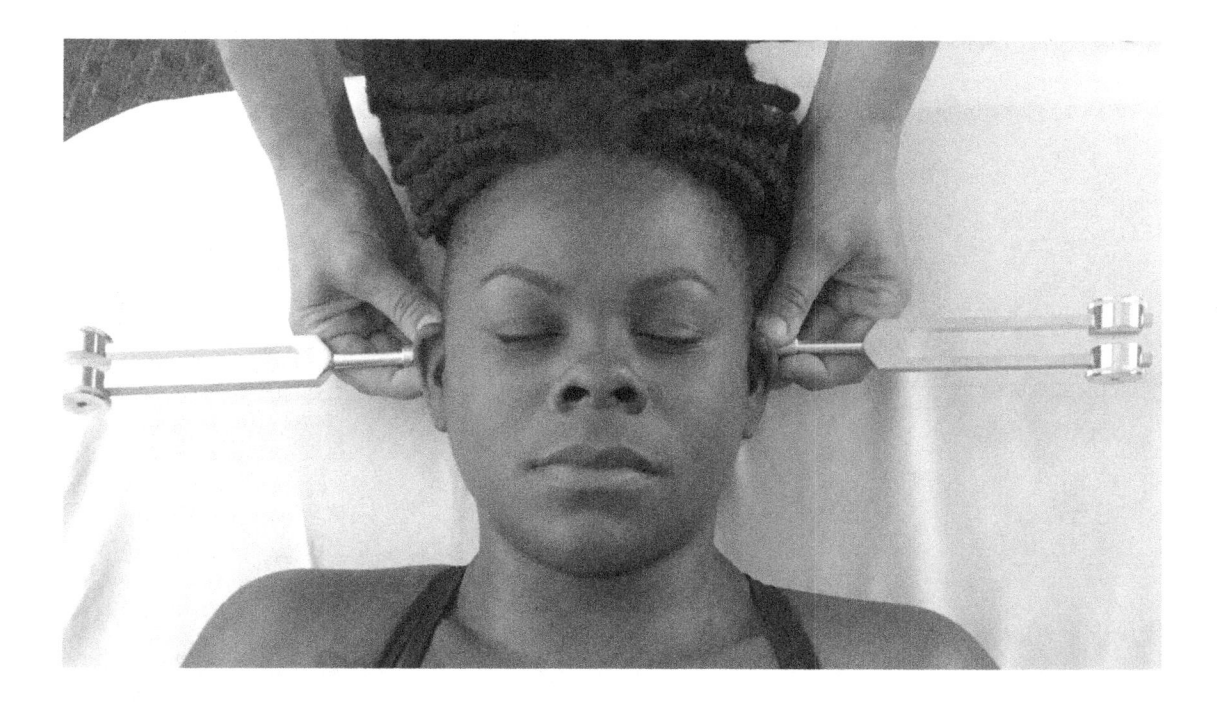

1-3b. Hold the activated tuning forks at the mastoid process on either side of the head.

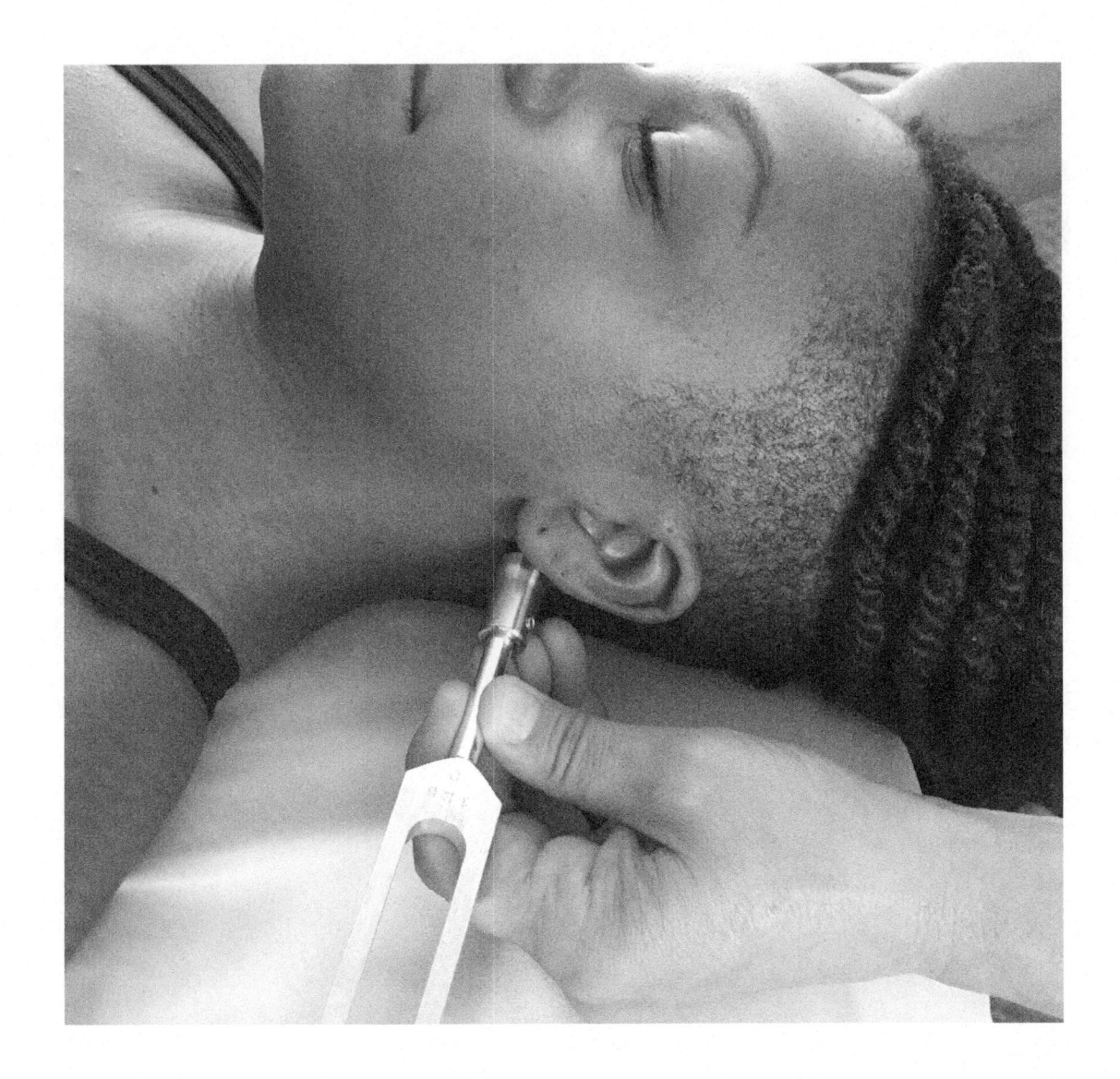

1-4a. Position the activated tuning forks behind the sternocleidomastoid and gently glide down to the collarbone. (*Two pictures: 1-4a and 1-4b*)

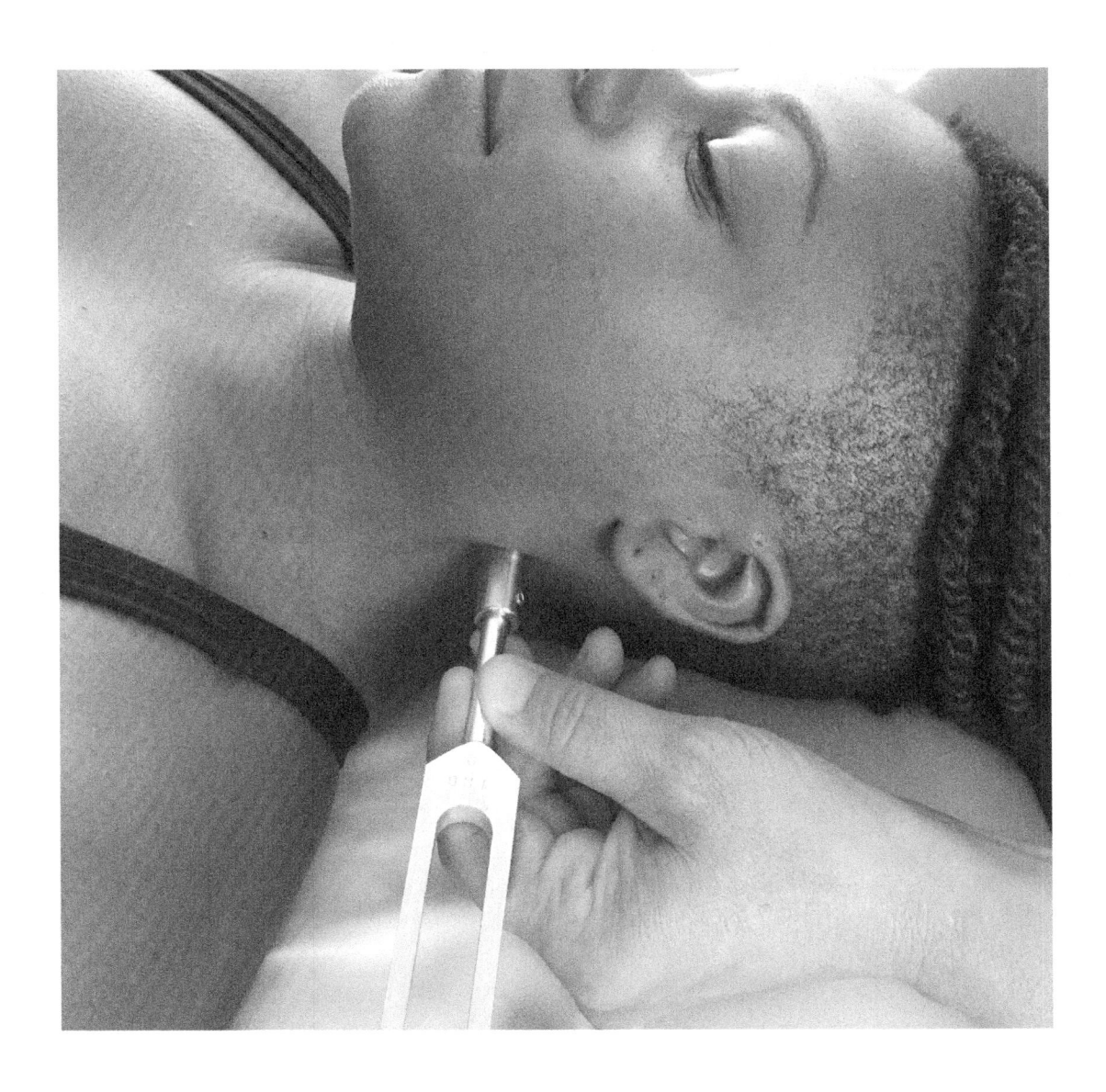

1-4b. Pause here for a few beats.

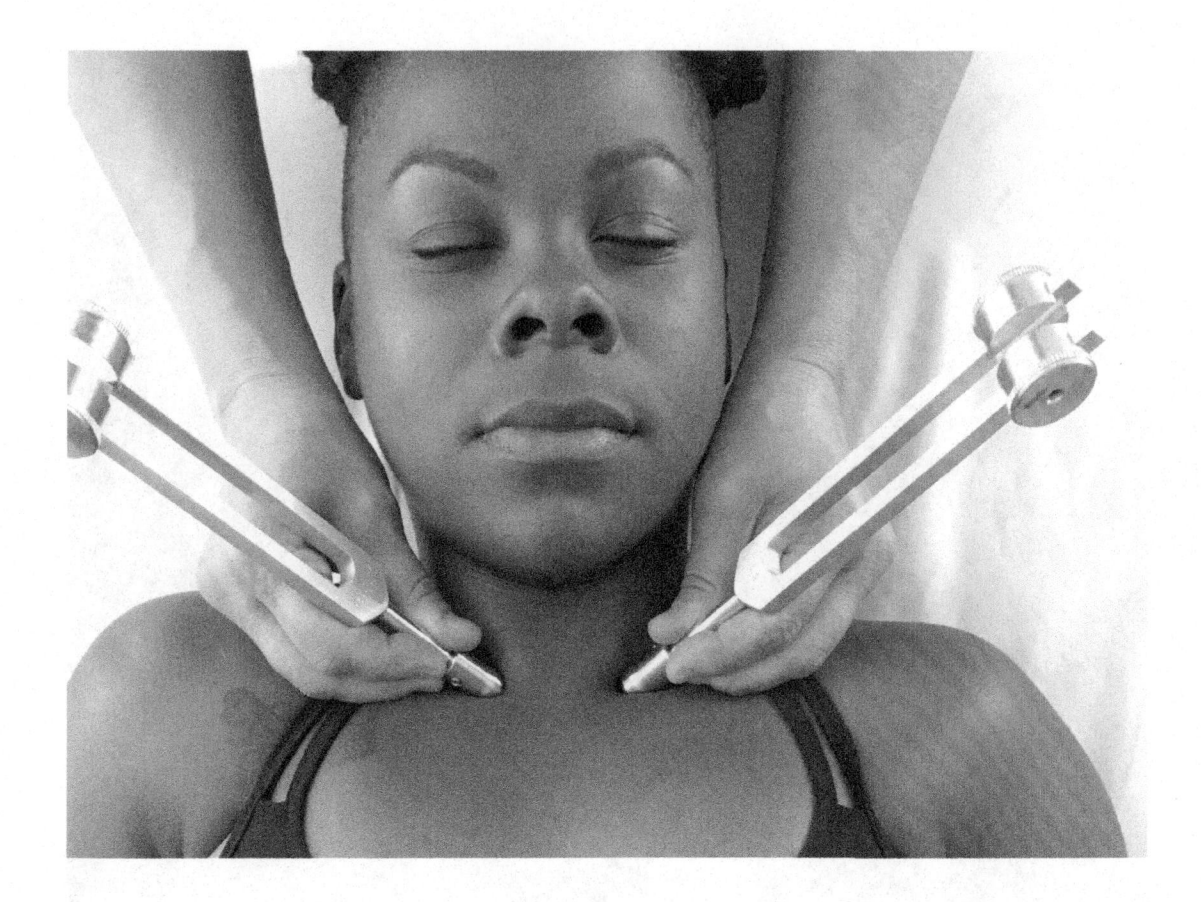

1-5a. Position both activated tuning forks at the midline of the forehead, just at the hairline. Glide out to the temples and pause on both sides. (*Two pictures: 1-5a and 1-5b*)

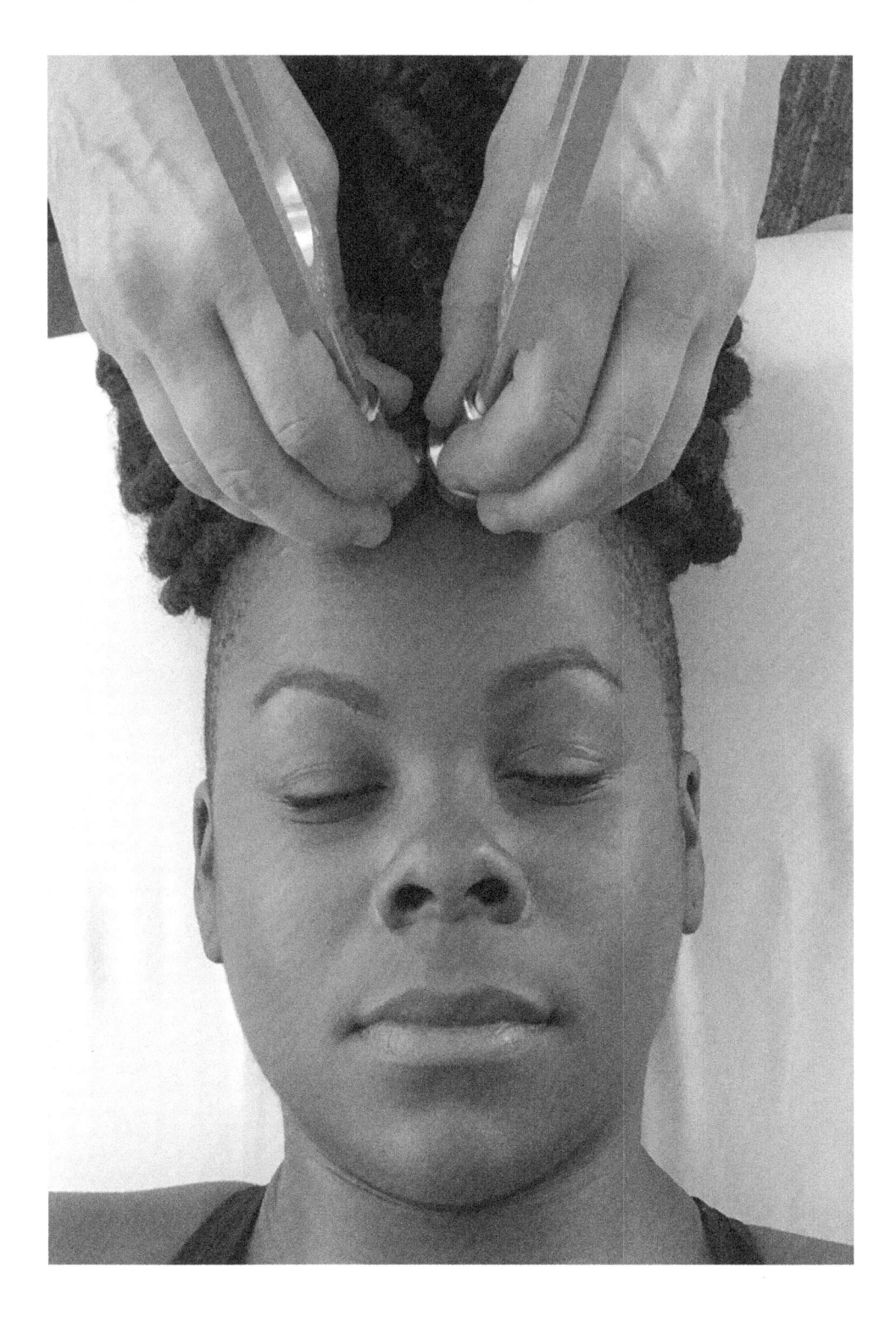

1-5b. Pause on both sides of the temples for a few beats.

1-6. Make gentle, clockwise circles on the temples (*NO PICTURE*)

1-7. Position both activated tuning forks at the midline of the forehead, 1½ inches below the hairline. Glide out to the temples and pause on both sides.

1-8. Make gentle, clockwise circles on the temples with activated tuning forks. (*NO picture*)

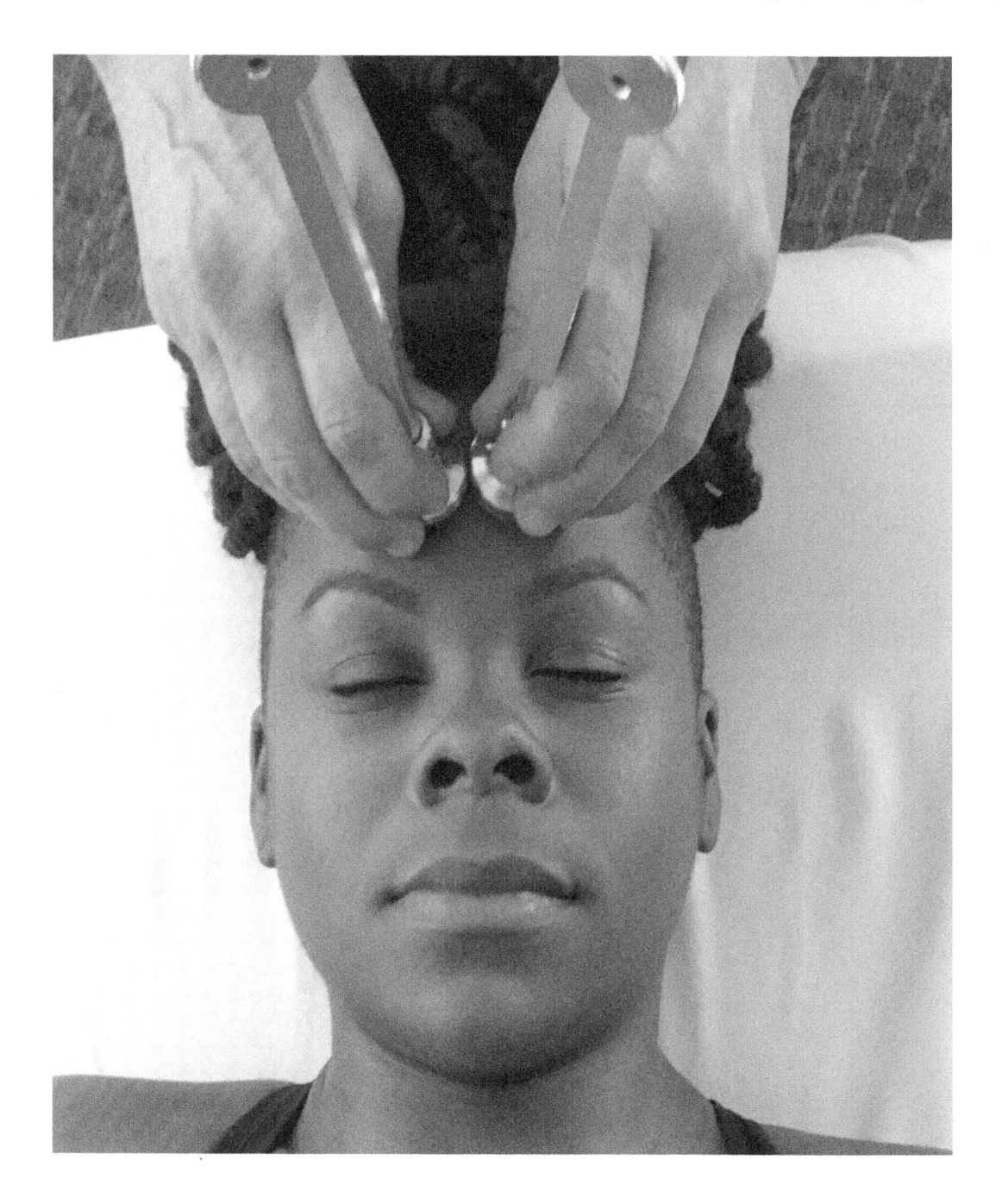

1-9a. Position both tuning forks between the eyebrows and lightly glide over them. Pause at the ends of the eyebrows (*Two pictures: 1-9a and 1-9b*)

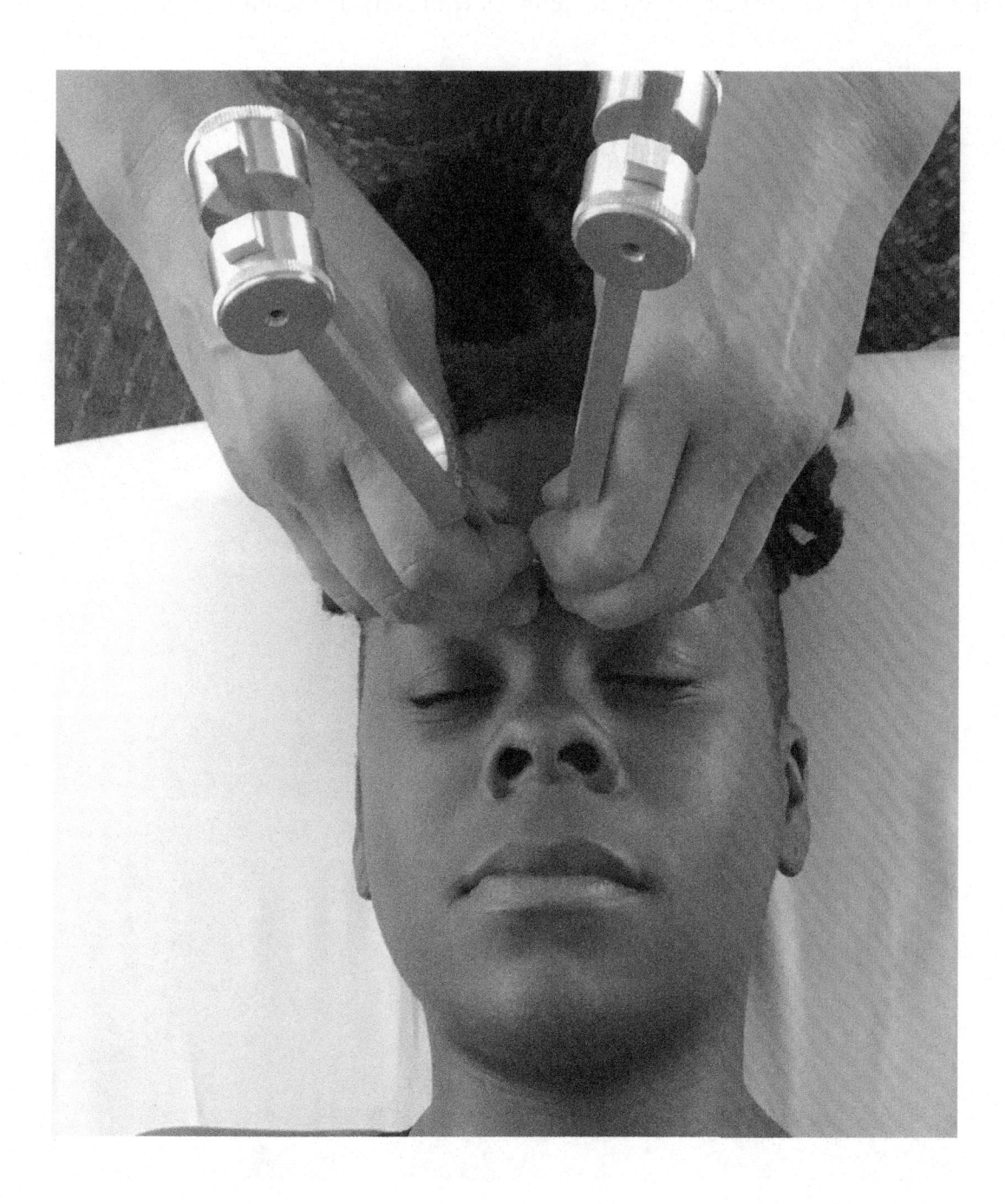

1-9b. Pause at the end of the eyebrows.

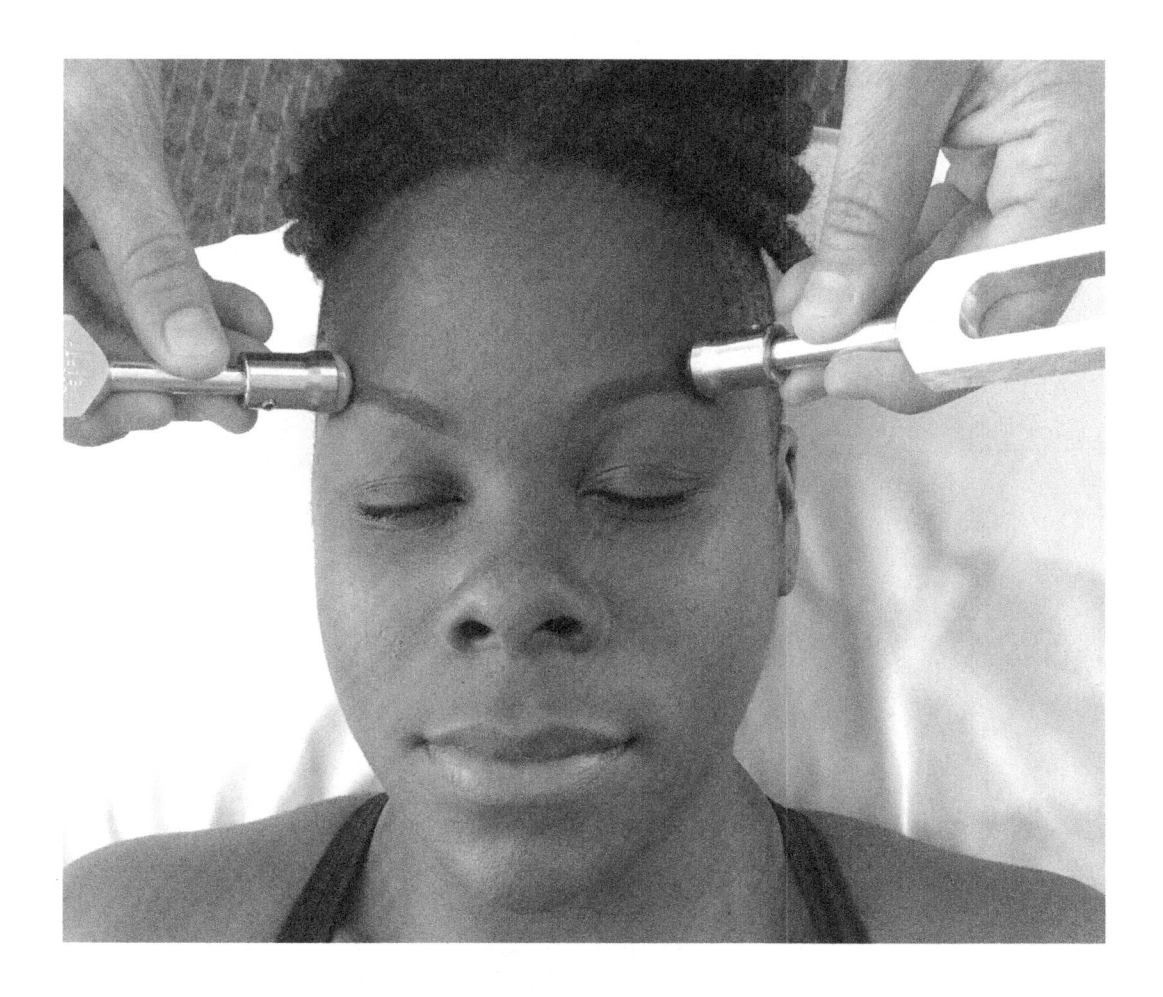

1-10a. Position both activated tuning forks on either side of the nose, just below the inside corners of the eyes. Glide down either side of the nose then just under the cheekbones and out to the temporal mandibular joint. Pause here for a beat or two.

(*Three pictures: 1-10a, 1-10b, 1-10c*)

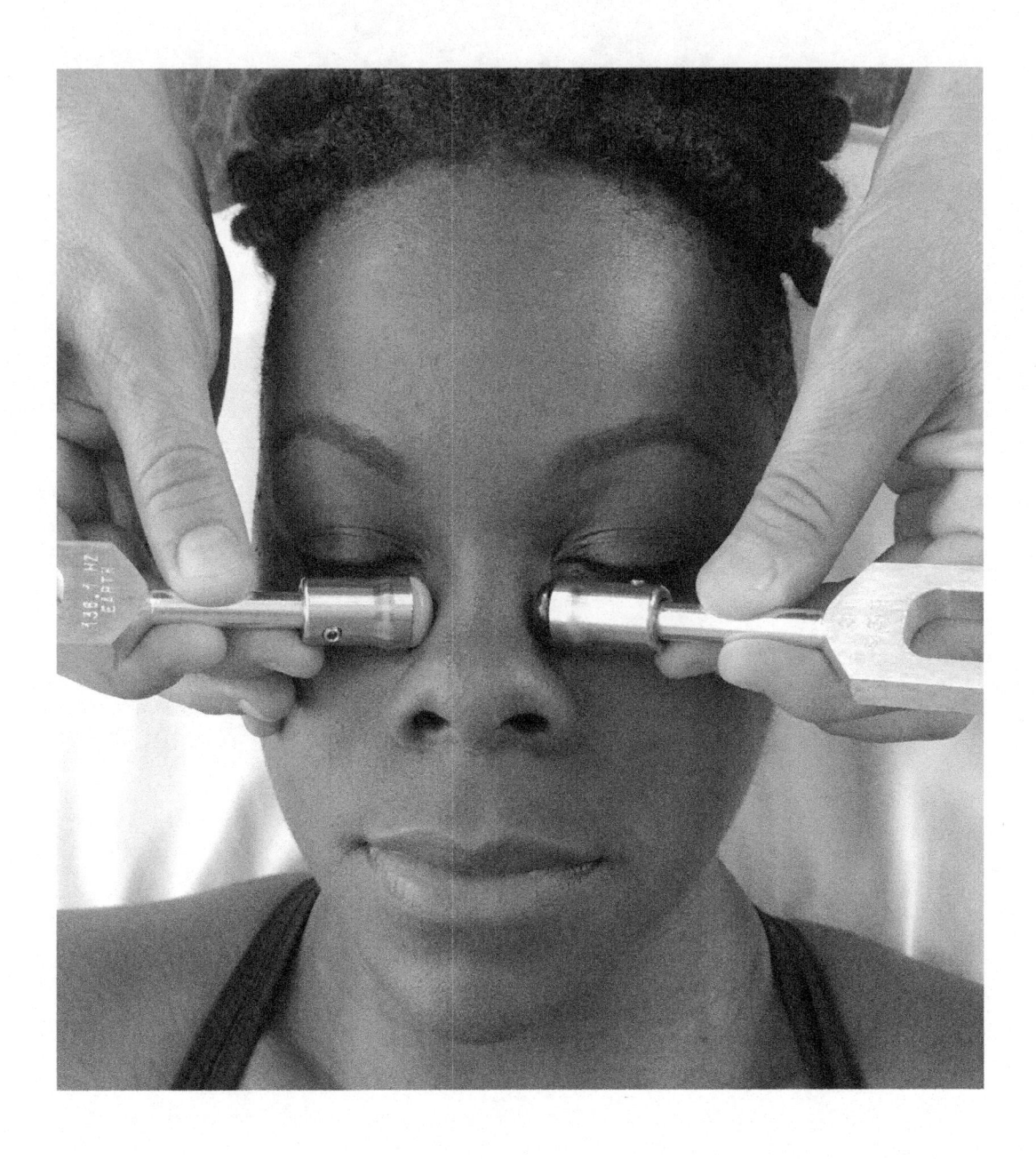

1-10b. Glide down either side of the nose then just under the cheekbones and out to the temporal mandibular joint. Reactivate the tuning forks if necessary.

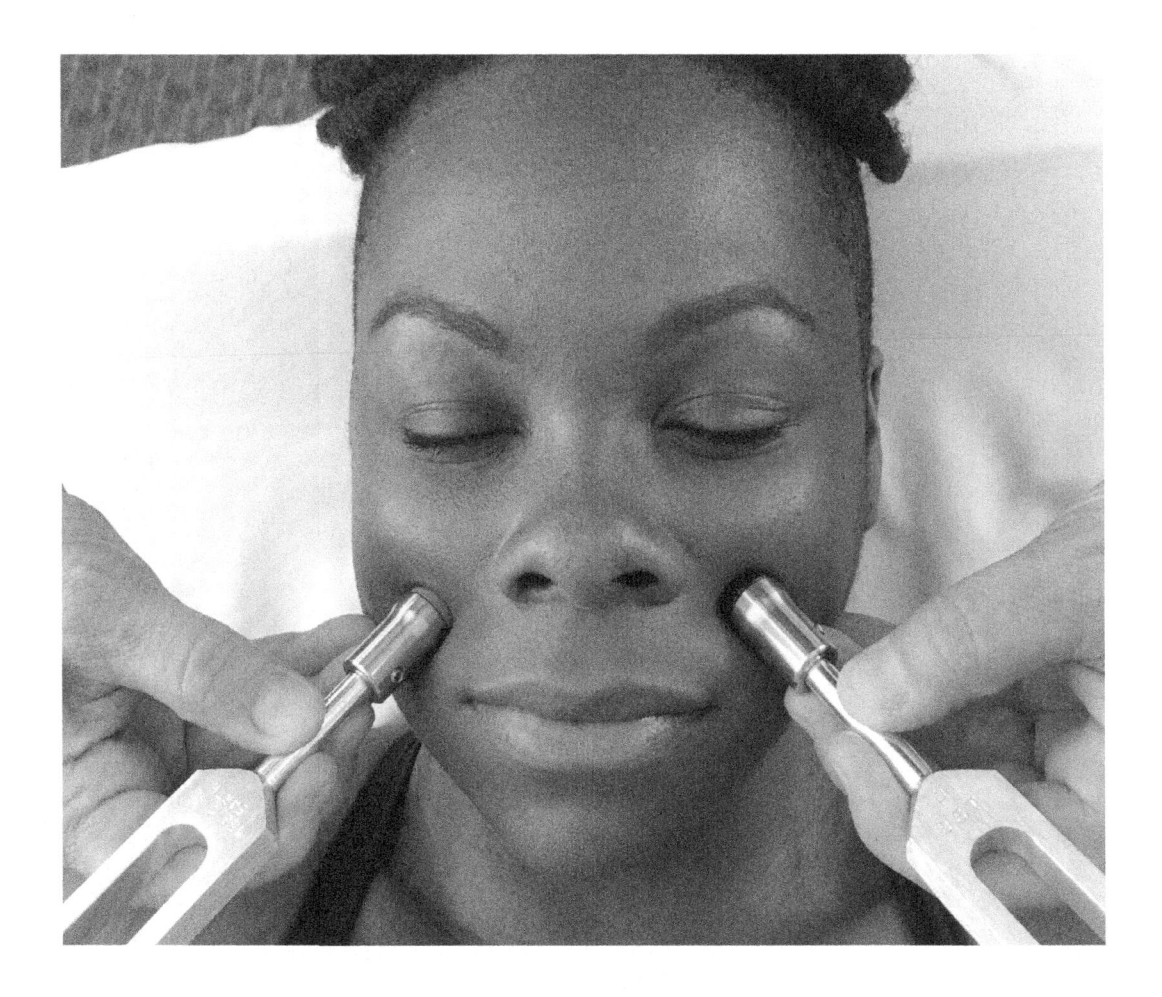

1-10c. Pause at temporal mandibular joint for a beat or two, with activated tuning forks.

1-11a. Position both activated tuning forks at the midline of the chin. Glide up either side of the jaw to the temporal mandibular joint. Pause there for a beat or two.

(*Two pictures: 1-11a and 1-11b*)

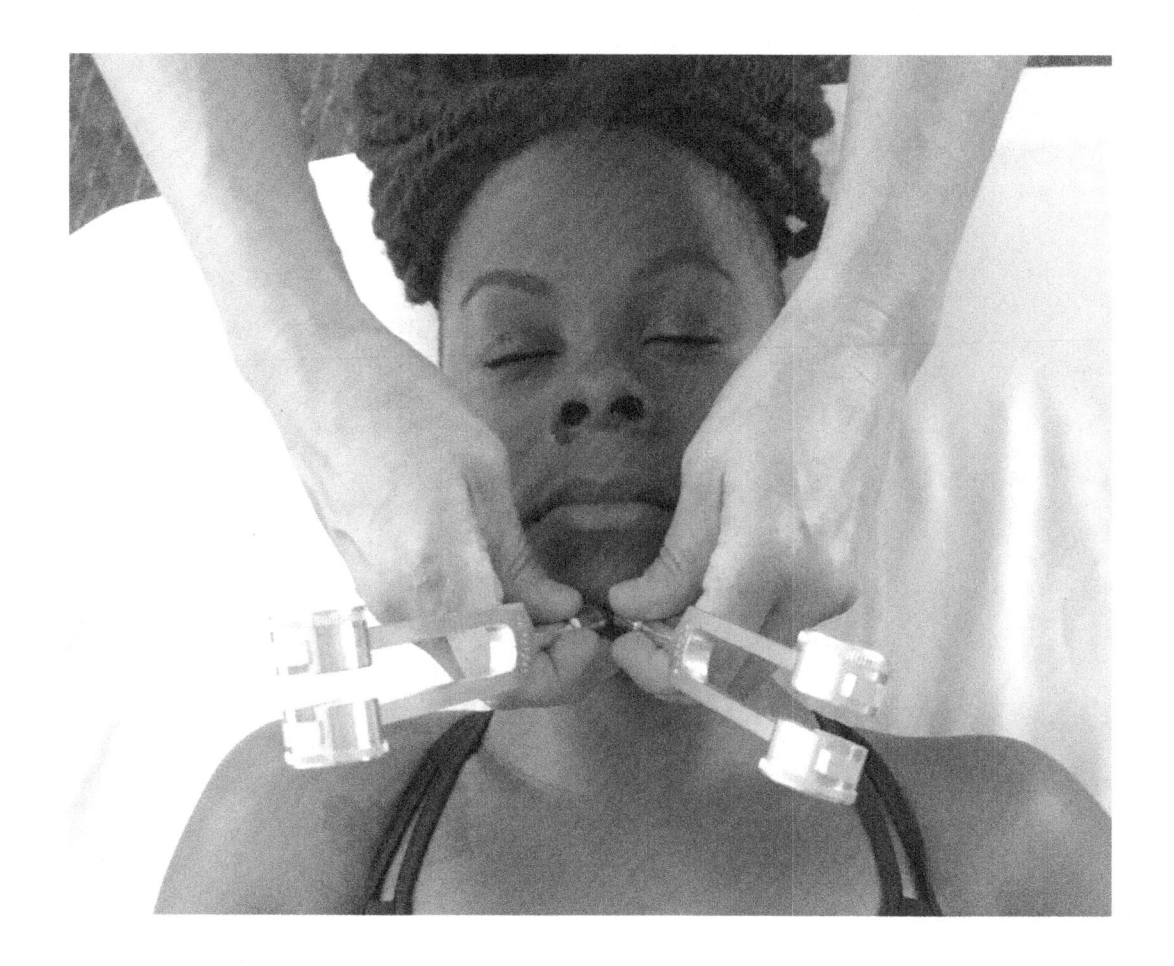

1-11b. Pause at temporal mandibular joint for a beat or two.

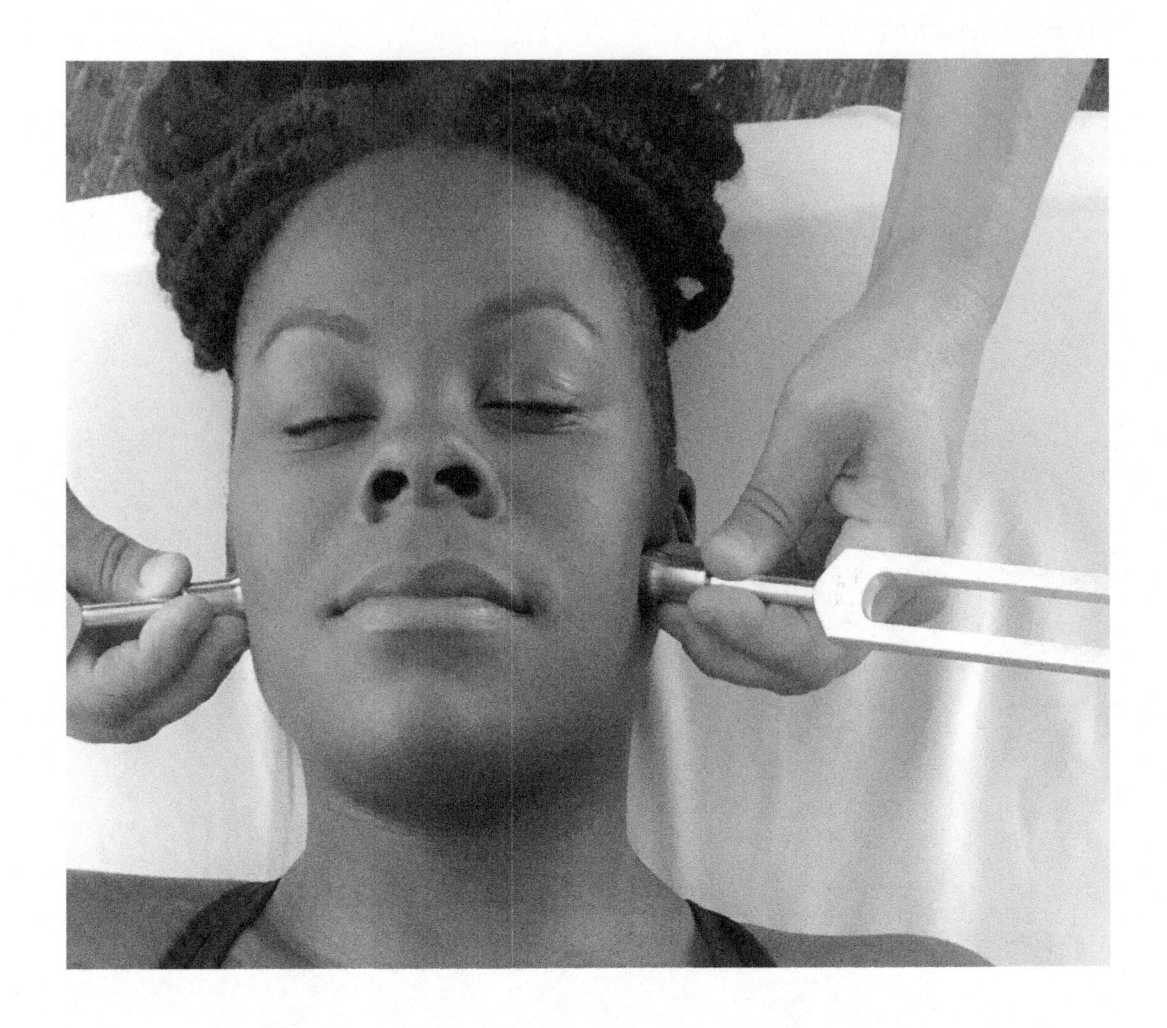

1-12a. Position both activated tuning fork ends, one at a time and gently, next to each other above the upper lip and just below the nose (specifically, the philtrum). Glide around the upper lip out towards ears. Pause at the corners of the mouth on either side.

(*Two pictures: 1-12a and 1-12b*)

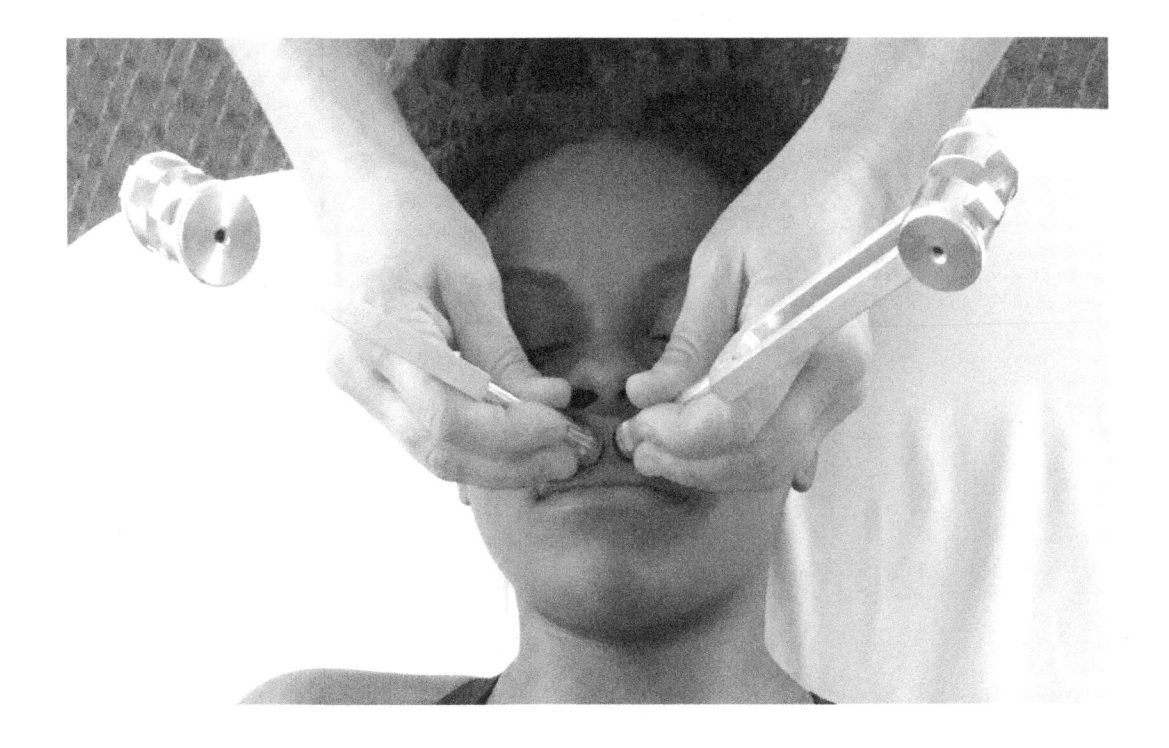

1-12b. Glide around the upper lip out towards ears. Pause at the corners of the mouth on either side.

1-13a. Position both activated tuning fork ends next to each other below the lower lip. Glide around the lower lip out towards the ears. Pause at, or before, the corners of the mouth on either side. *(Two pictures: 1-13a and 1-13b)*

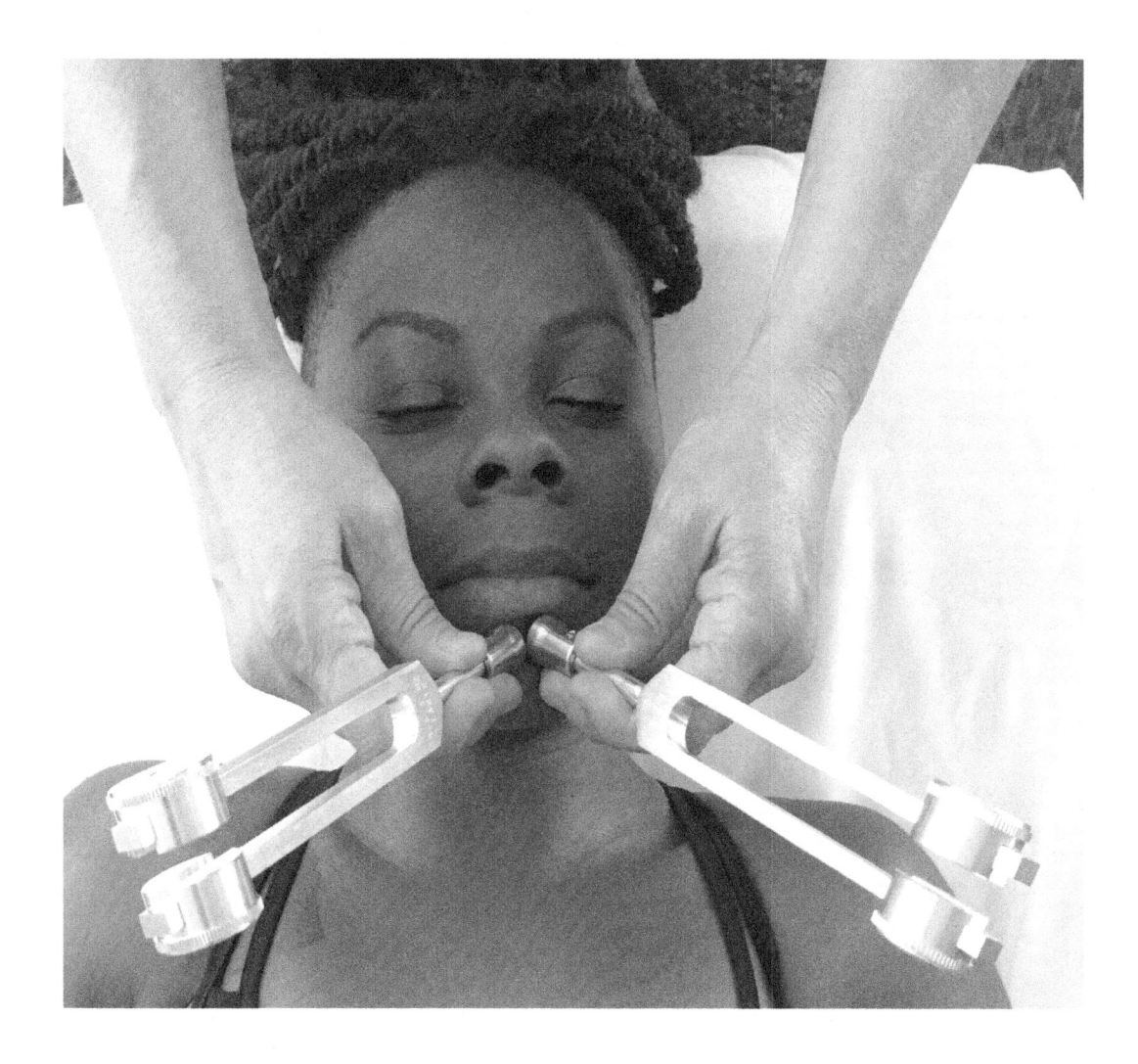

1-13b. Pause at, or before, the corners of the mouth on either side.

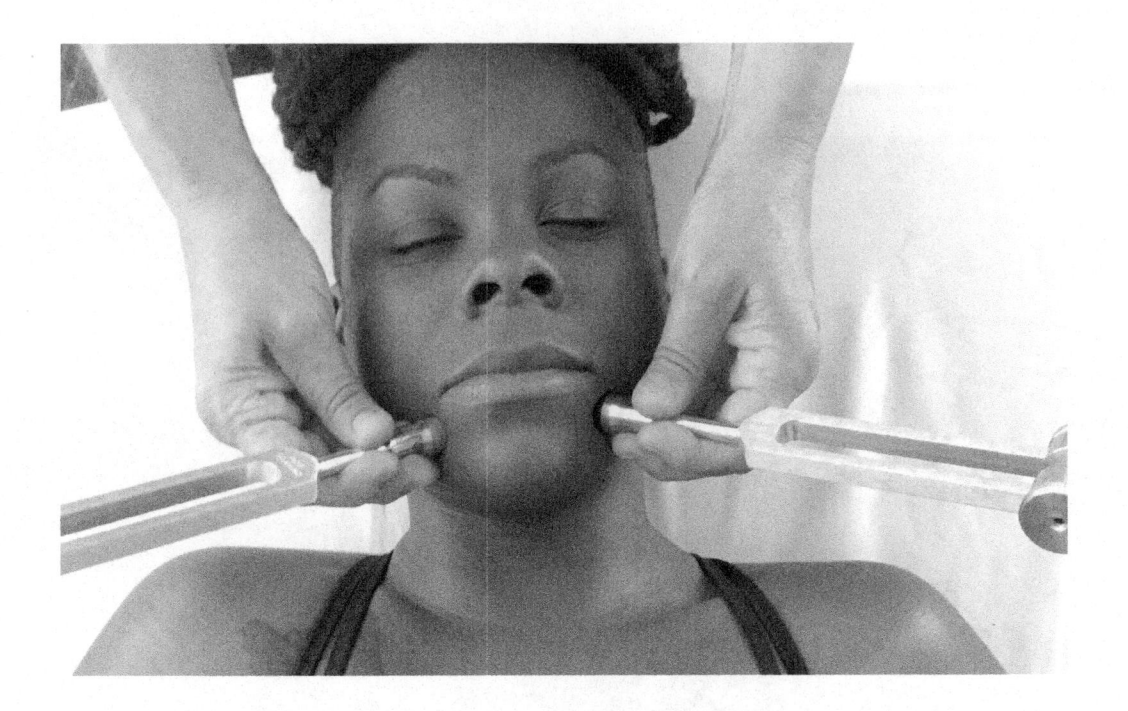

2. Protocol for Head/Neck (prone)

2-1. Position one activated tuning fork end on top of the head and the other activated tuning fork end on the sacrum.

2-2. Position the activated tuning forks on either side of the head (above and just forward of the ears). This creates a beat frequency. It brings awareness to vibration and flow in the body. Plus it's super relaxing. Repeat this a few times.

2-3. Position both activated tuning forks in the midline of the occipital ridge. Slowly glide out to the sides. Pause on either side for a moment or two. (*Two pictures: 2-3a and 2-3b*)

2-4. Move down the neck 1 inch or so at a time and glide from the midline to the sides of the neck. Pause on either side. (*Two pictures: 2-4a and 2-4b*)

2-5. Move down the neck another 1 inch or so and repeat this until reaching C7.

2-6. Position one activated tuning fork in the midline of the occipital ridge and the other on C7.

2-7. Glide over the top of the trapezius muscle with activated tuning forks. Continue along the trapezius until reaching the shoulder. (*Two pictures: 2-7a and 2-7b*)

2-1. Position one activated tuning fork end on top of the head and the other activated tuning fork end on the sacrum.

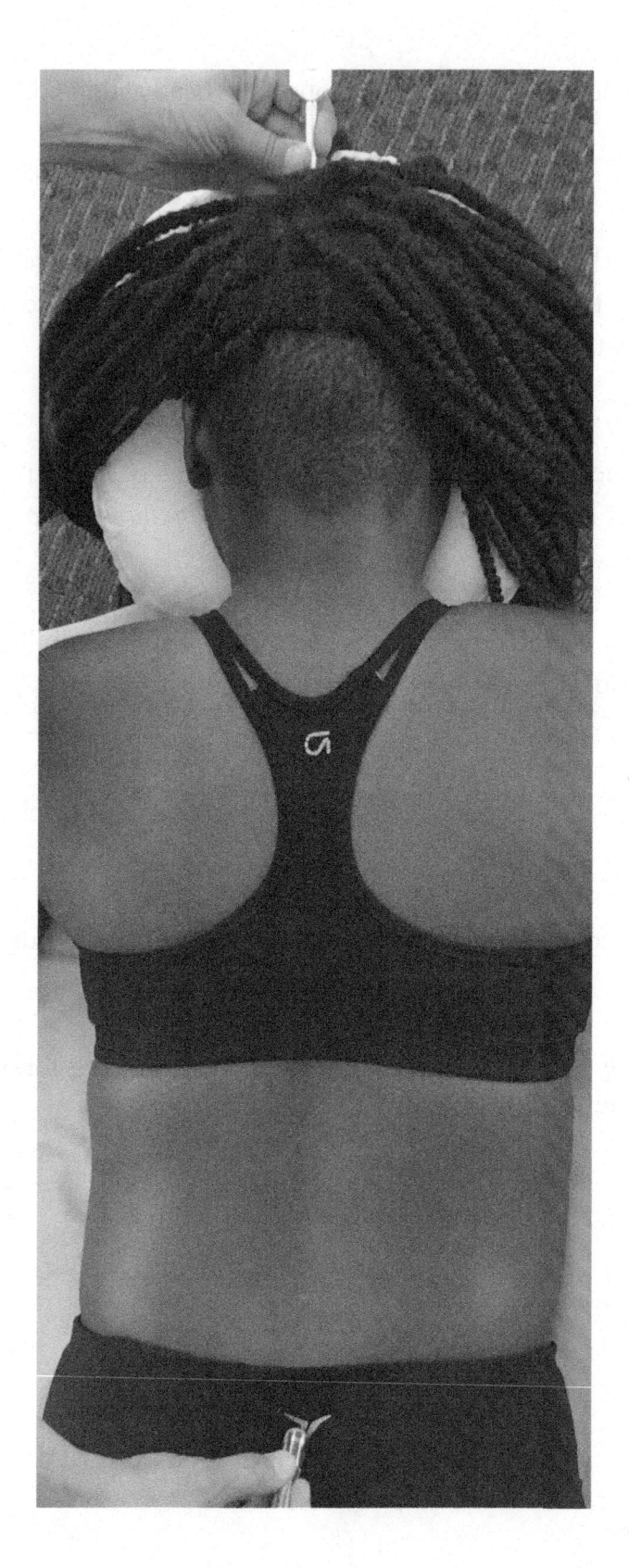

2-2. Position the activated tuning forks on either side of the head (above and just forward of the ears). This creates a beat frequency. It brings awareness to vibration and flow in the body. Plus it's super relaxing. Repeat this a few times.

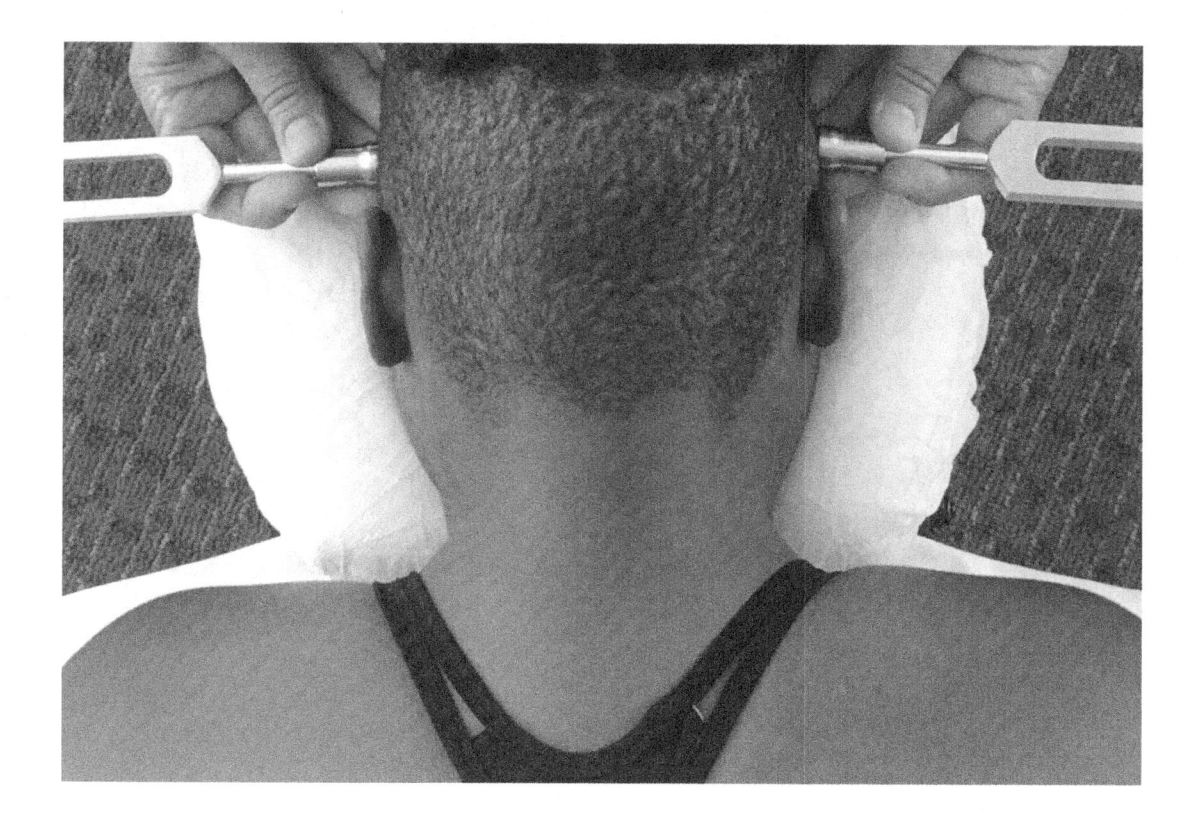

2-3a. Position both activated tuning forks in the midline of the occipital ridge. Slowly glide out to the sides. (*Two pictures: 2-3a and 2-3b*)

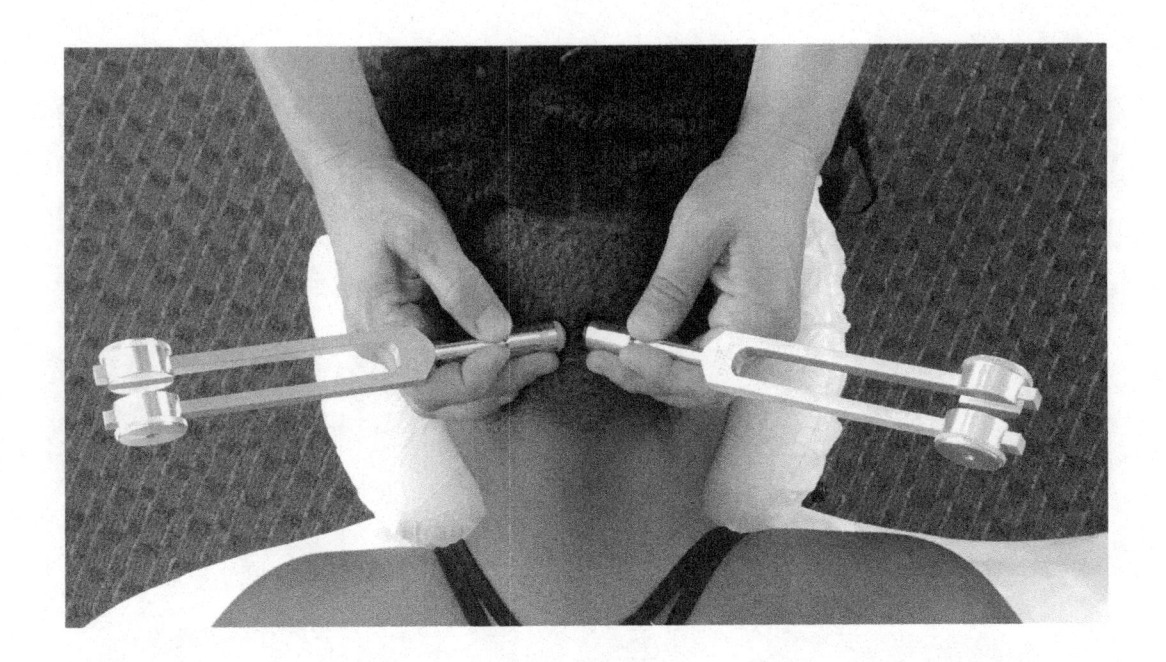

2-3b. Reactivate the tuning forks and pause on either side of occiput for a moment or two.

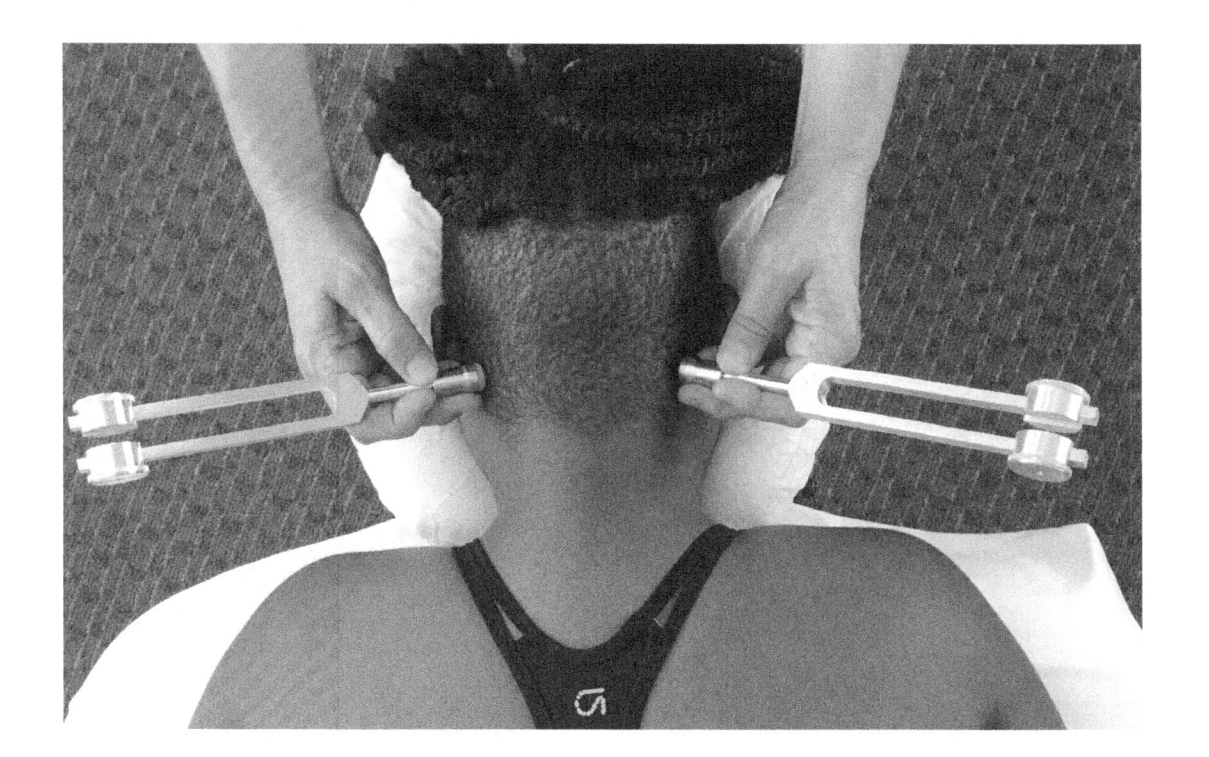

2-4a. Move down the neck 1 inch or so at a time and glide from the midline to the sides of the neck (*Two pictures: 2-4a and 2-4b*)

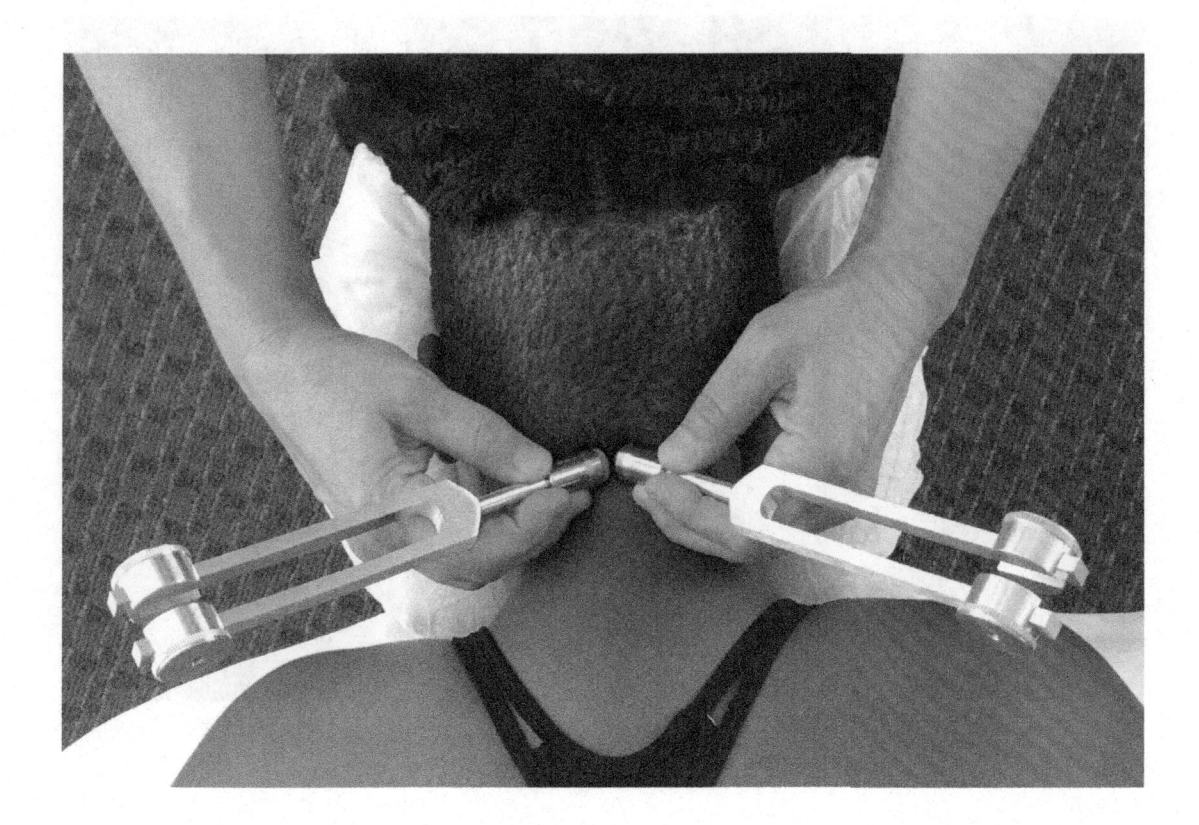

2-4b. Pause on either side of the neck.

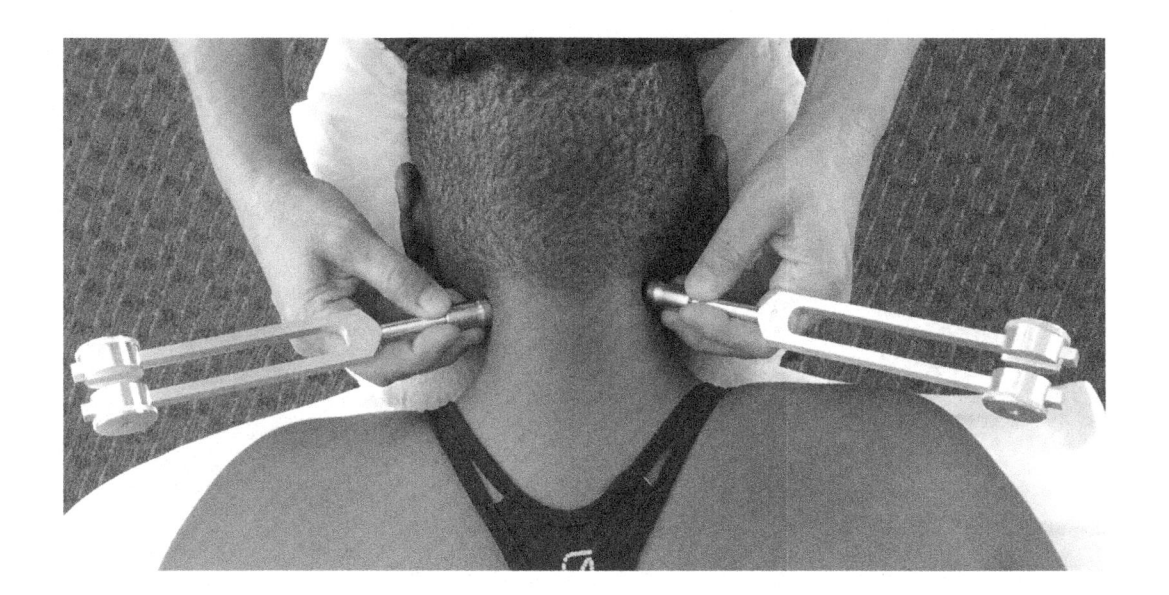

2-5. Move down the neck another 1 inch or so and repeat this until reaching C7.

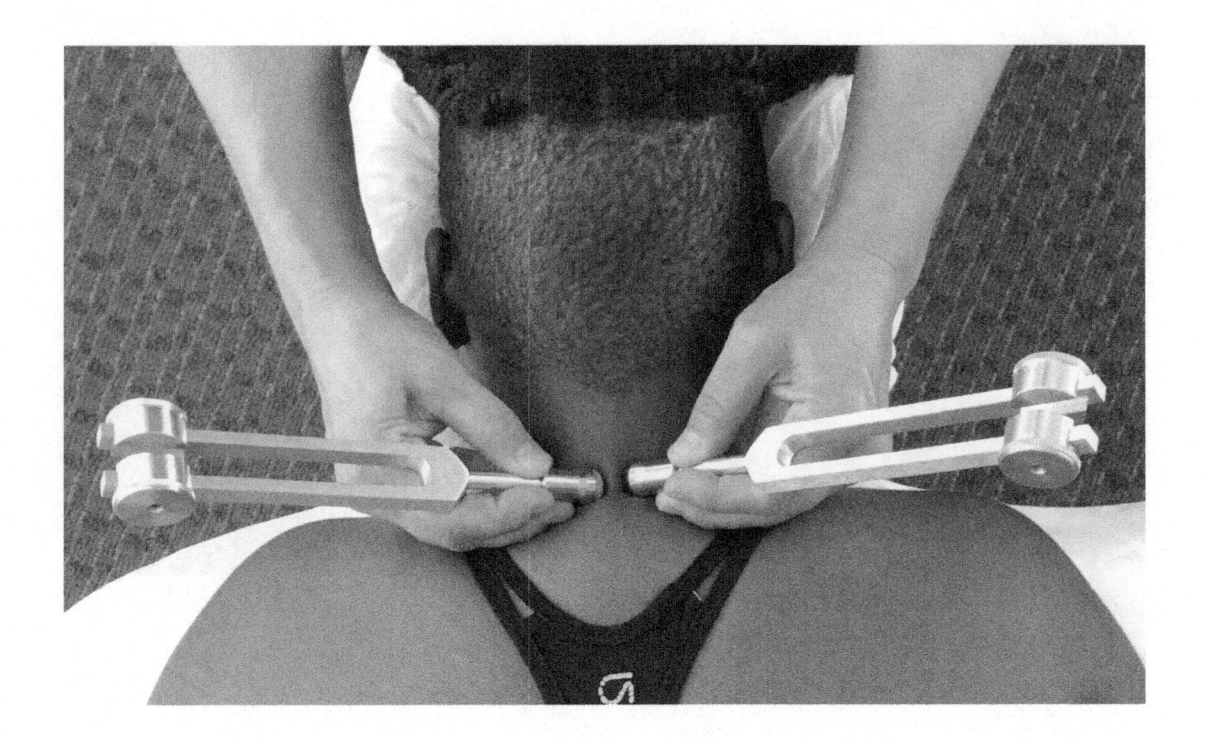

2-6. Position one activated tuning fork in the midline of the occipital ridge and the other activated tuning fork on C7.

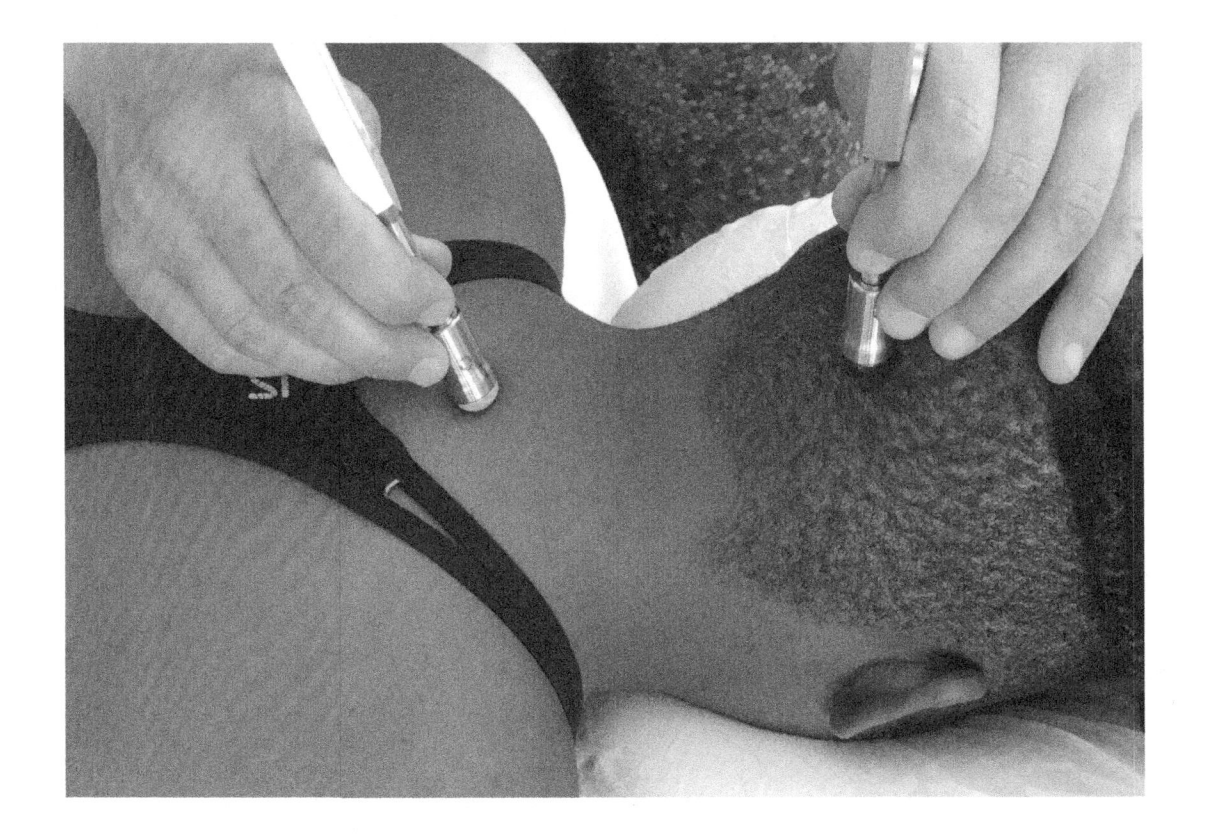

2-7a. Glide over the top of the trapezius muscle with activated tuning forks.

(*Two pictures: 2-7a and 2-7b*)

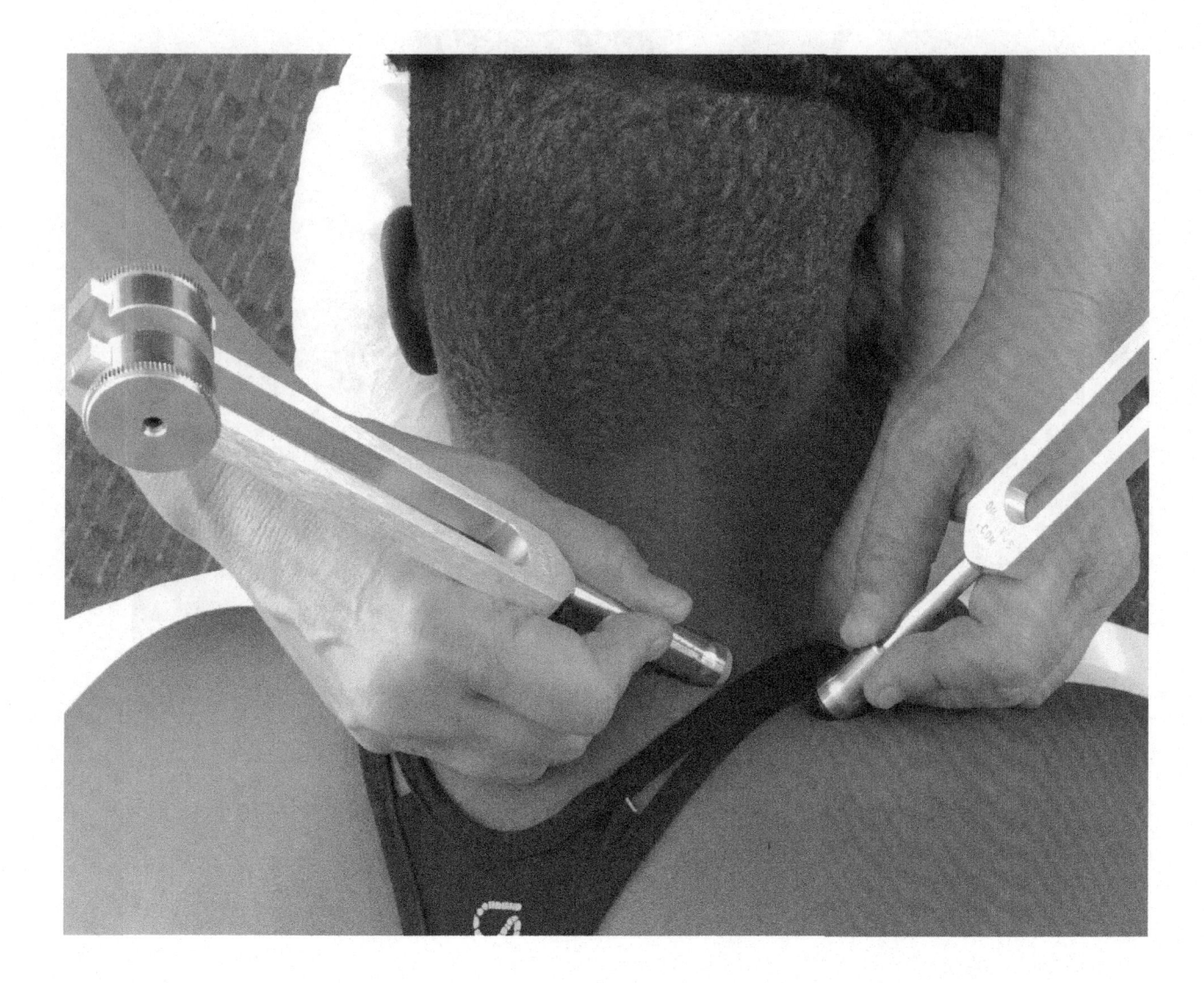

2-7b. Reactivate the tuning forks and continue along trapezius until reaching the shoulder.

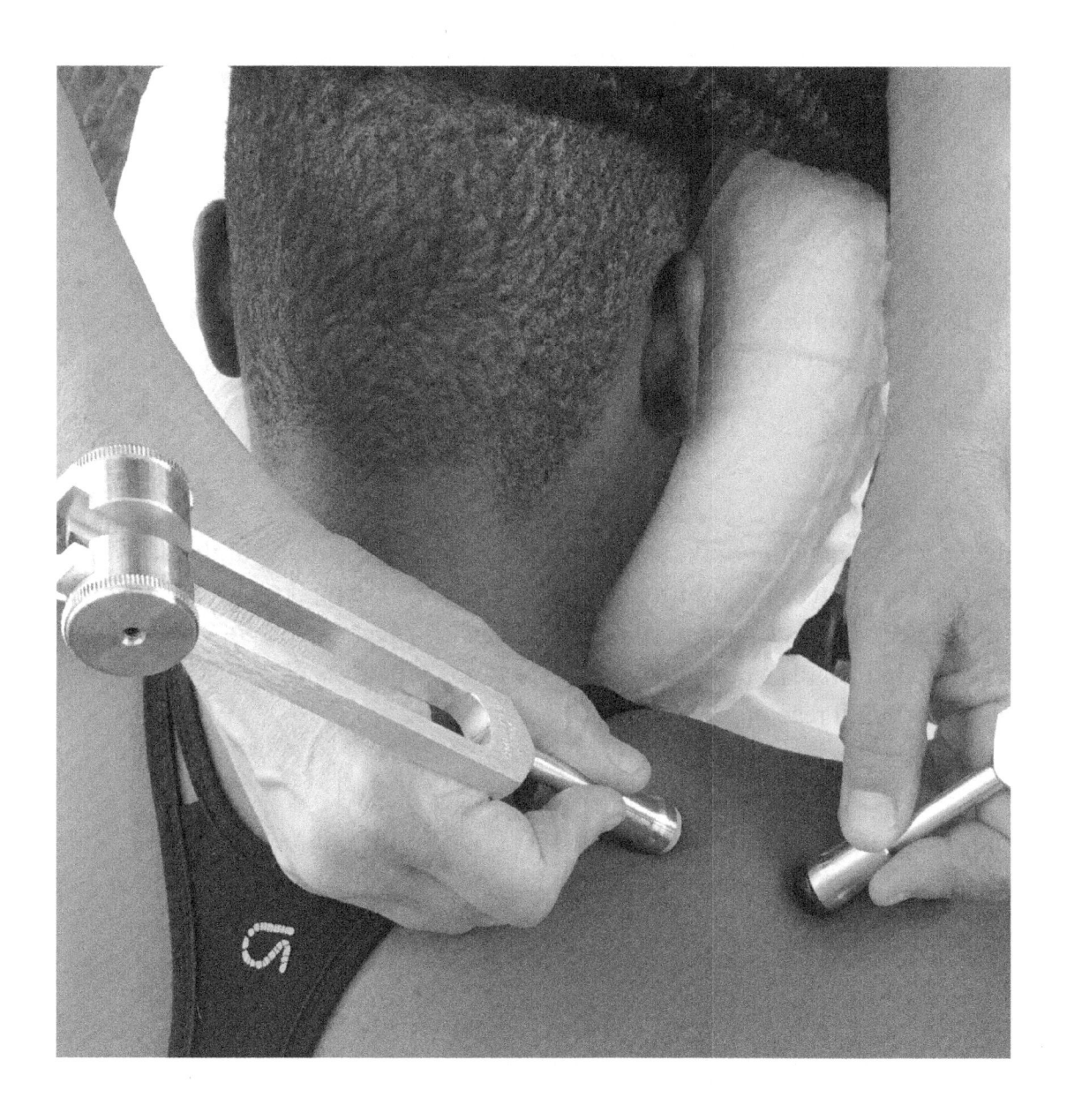

3. **Protocol for Neck (supine)**

3-1. Position the activated tuning forks just under the sternocleidomastoid (SCM) muscle. Glide from the mastoid process down to the collarbone. Proceed gently in this area.

(Two pictures: 3-1a and 3-2b)

3-2. Pinch the SCM gently between two activated tuning forks starting just below the mastoid process Release then move down 1 inch or so and repeat until close to the collarbone.

(Two pictures: 3-2a and 3-2b)

3-3. Angle the activated tuning forks so that the ends are on the midline of the occipital ridge and slowly glide out to the sides of neck. (Depending on the client, it may be difficult to locate the back of the neck from a supine position). Begin again 1 inch or so below the starting point and glide out again towards side of the neck. Repeat this process each time 1 inch or so below where you left off until reaching C6/C7.

3-4. Position the activated tuning fork ends ABOVE the midline of the collarbone. Glide out towards the shoulders to the lung points. Pause here for a few moments.

(Two pictures: 3-4a and 3-4b)

3-5. Position the activated tuning fork ends BELOW the midline of the collarbone. Glide out towards the shoulders to the lung points. Pause here for a few moments.

3-6. Position an activated tuning fork end on either side of the base of the neck and glide or walk, point by point, the activated fork ends over the trapezius muscle. End with an activated tuning fork on the back of the shoulder. An activated tuning fork can also be applied to the front of the shoulder joint at the same time. *(Two pictures: 3-6a and 3-6b)*

3-1a. Position the activated tuning forks just under the sternocleidomastoid (SCM) muscle.

(Two pictures: 3-1a and 3-2b)

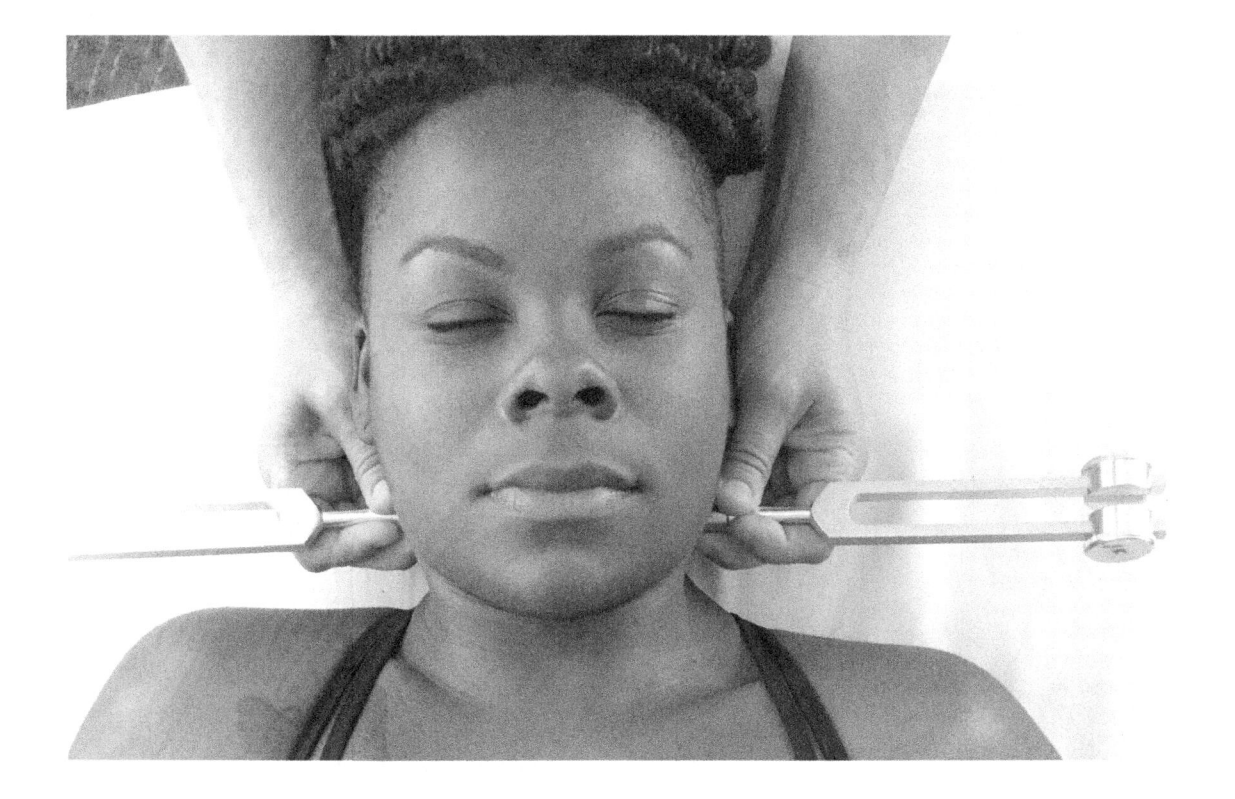

3-1b. Glide from the mastoid process down to the collarbone. Proceed gently in this area.

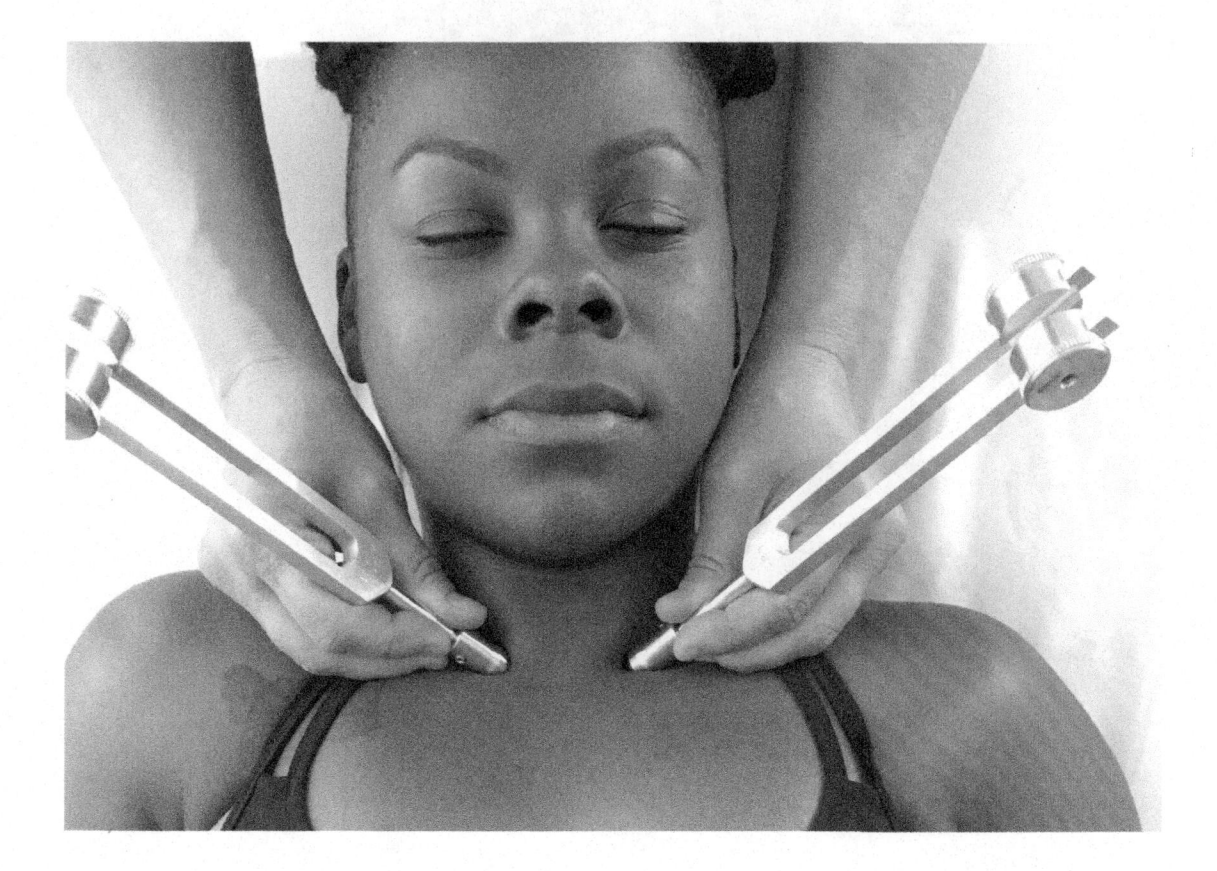

3-2a. Gently pinch the SCM between two tuning forks, starting just below the mastoid process. Release then move down 1 inch or so and repeating until close to the collarbone.

(Two pictures: 3-2a and 3-2b)

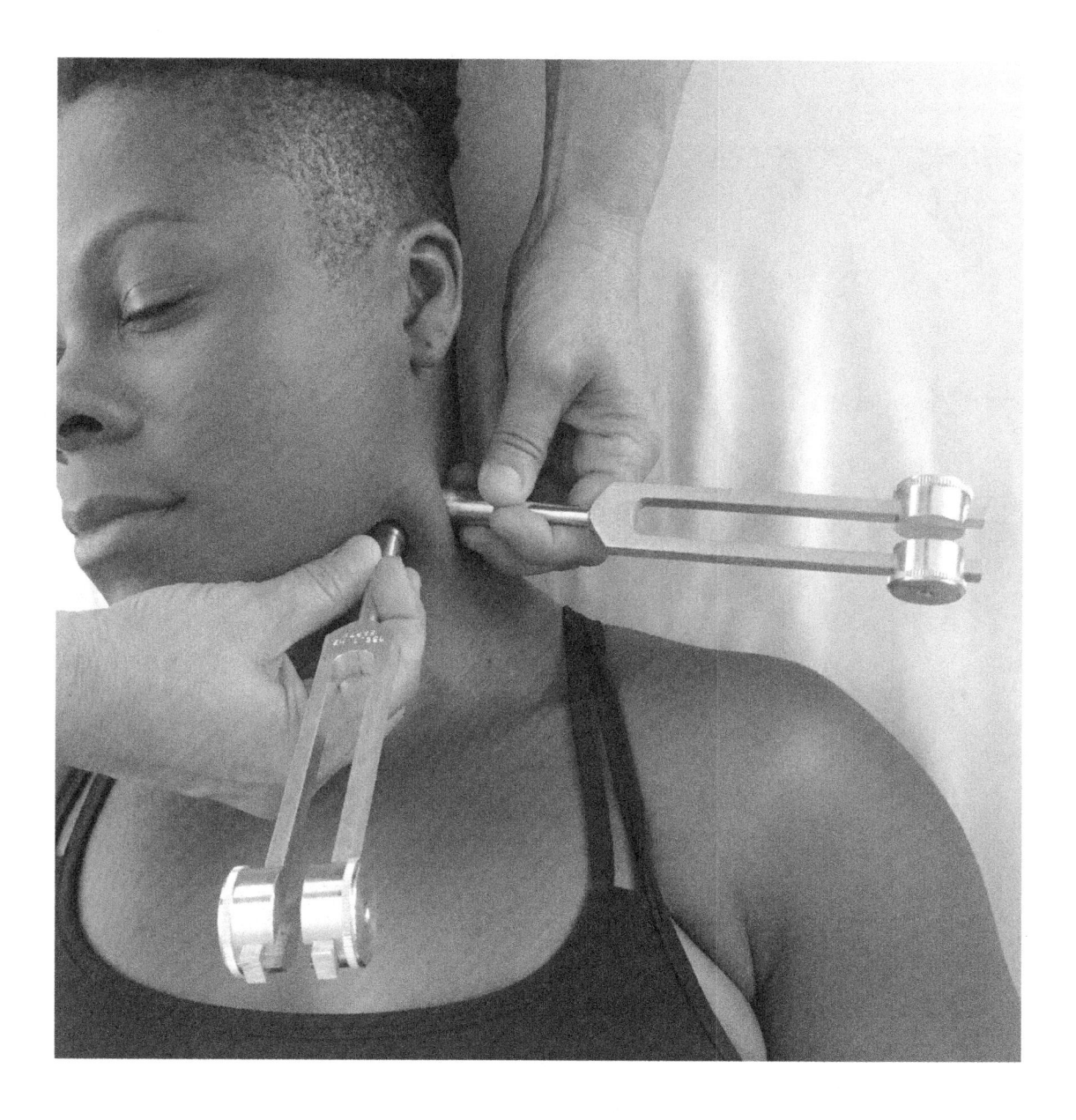

3-2b. Pause here for a few beats.

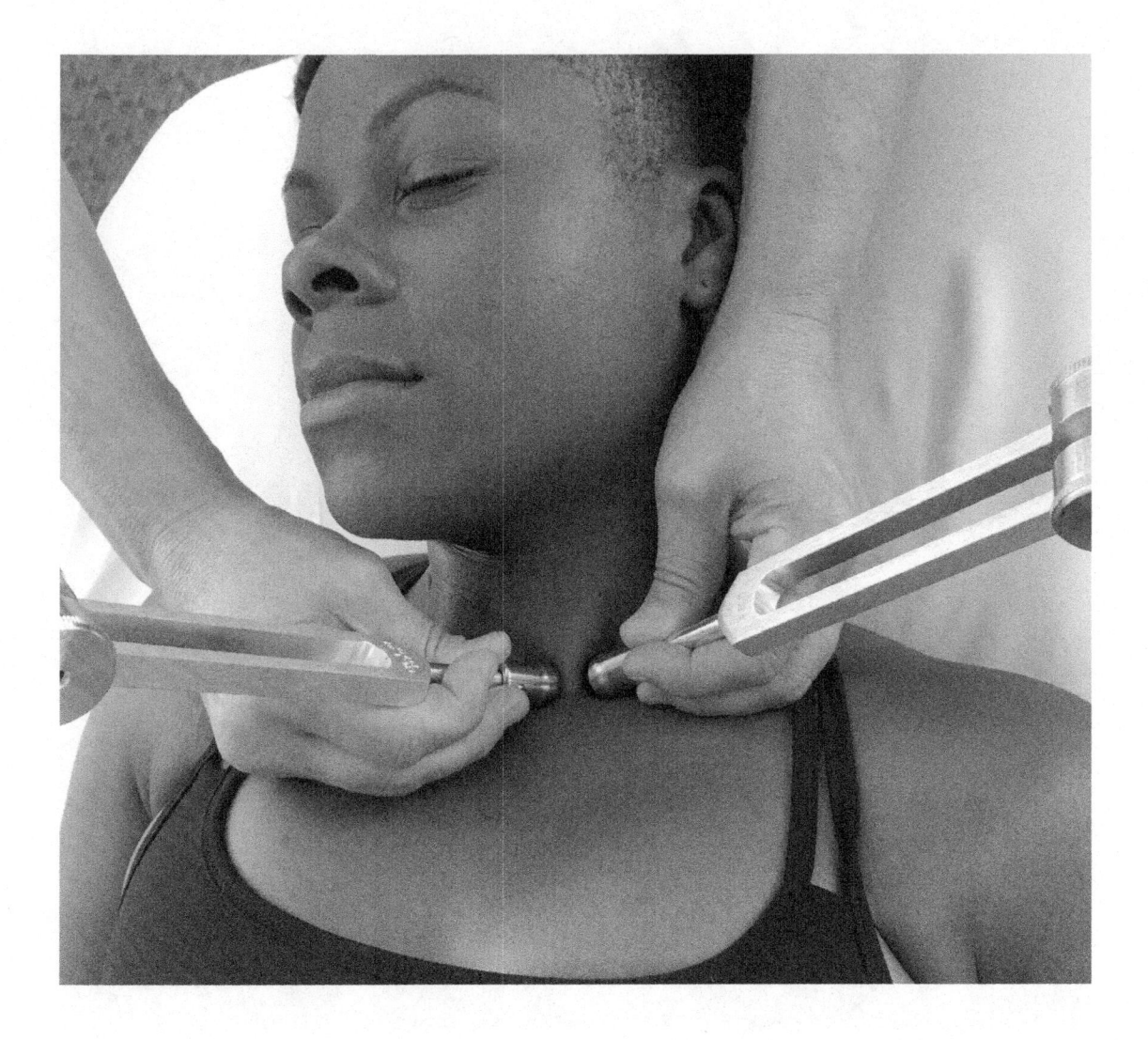

3-3. Angle the activated tuning forks so that the ends are on the midline of the occipital ridge and slowly glide out to the sides of neck. (Depending on the client, it may be difficult to locate the back of the neck from a supine position). Begin again 1 inch or so below the starting point and glide out again towards side of the neck. Repeat this process each time 1 inch or so below where you left off until reaching C6/C7.

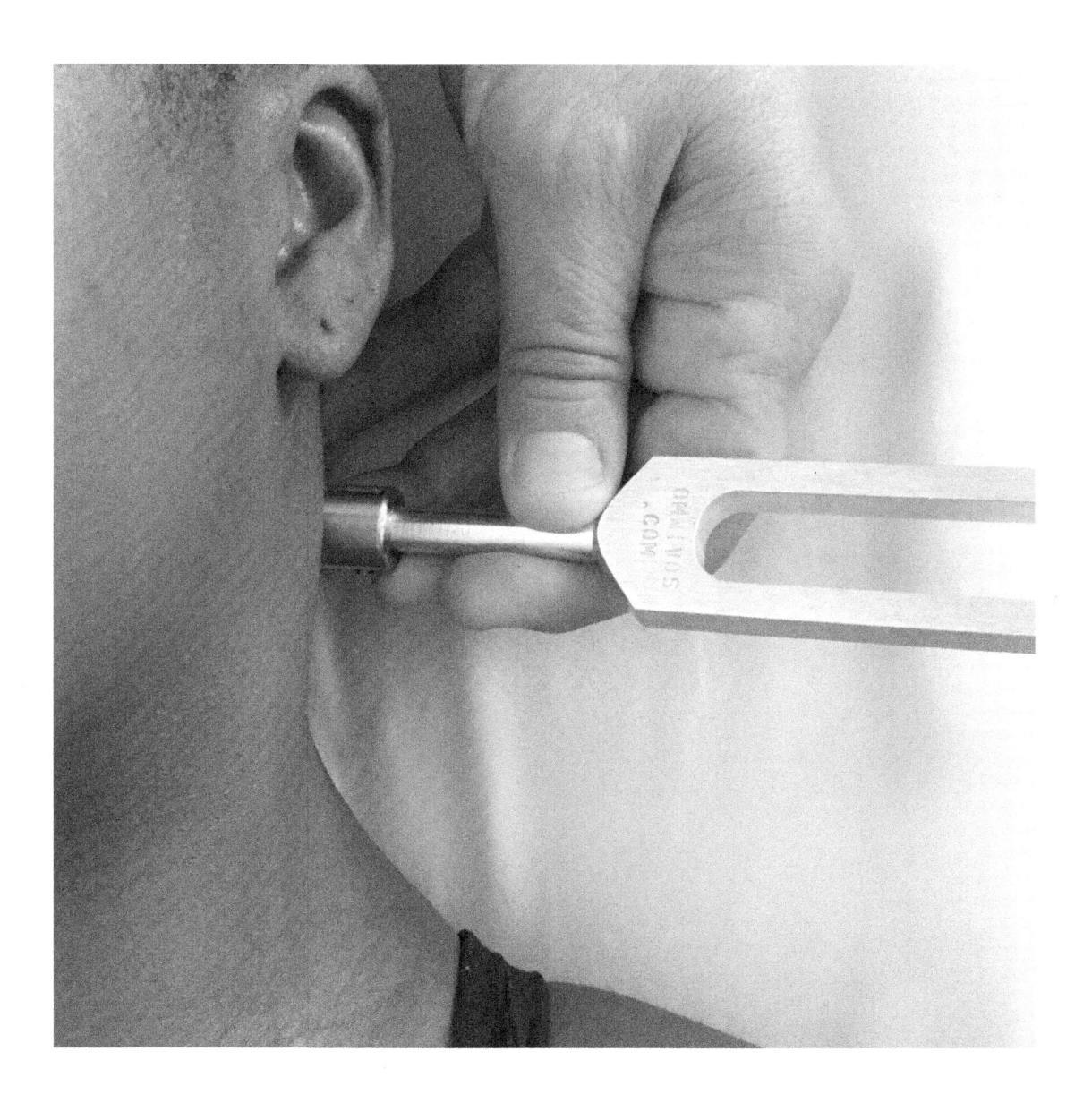

3-4a. Position the activated tuning fork ends ABOVE the midline of the collarbone. Glide out towards the shoulders. *(Two pictures: 3-4a and 3-4b)*

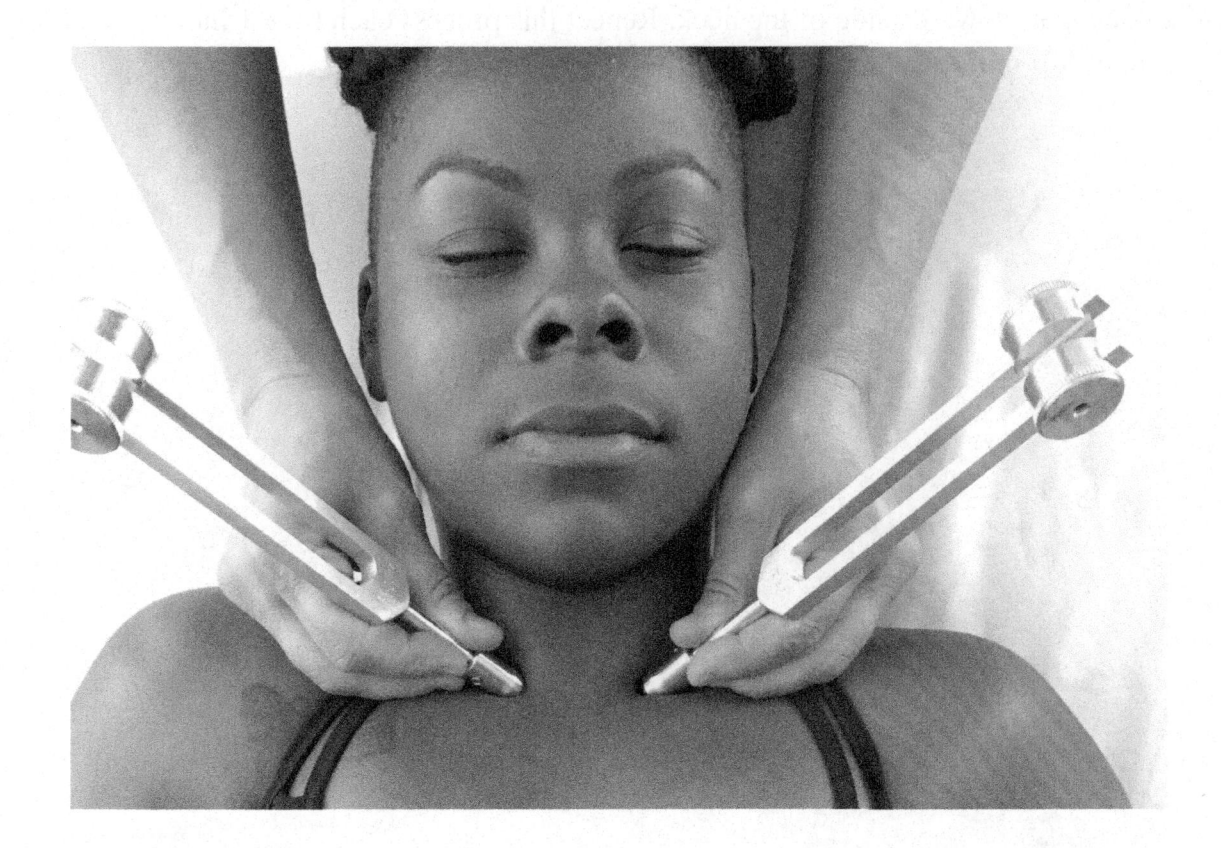

3-4b. Pause for a few beats on the lung points.

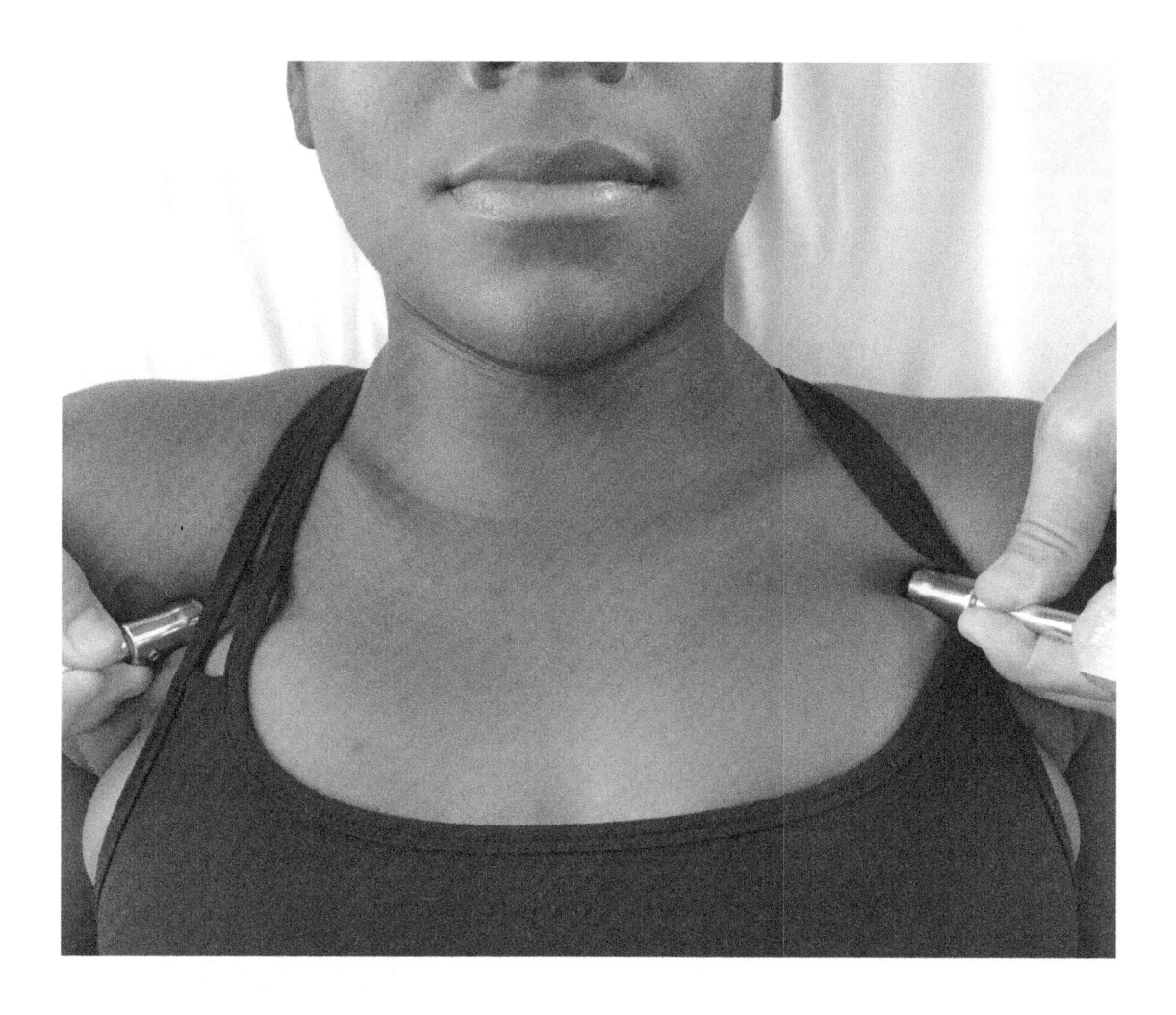

3-5. Position the activated tuning fork ends BELOW the midline of the collarbone. Glide out towards the shoulders to the lung points. Pause for a few beats on the lung points.

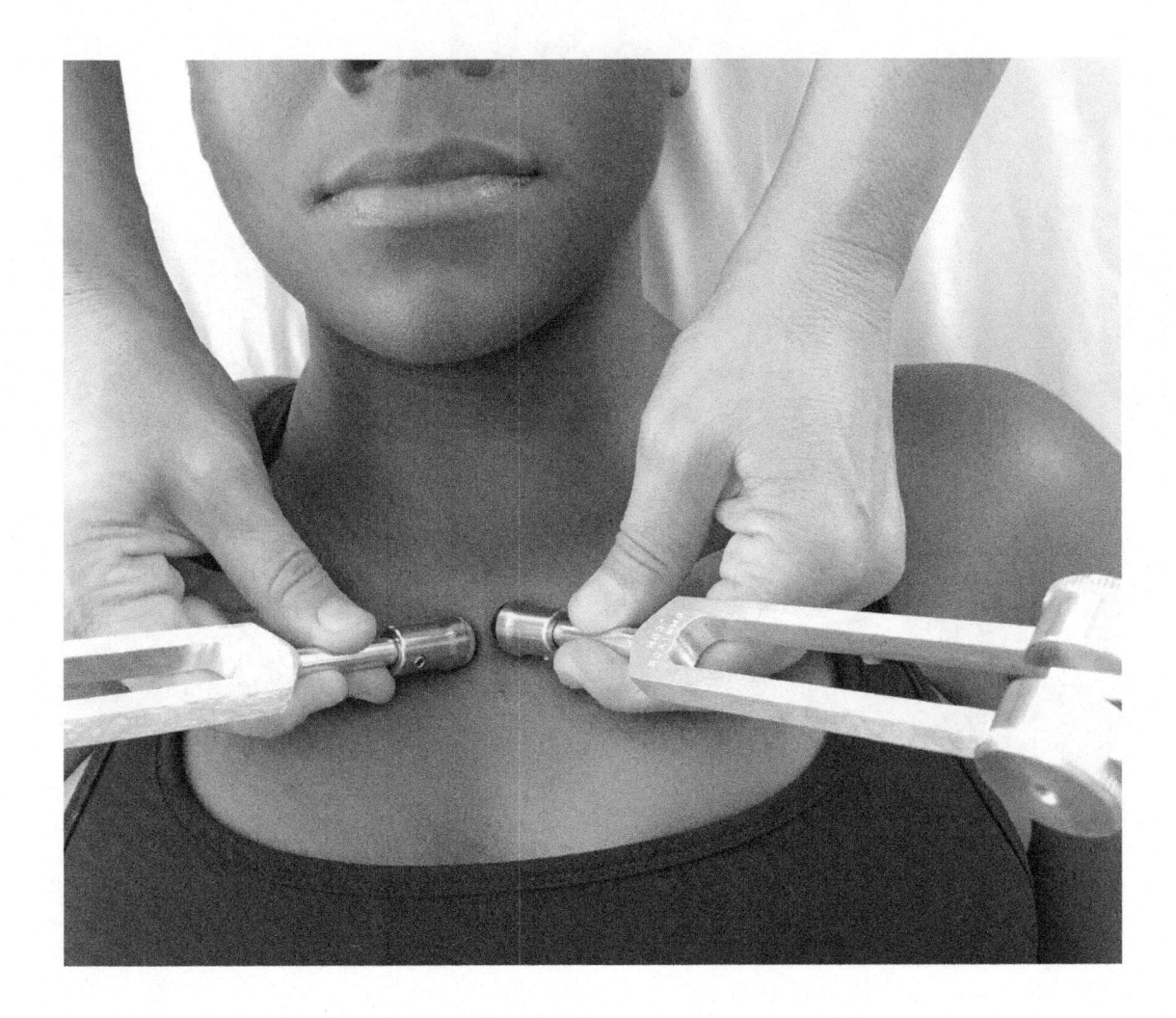

3-6a. Position an activated tuning fork end on either side of the base of the neck and glide or walk, point by point, the activated tuning fork ends over the trapezius muscle.

(Two pictures: 3-6a and 3-6b)

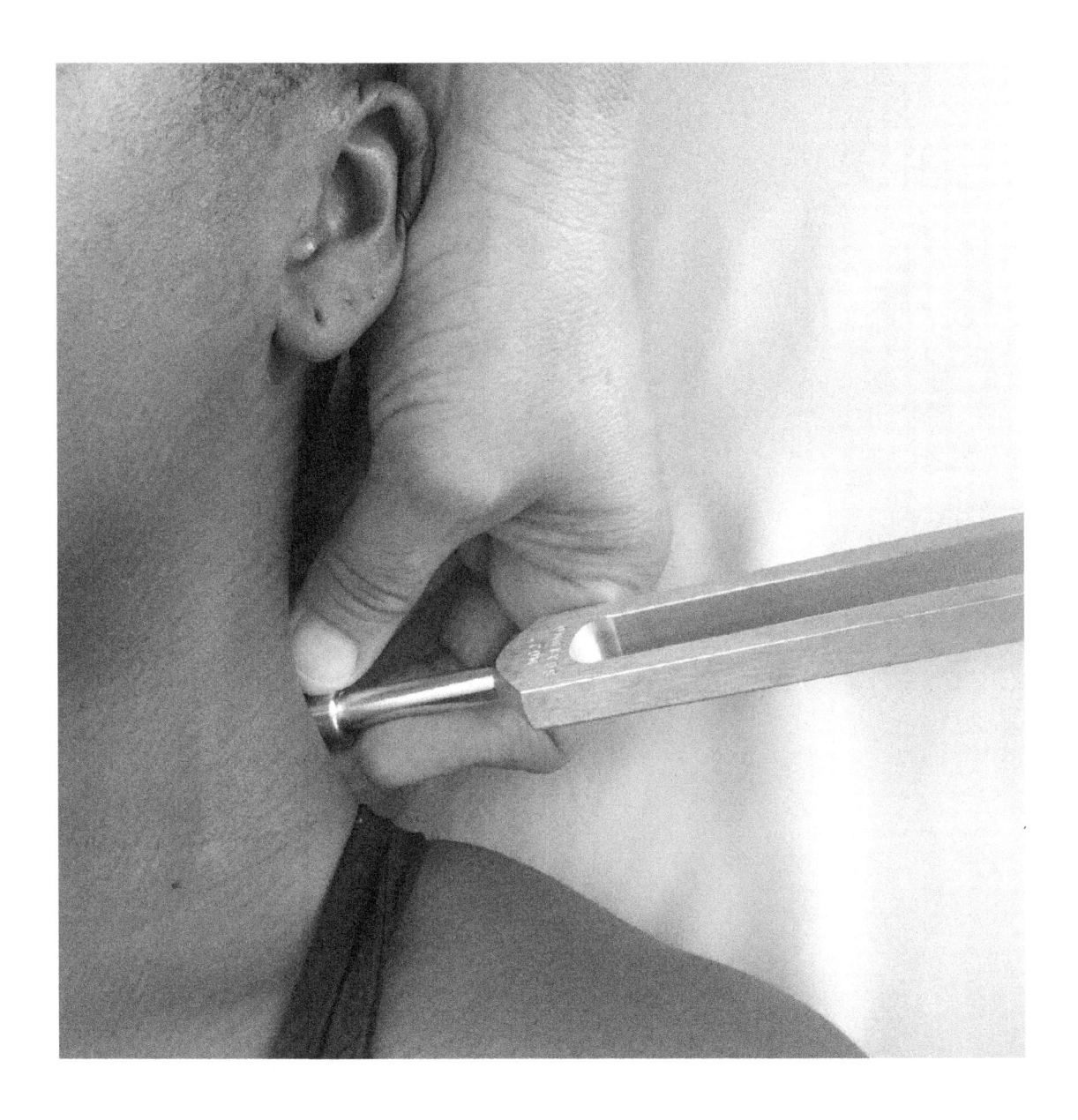

3-6b. End with an activated tuning fork on the back of the shoulder. An activated tuning fork can also be applied to the front of the shoulder joint at the same time.

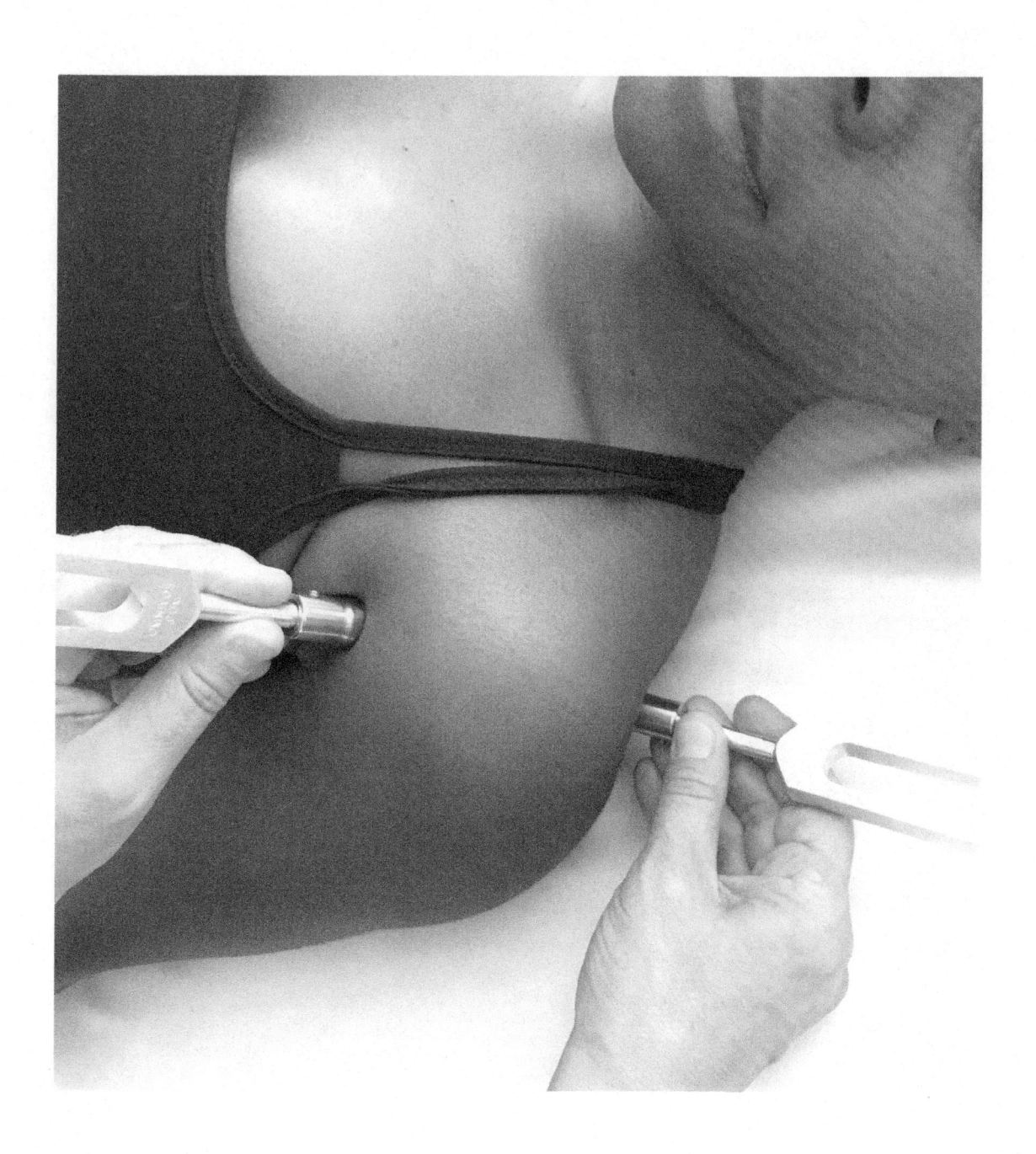

4. **Protocol for Neck (prone)**

4-1. Position both activated tuning fork ends on the midline of the occipital ridge. Glide along the occipital ridge from the midline to the sides of the occiput. Pause on either side of the occiput. *(Two pictures: 4-1a and 4-1b)*

4-2. Position both activated tuning fork ends about 1 inch or so below the starting point and glide out again towards sides of the neck. Repeat this process about 1 inch below where you left off until reaching the base of the neck (C6/C7). *(Two pictures: 4-2a and 4-2b)*

4-3. Walk or glide the activated tuning fork ends down the cervical vertebrae in the lamina groove. Pause where the neck meets the shoulders. *(Two pictures: 4-3a and 4-3b)*

4-4. Position the activated tuning fork ends at the midline of the base of the neck (C6/7). Glide out along the trapezius muscle. Pause at the outer edge of the trapezius muscle.

(Two pictures: 4-4a and 4-4b)

4-5. Apply pressure with the activated tuning fork end on the origin of the levator scapulae muscle (on the superior angle of scapula). Use your other hand to push up a bit from the bottom of the scapula.

4-6. Work a few points in and around this area with the activated tuning forks, as this muscle is usually overworked and grateful for the attention. *(No picture)*

4-1a. Position both activated tuning fork ends on the midline of the occipital ridge. Glide along the occipital ridge from the midline to the sides of the occiput. *(Two pictures: 4-1a and 4-1b)*

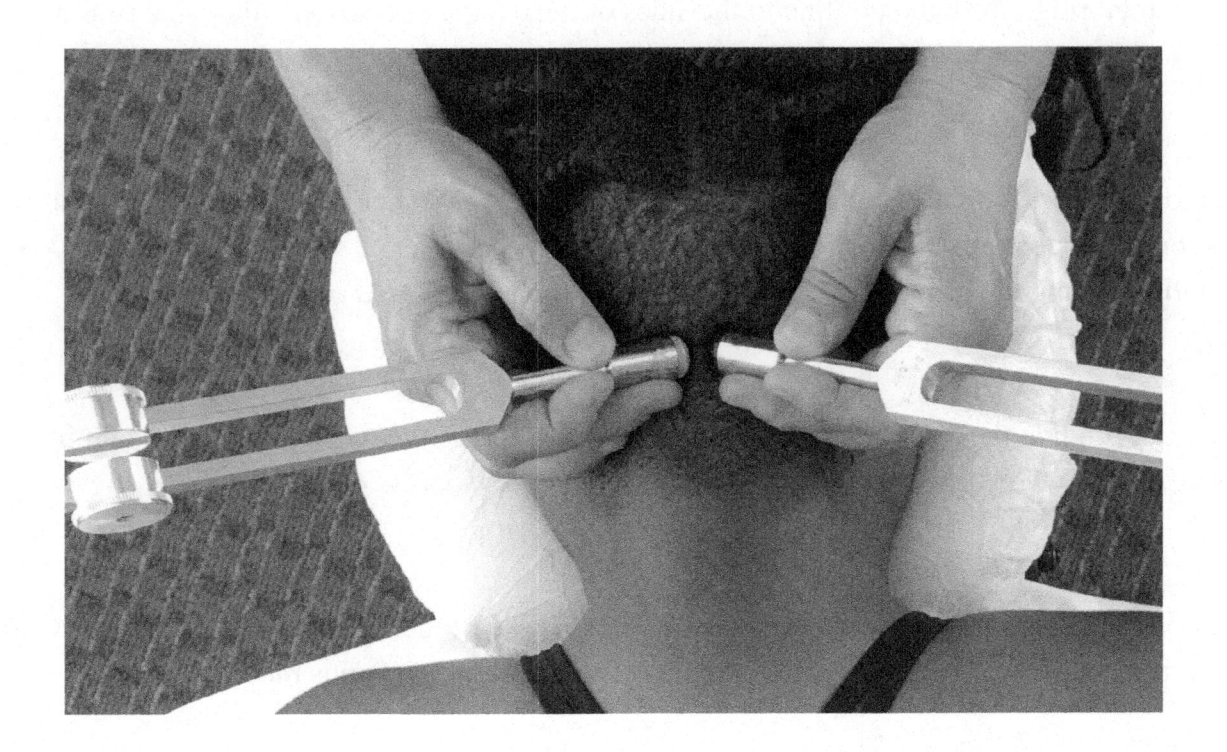

4-1b. Pause on either side of the occiput.

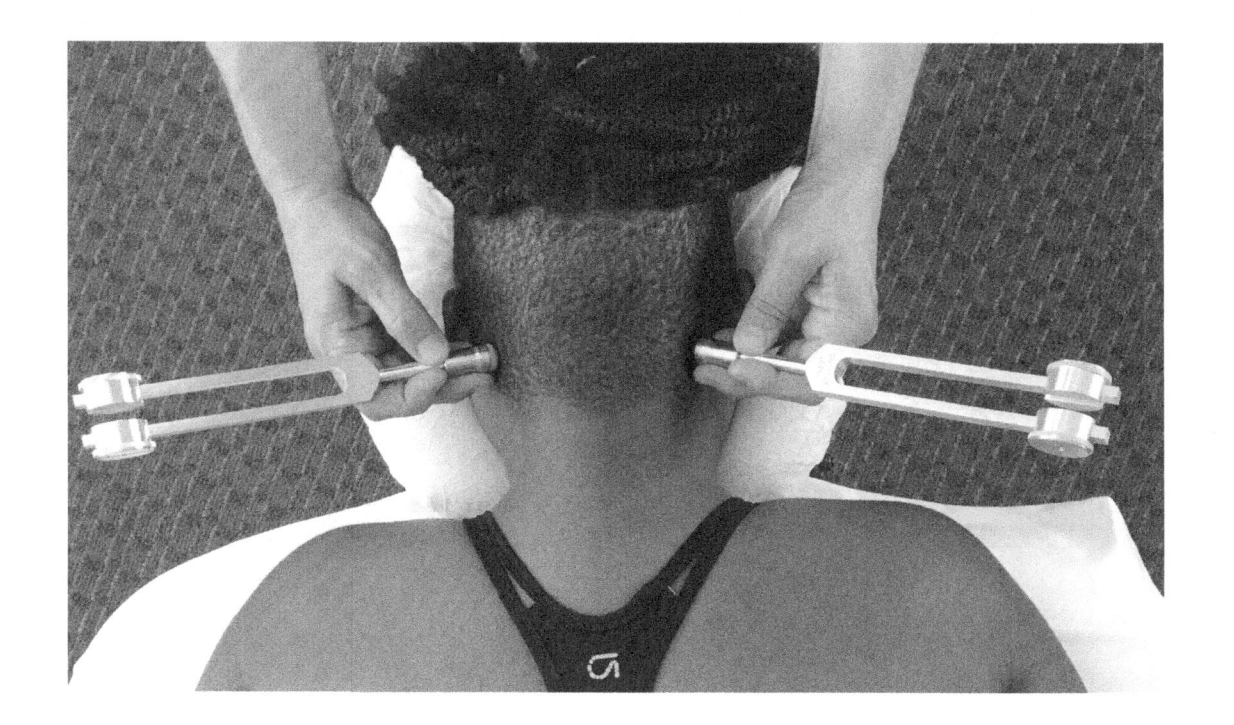

4-2a. Position both activated tuning fork ends about 1 inch or so below the starting point and glide out again towards sides of the neck. *(Two pictures: 4-2a and 4-2b)*

4-2b. Repeat this process about 1 inch below where you left off until reaching the base of the neck (C6/C7).

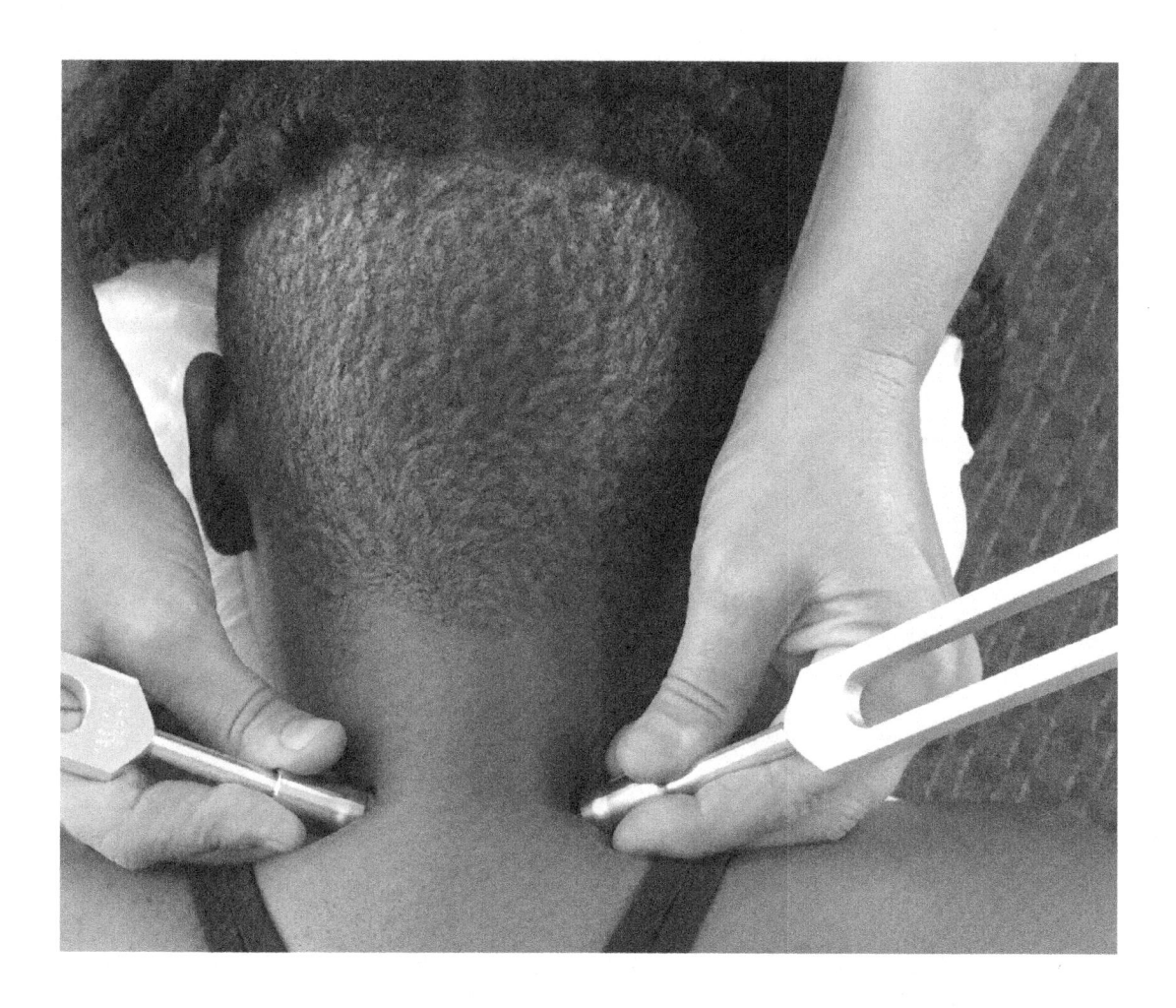

4-3a. Walk or glide the activated tuning fork ends down the cervical vertebrae in the lamina groove. *(Two pictures: 4-3a and 4-3b)*

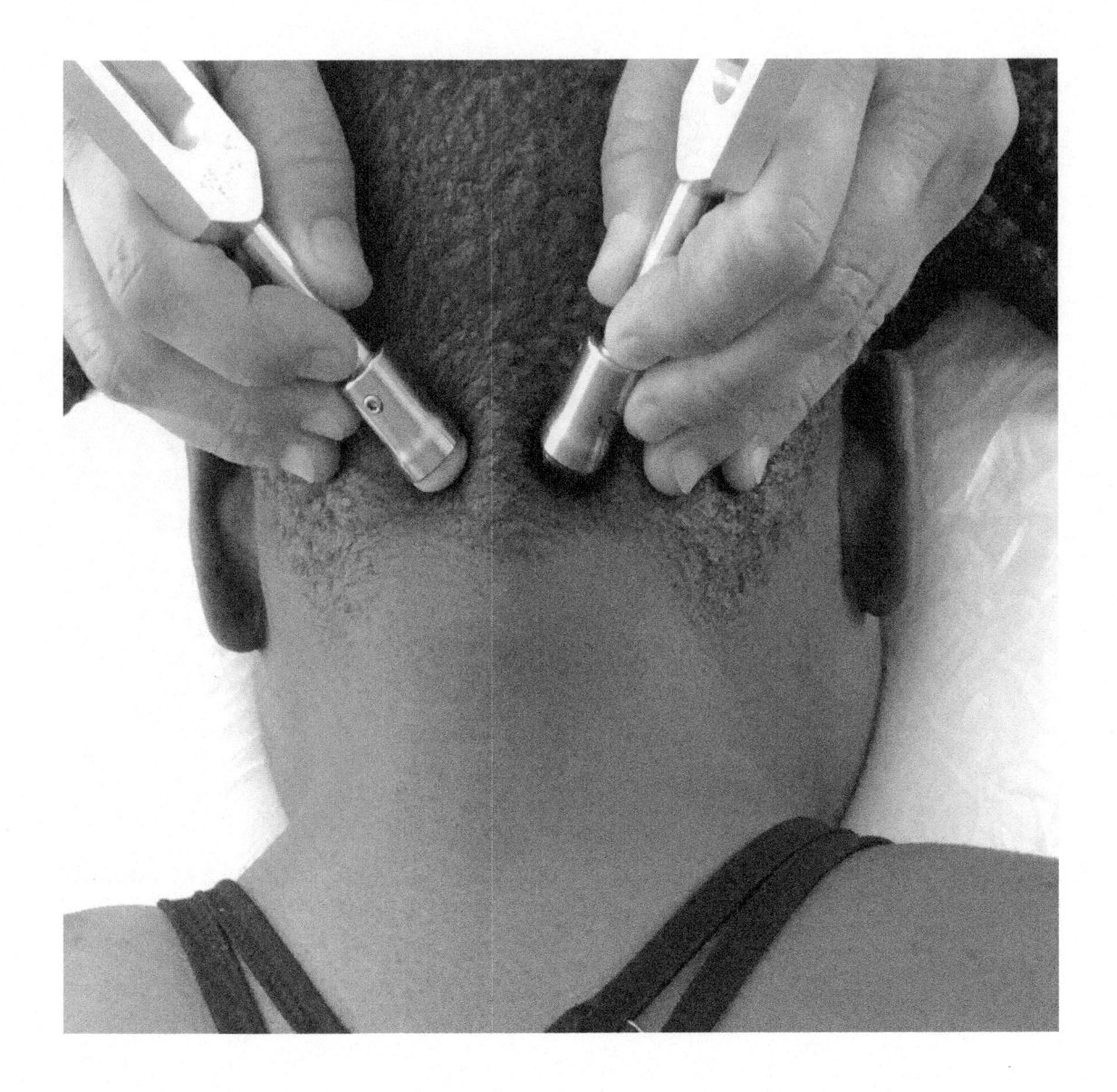

4-3b. Pause where the neck meets the shoulders.

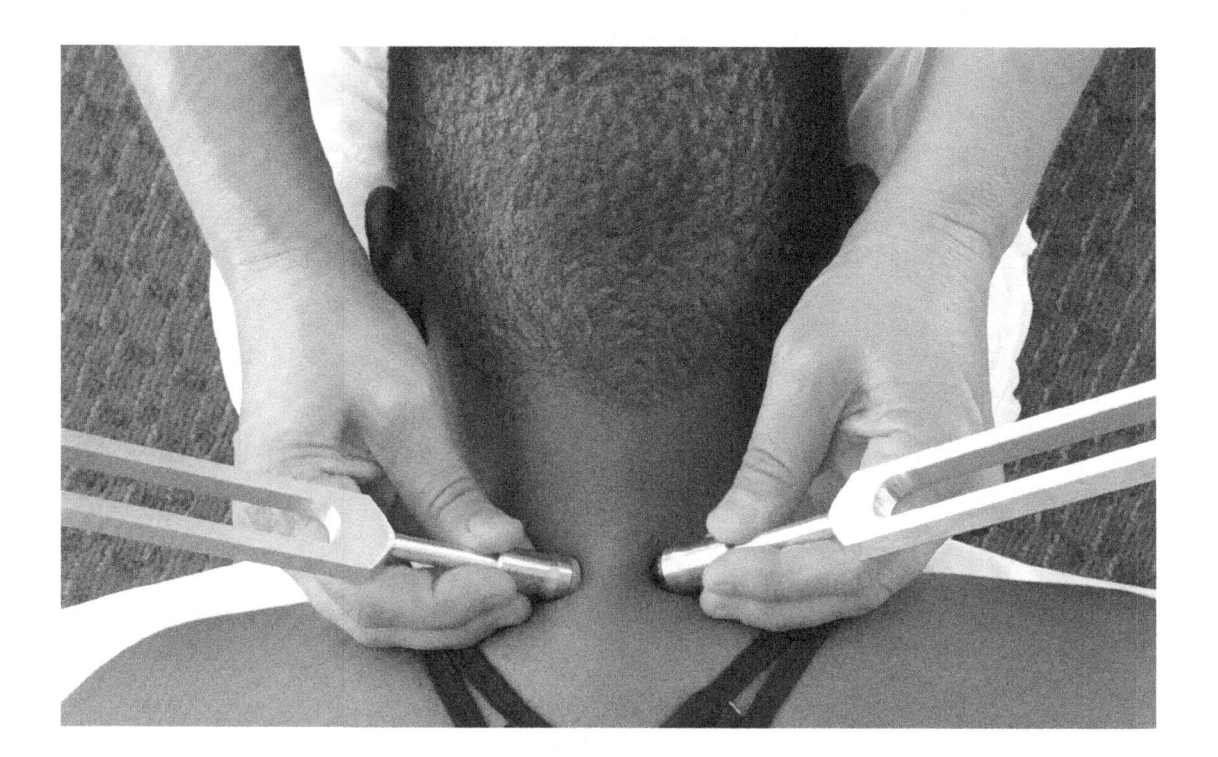

4-4a. Position the activated tuning fork ends at the midline of the base of the neck (C6/7). Glide out along the trapezius muscle. *(Two pictures: 4-4a and 4-4b)*

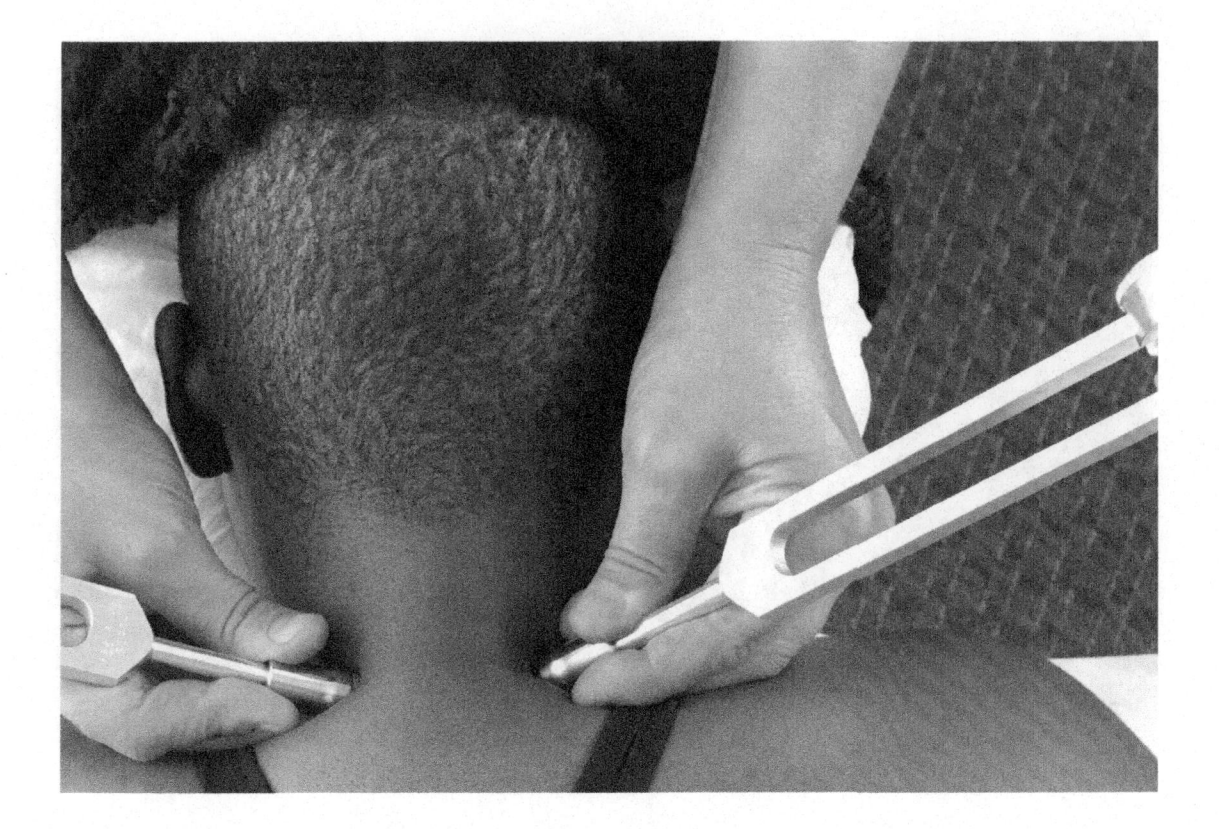

4-4b. Pause at the outer edge of the trapezius muscle.

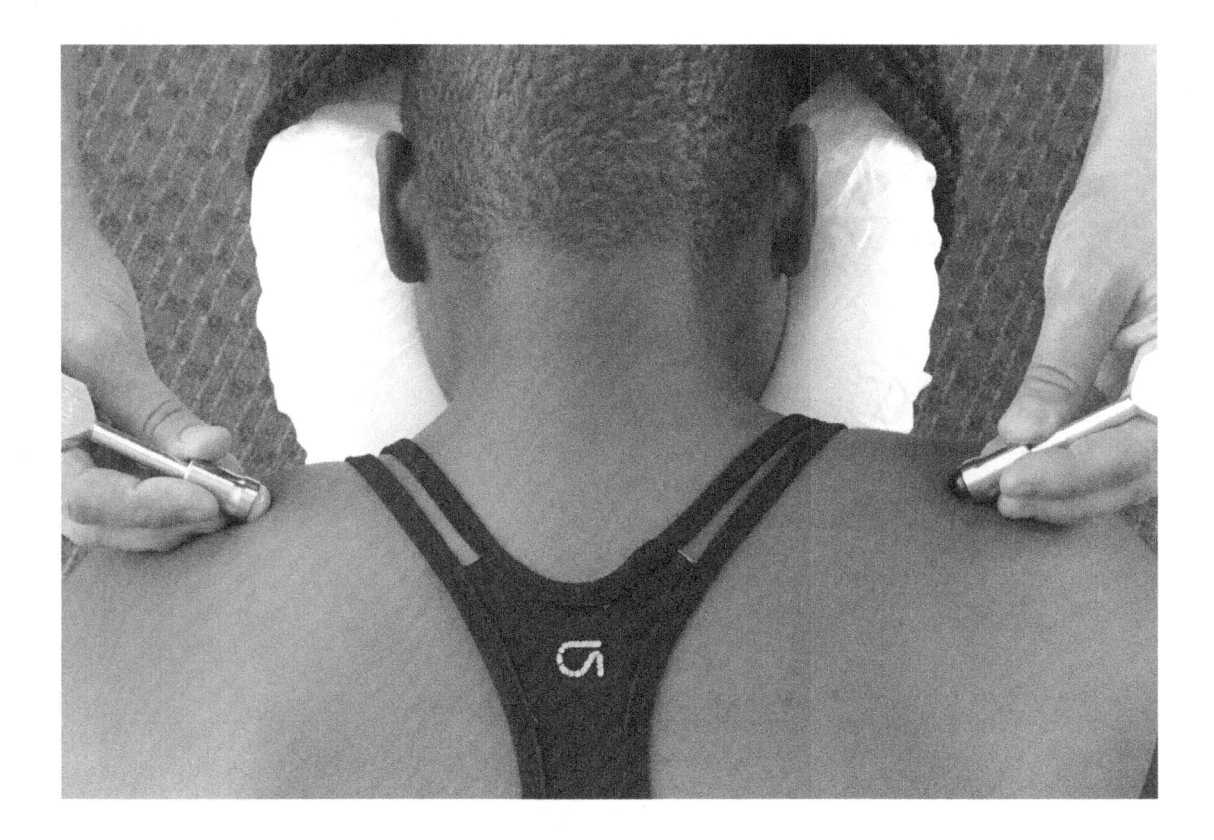

4-5. Apply pressure with the activated tuning fork end on the origin of the levator scapulae muscle (on the superior angle of scapula). Use your other hand to push up a bit from the bottom of the scapula.

4-6. Work a few points in and around this area with the activated tuning forks, as this muscle is usually overworked and grateful for the attention. *(No picture)*

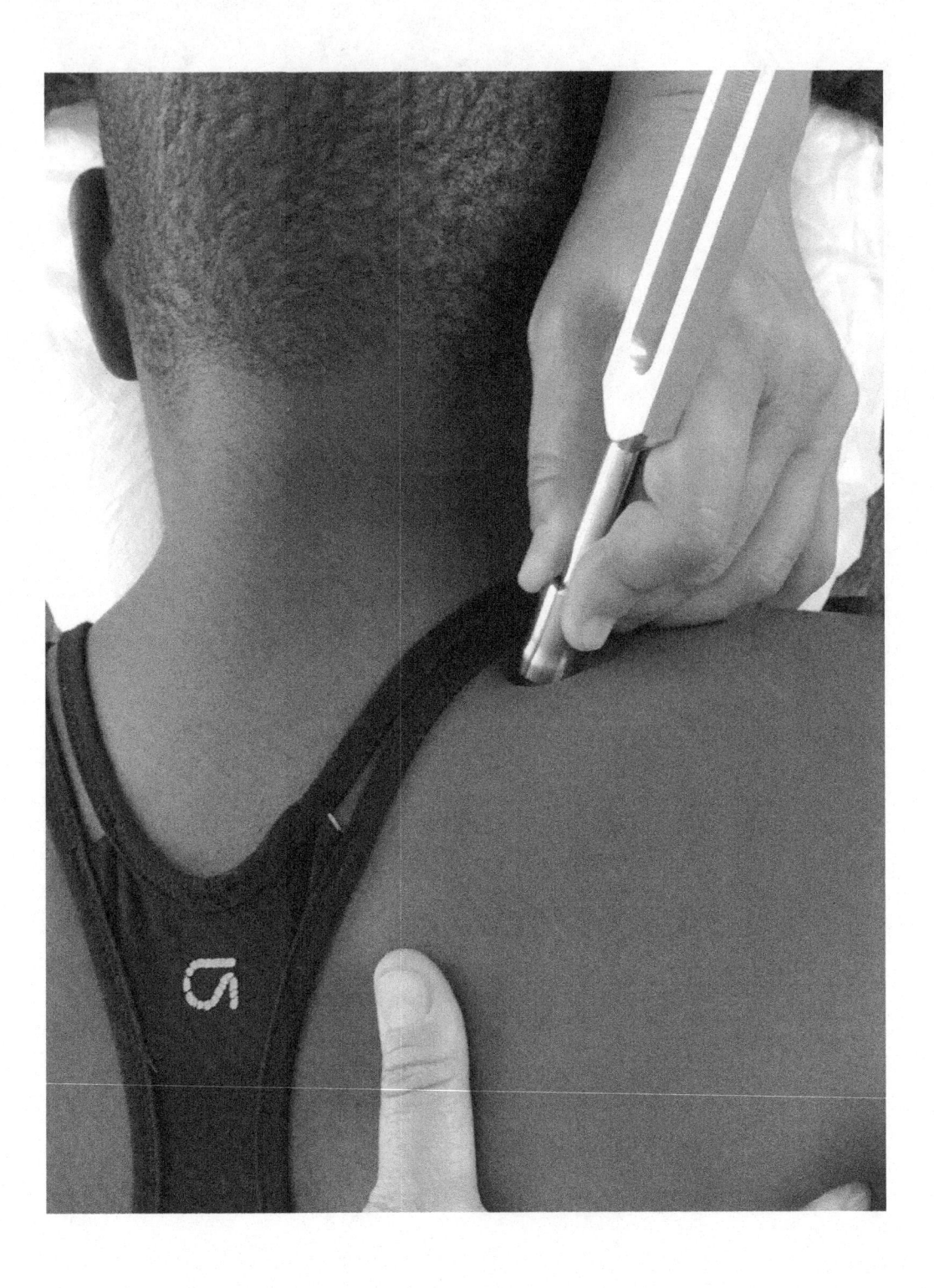

5. Protocol for Shoulders/Chest (supine)

5-1. Position the activated tuning fork ends below the midline of the collarbone. Glide out towards the shoulders to the lung points. Pause here for a few moments.

(Two pictures: 5-1a and 5-1b)

5-2. Position the activated tuning fork ends on the front and back of the shoulder joint.

5-3. Position the activated tuning forks at the top of the deltoid (front and side). Glide down the striations of the muscle from the top to the bottom, then side to side. Also, use a slight pinching motion with the tuning forks. *(Three pictures: 5-3a, 5-3b and 5-3c)*

5-4. Position the activated tuning fork end on the pectoral insertion.

5-1a. Position the activated tuning fork ends below the midline of the collarbone.

(Two pictures: 5-1a and 5-1b)

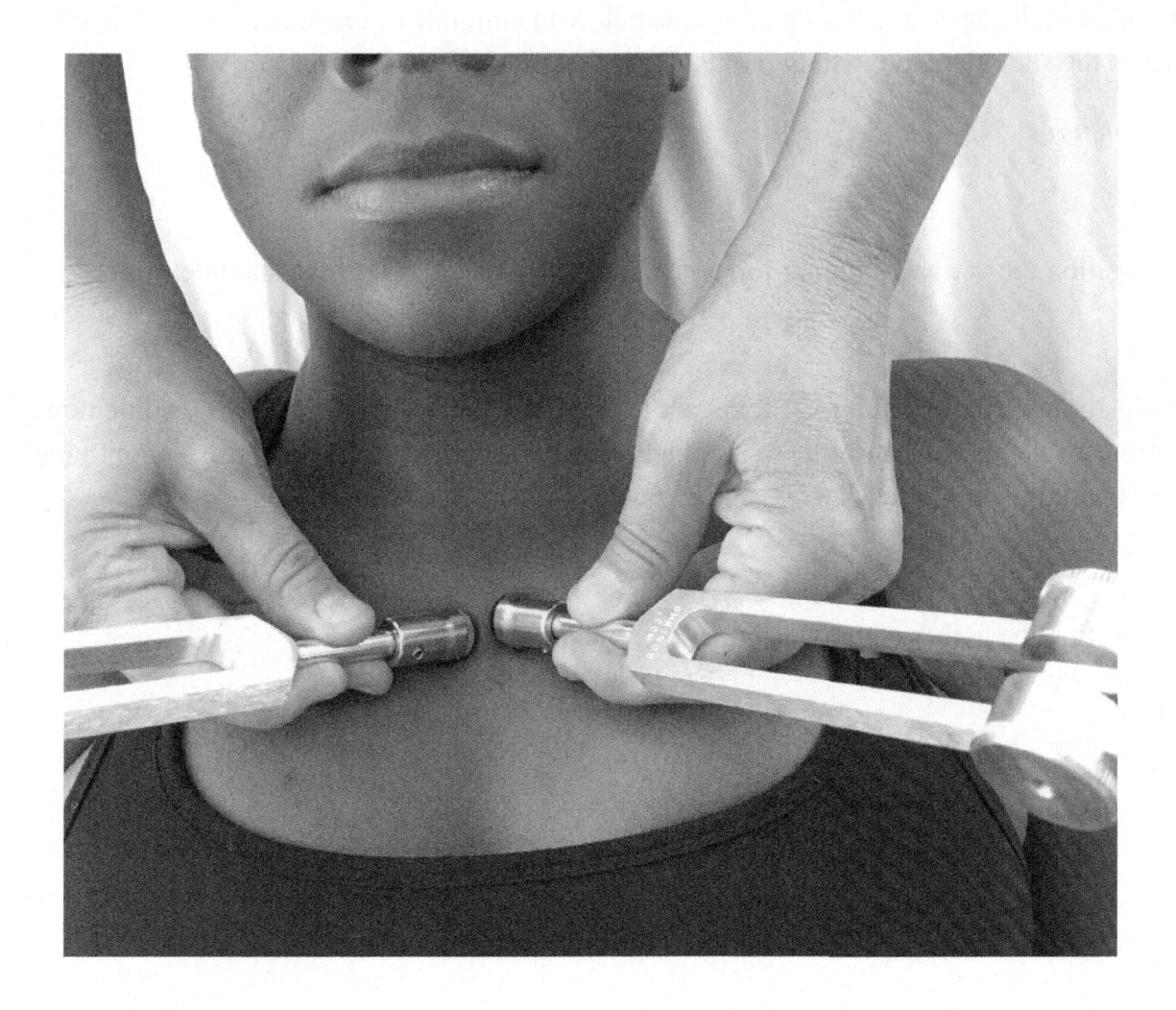

5-1b. Glide out towards the shoulders to the lung points. Pause here for a few moments.

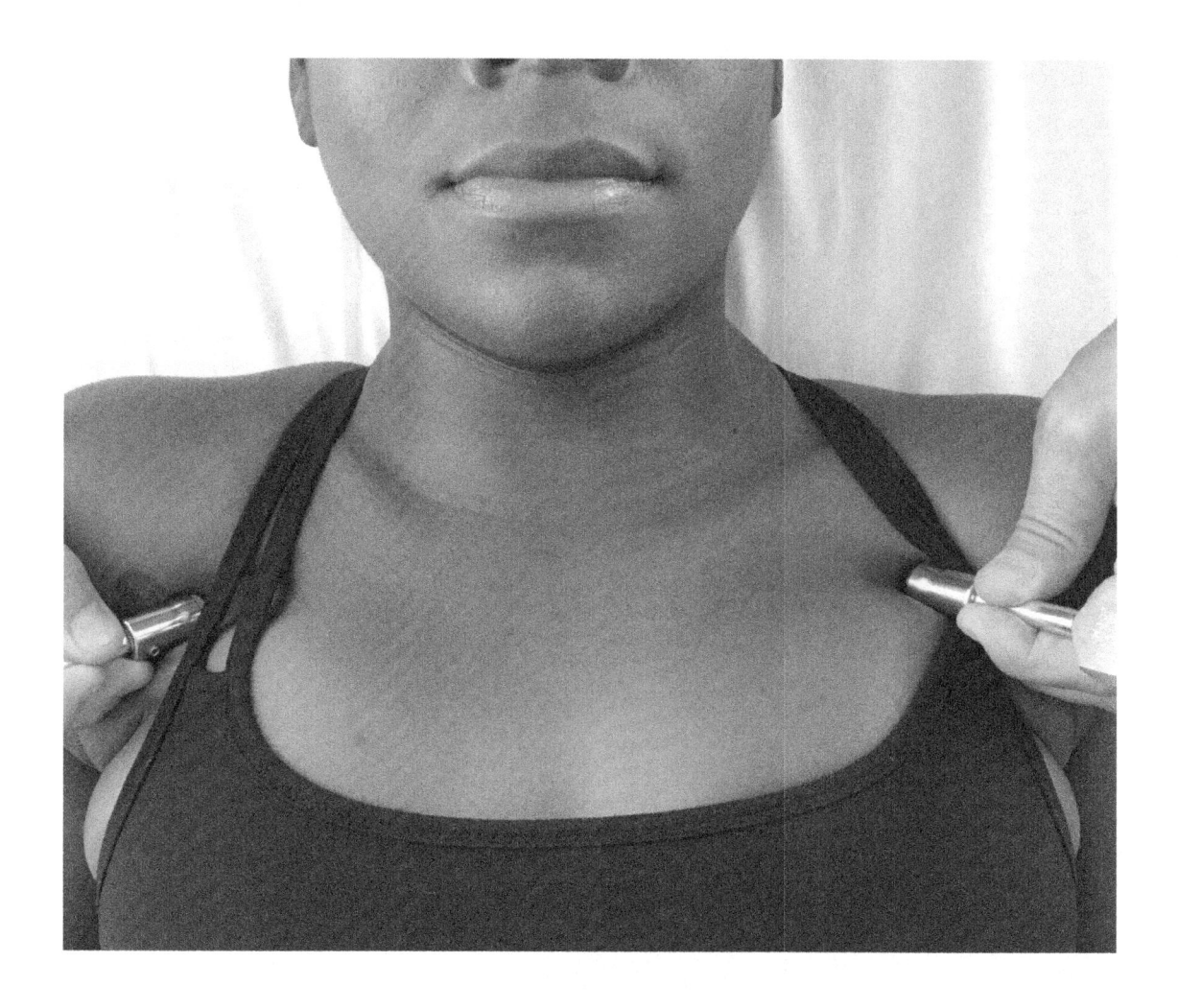

5-2. Position the activated tuning fork ends on the front and back of the shoulder joint.

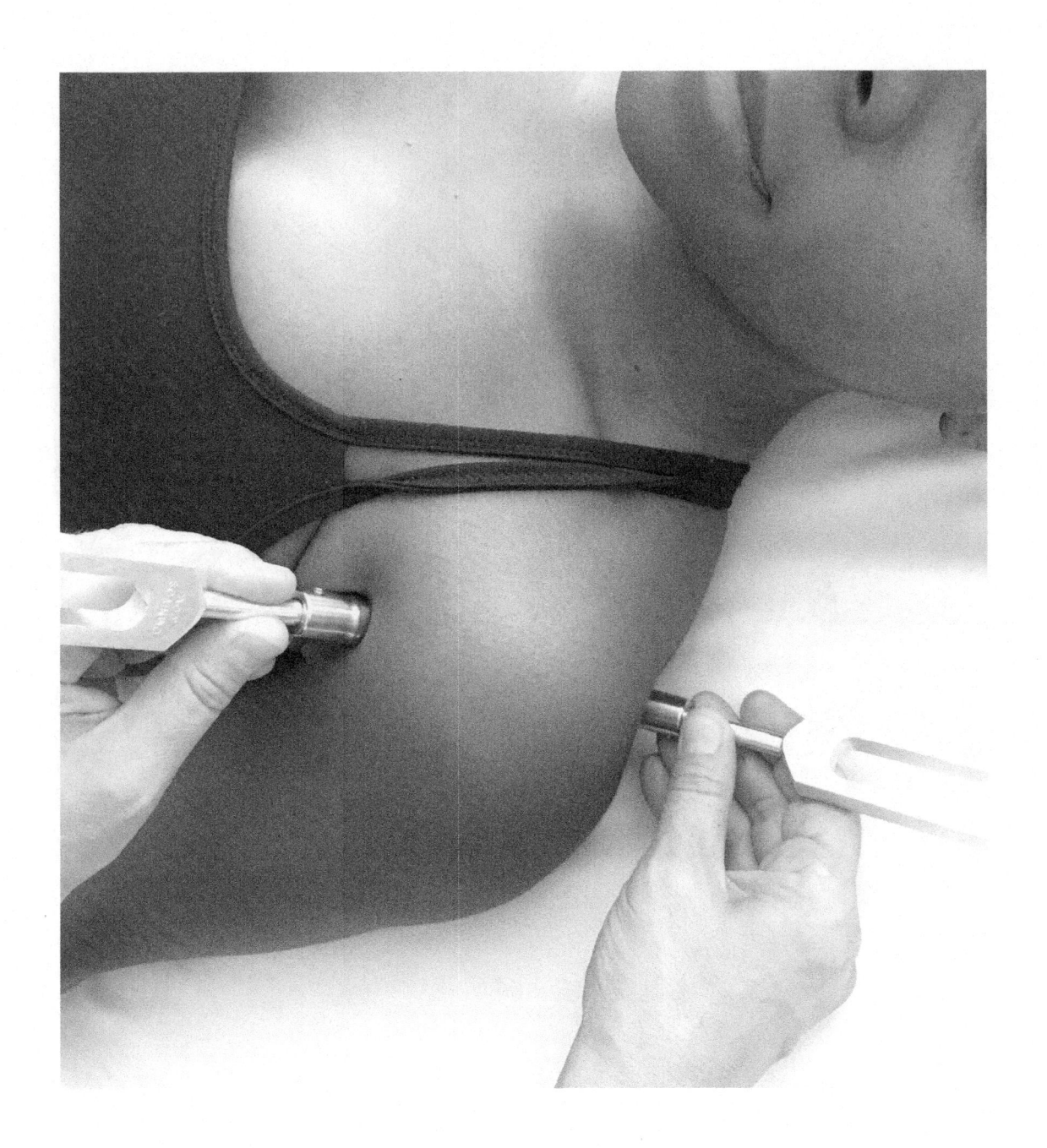

5-3a. Position the activated tuning forks at the top of the deltoid (front and side).

(Three pictures: 5-3a, 5-3b and 5-3c)

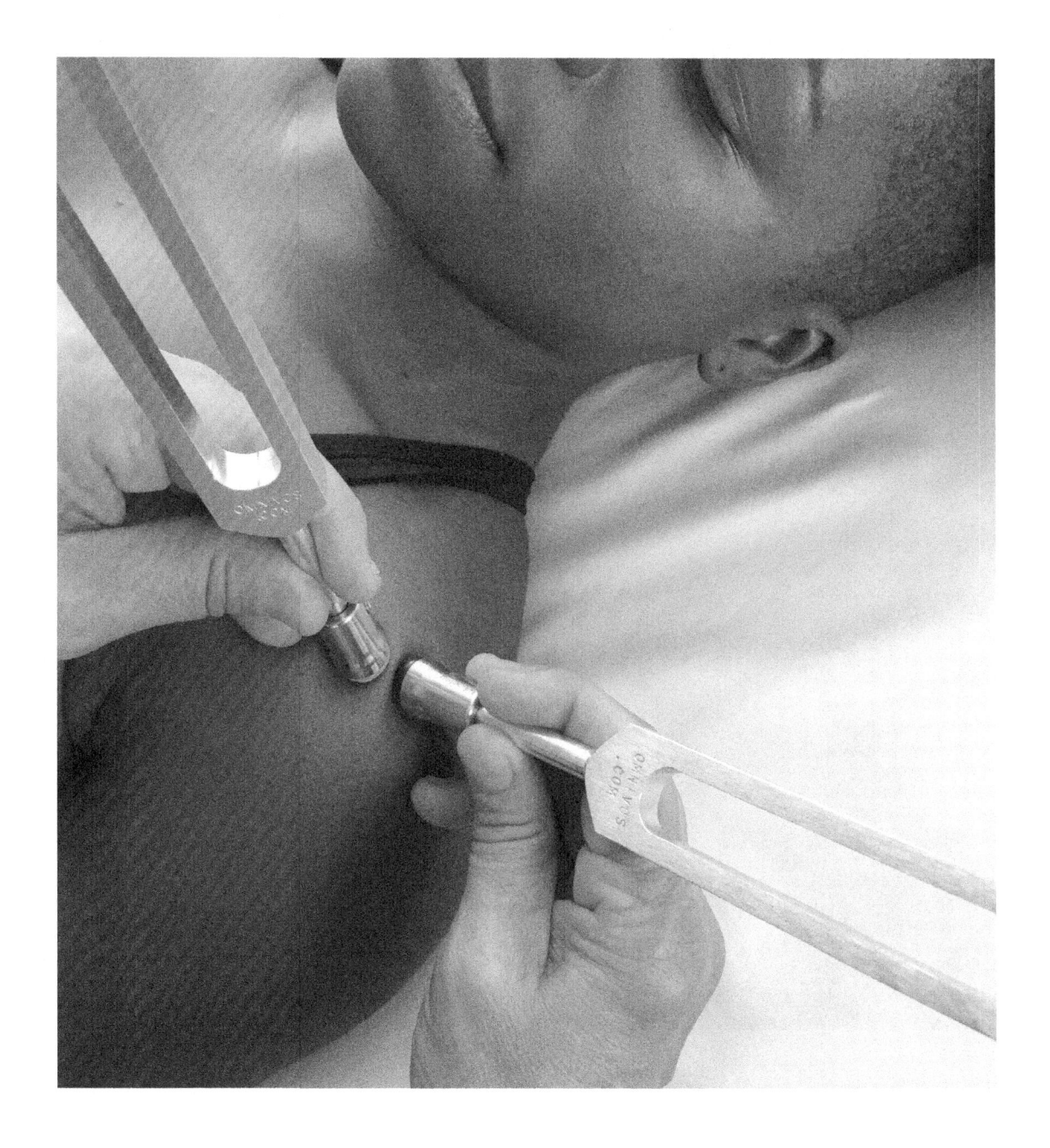

5-3b. Glide down the striations of the muscle from the top to the bottom, then side to side.

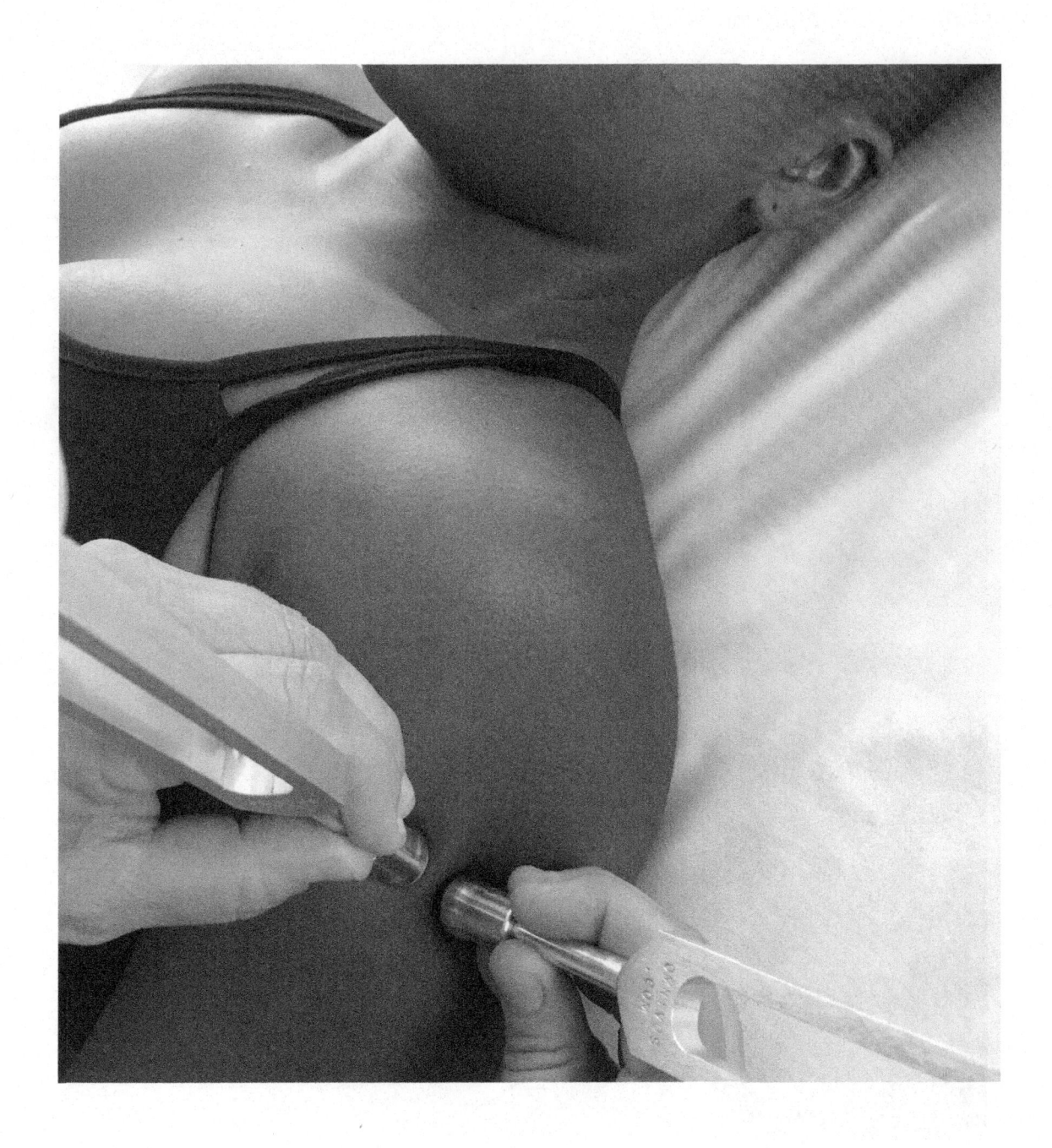

5-3c. Also, use a slight pinching motion with the tuning forks.

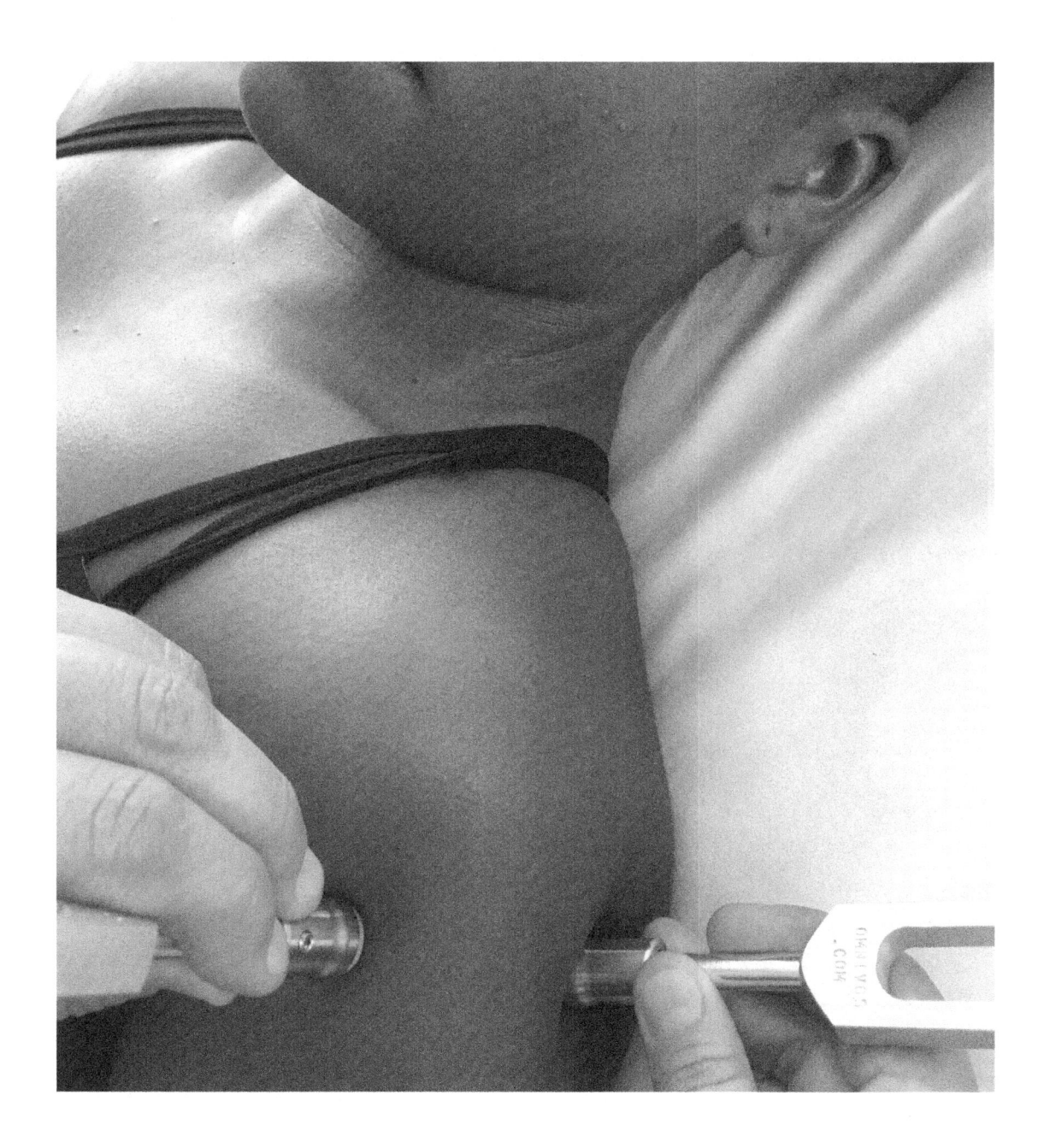

5-4. Position the activated tuning fork on the pectoral insertion.

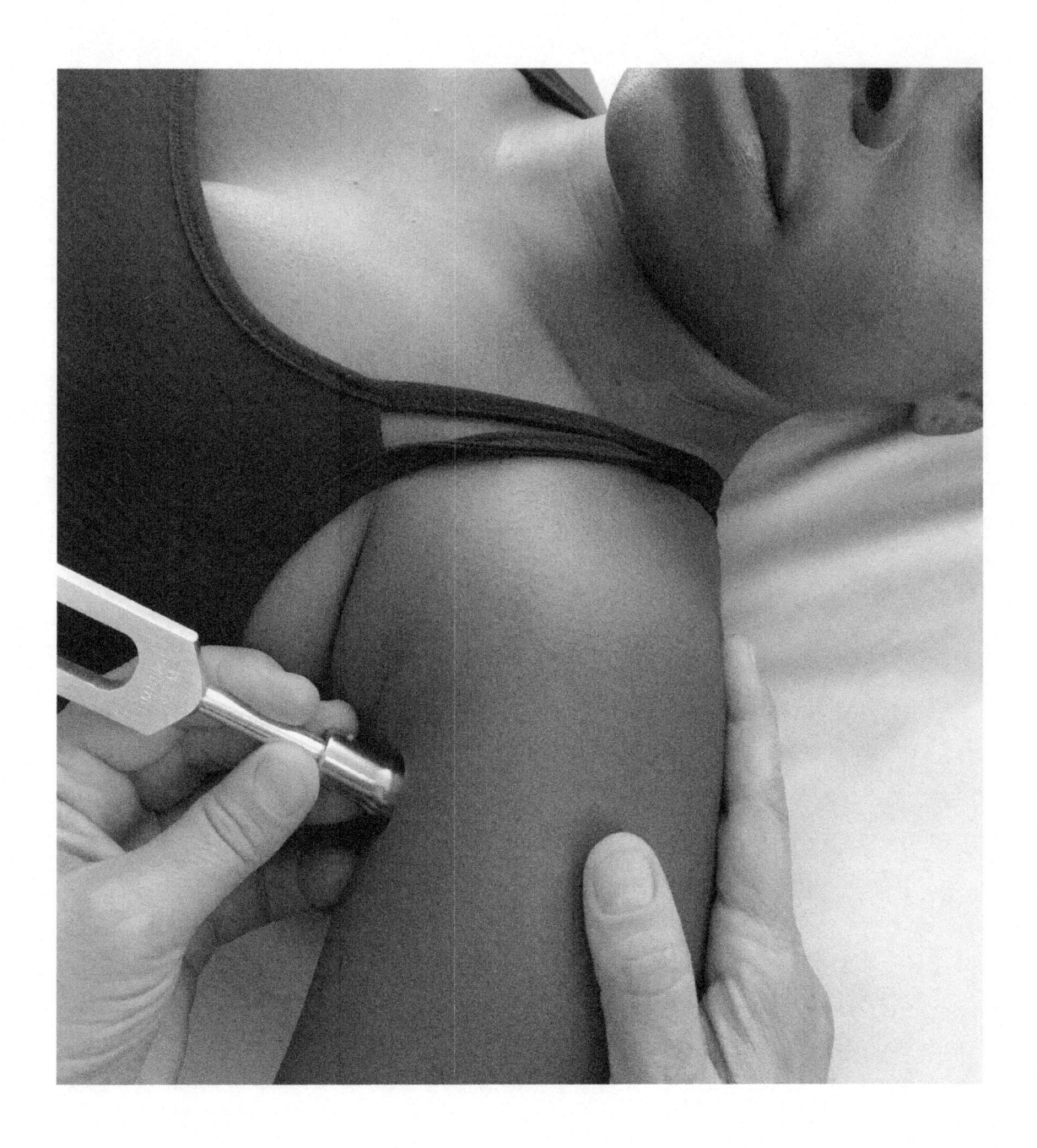

6. Protocol for Shoulders (prone)

6-1. Position the activated tuning forks on either side of the neck/upper back junctions (trapezius and C6/C7 area).

6-2. Glide the activated tuning forks from the neck/shoulder junctions along the upper trapezius and end just before the shoulder joints.

6-3. Position one activated tuning fork at the neck/upper back junction (trapezius/C7 lateral) and the other activated tuning fork on the shoulder joint.

6-4. Glide or walk from the neck/shoulder junction along the medial border of the scapula, with one activated tuning fork following the other. Repeat on the other side.

(Two pictures: 6-4a and 6-4b)

6-5. Position one activated tuning fork end to the top of the head, position the second activated tuning fork on the sacrum.

6-6. Glide the activated tuning forks down the lamina groove of vertebrae from C7 to mid back (or to the sacrum). *(Three pictures: 6-6a, 6-6b and 6-6c)*

6-7. Glide the activated tuning forks from the midline of the body to the edge of the scapula. use a back and forth motion with some pressure.

6-8. Position the activated tuning forks on top of the scapula. Glide towards the shoulder joint. This is about three or four passes on the scapula from the midline to the side.

(Two pictures: 6-8a and 6-8b)

6-1. Position the activated tuning forks on either side of the neck/upper back junctions (trapezius and C6/C7 area).

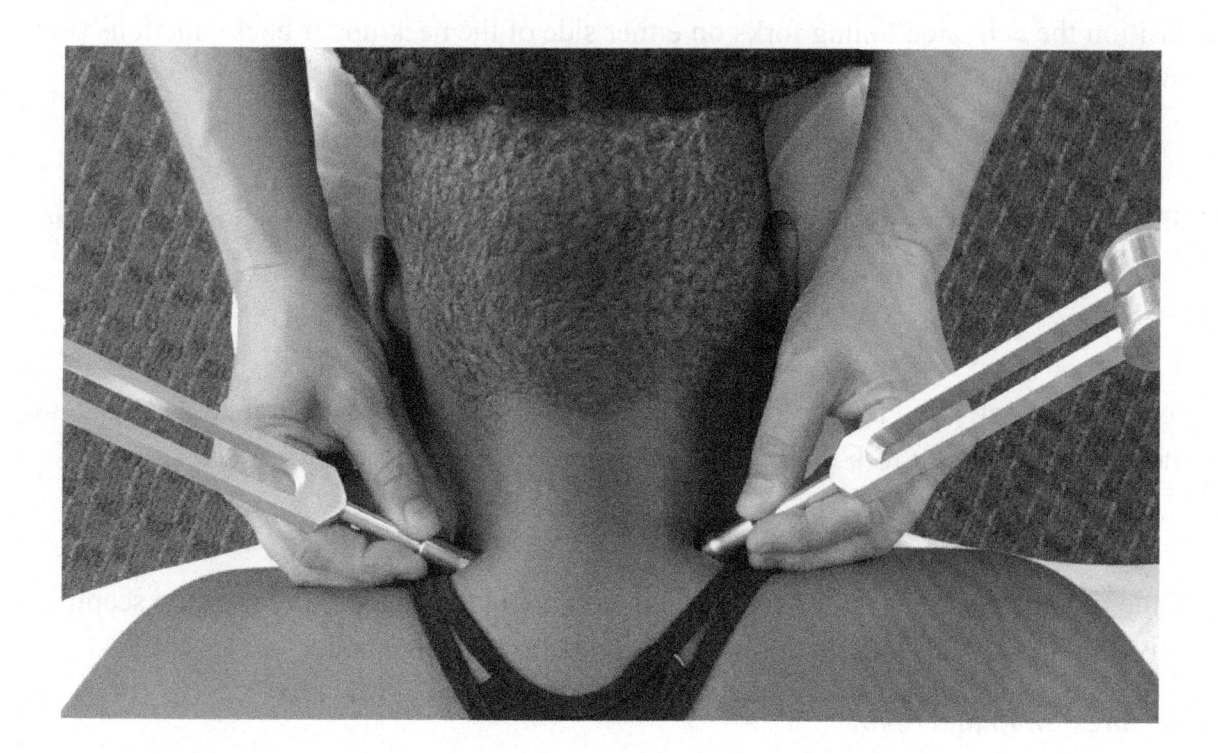

6-2. Glide the activated tuning forks from the neck/shoulder junctions along the upper trapezius and end just before the shoulder joints.

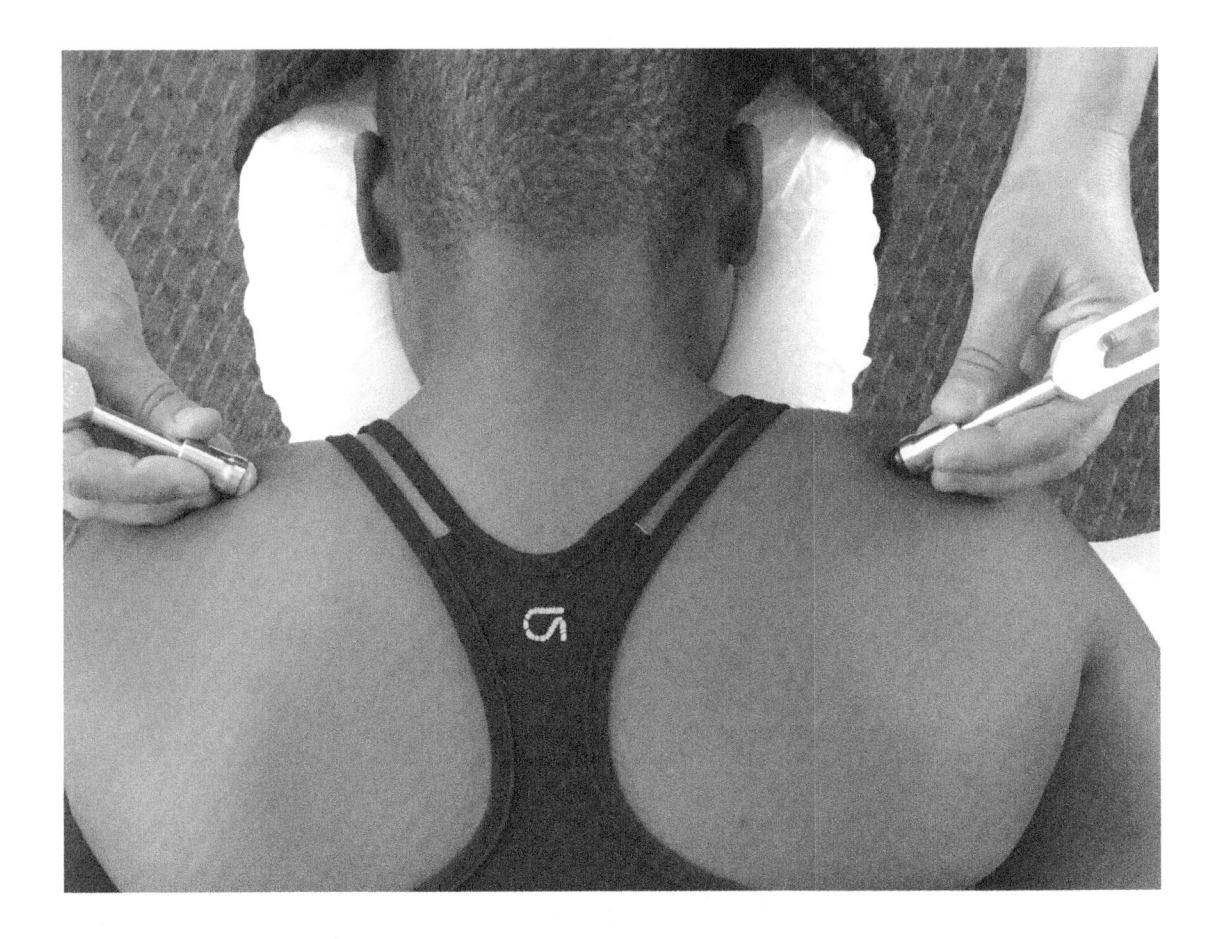

6-3. Position one activated tuning fork at the neck/upper back junction (trapezius/C7 lateral) and the other activated tuning fork on the shoulder joint.

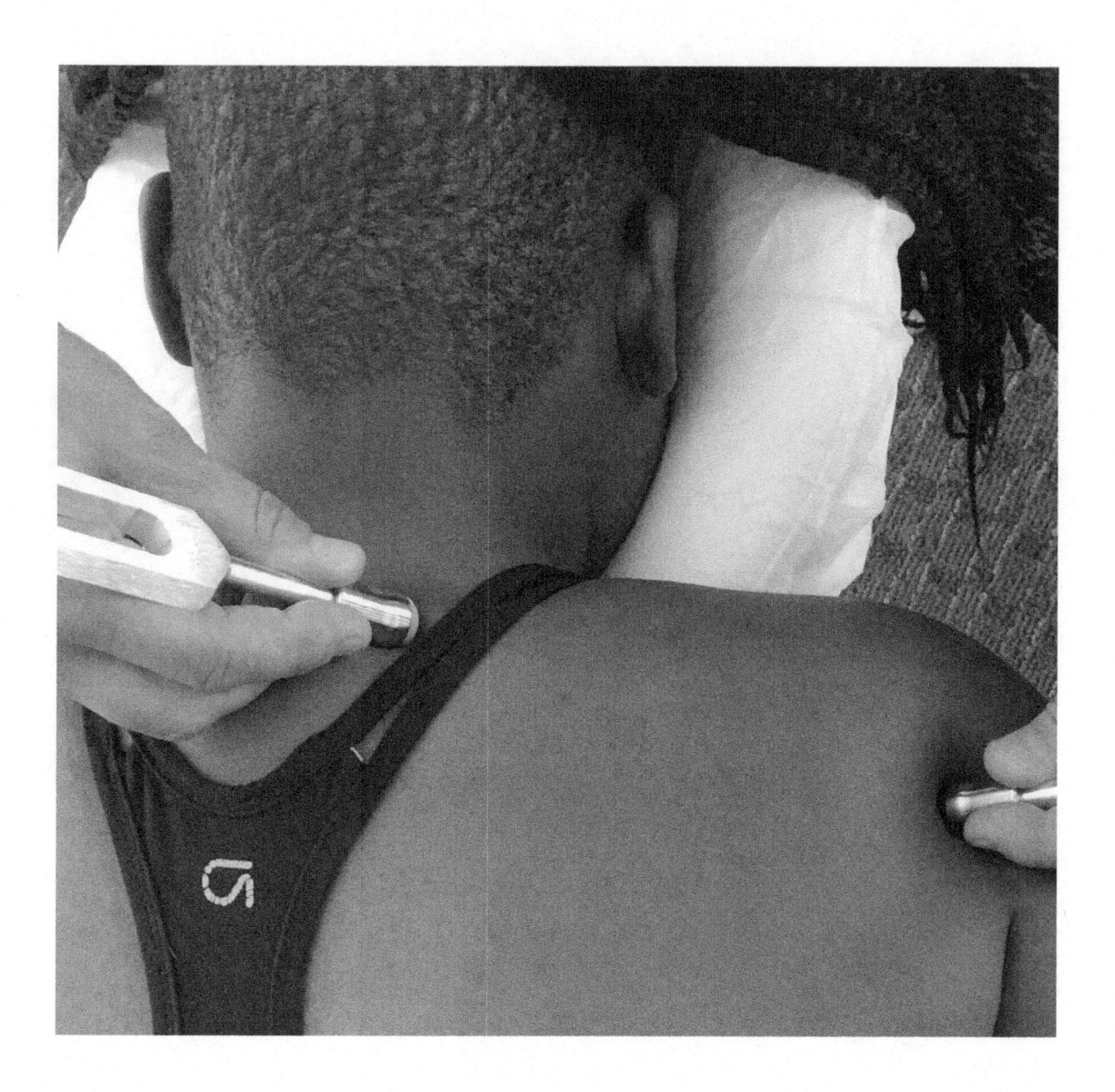

6-4a. Glide or walk from the neck/shoulder junction along the medial border of the scapula, with one activated tuning fork following the other. Repeat on the other side.

(Two pictures: 6-4a and 6-4b)

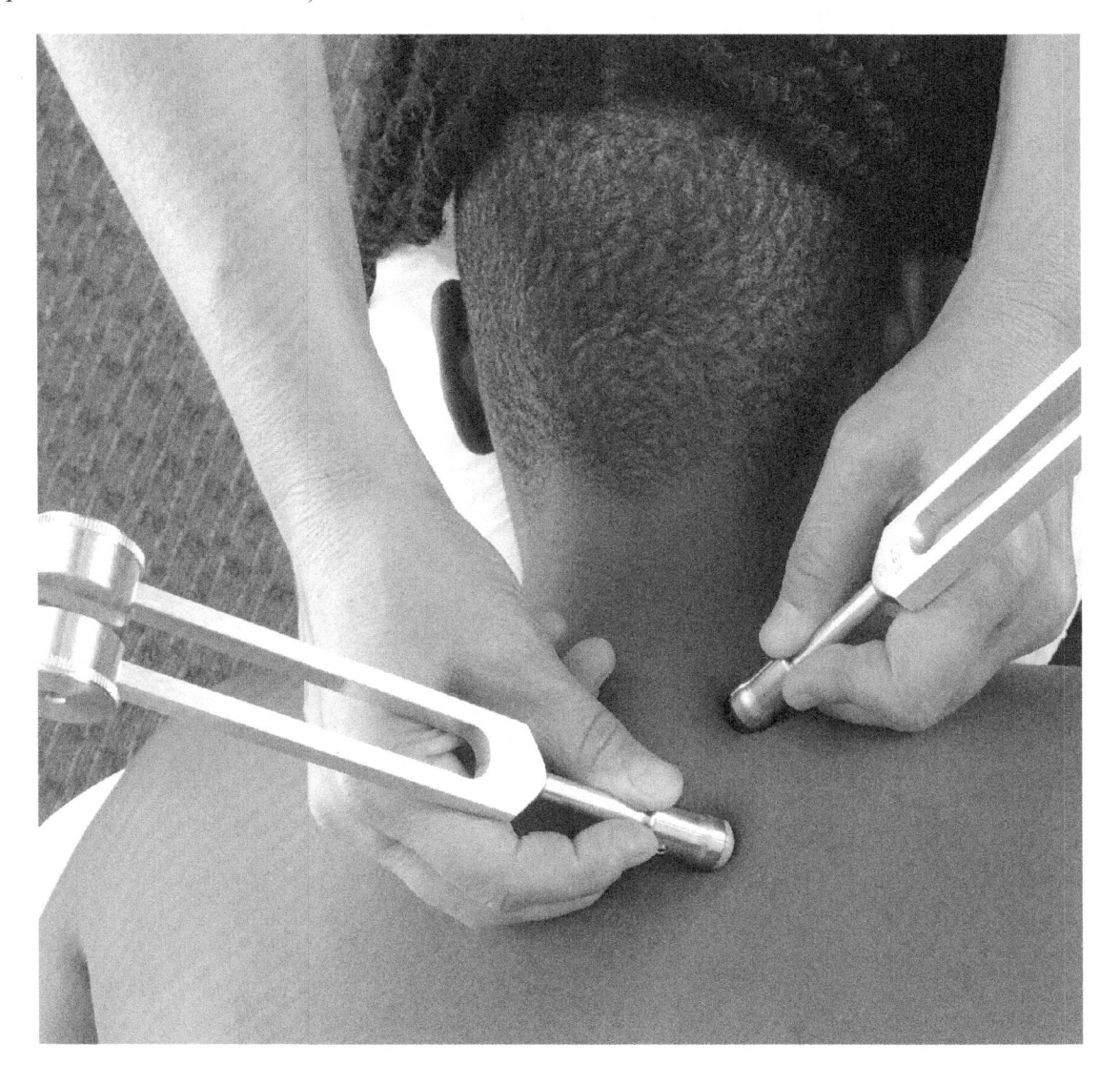

6-4b. Continue down just past the end of the scapula.

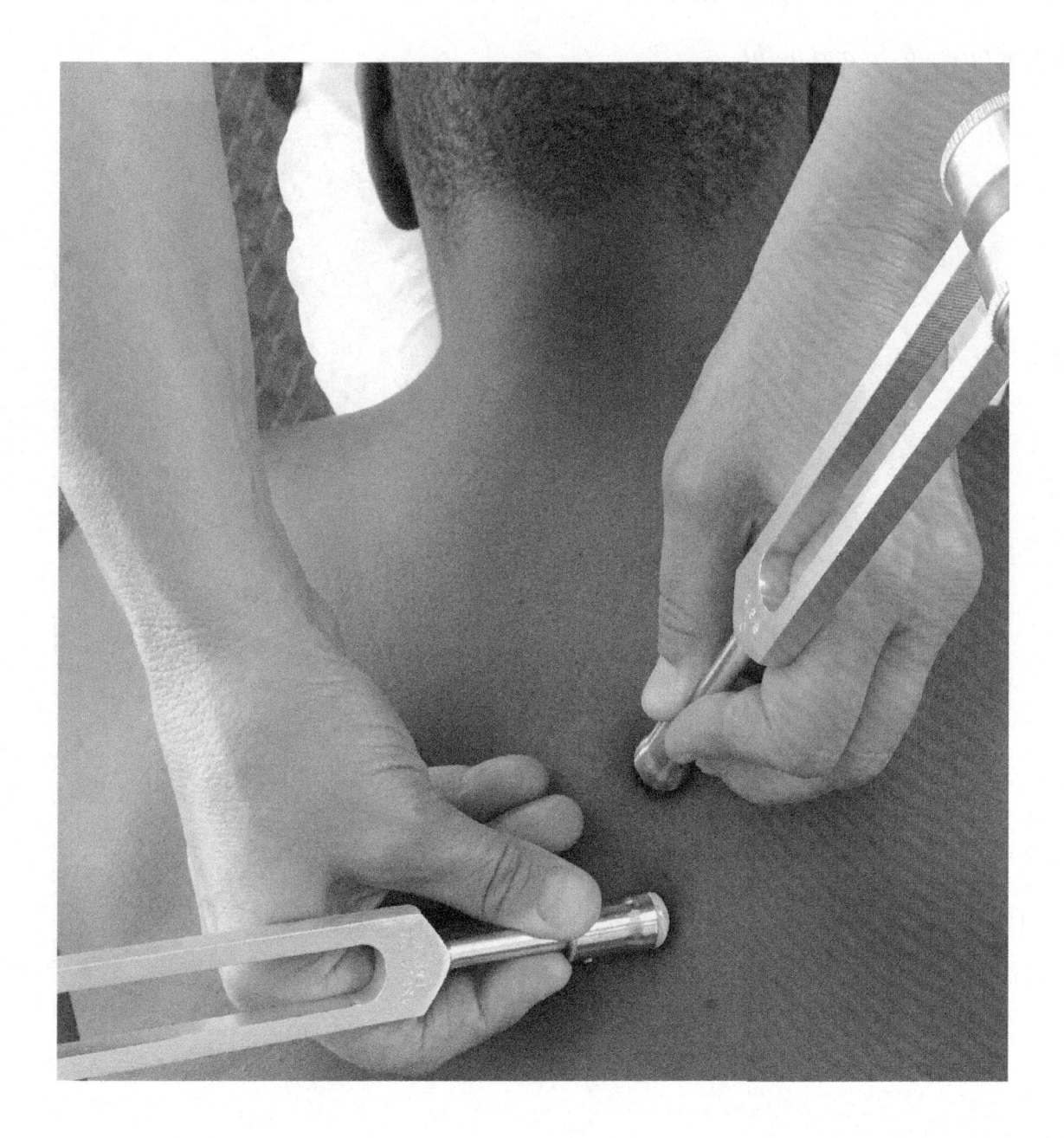

6-5. Position one activated tuning fork end to the top of the head, the other one on the sacrum.

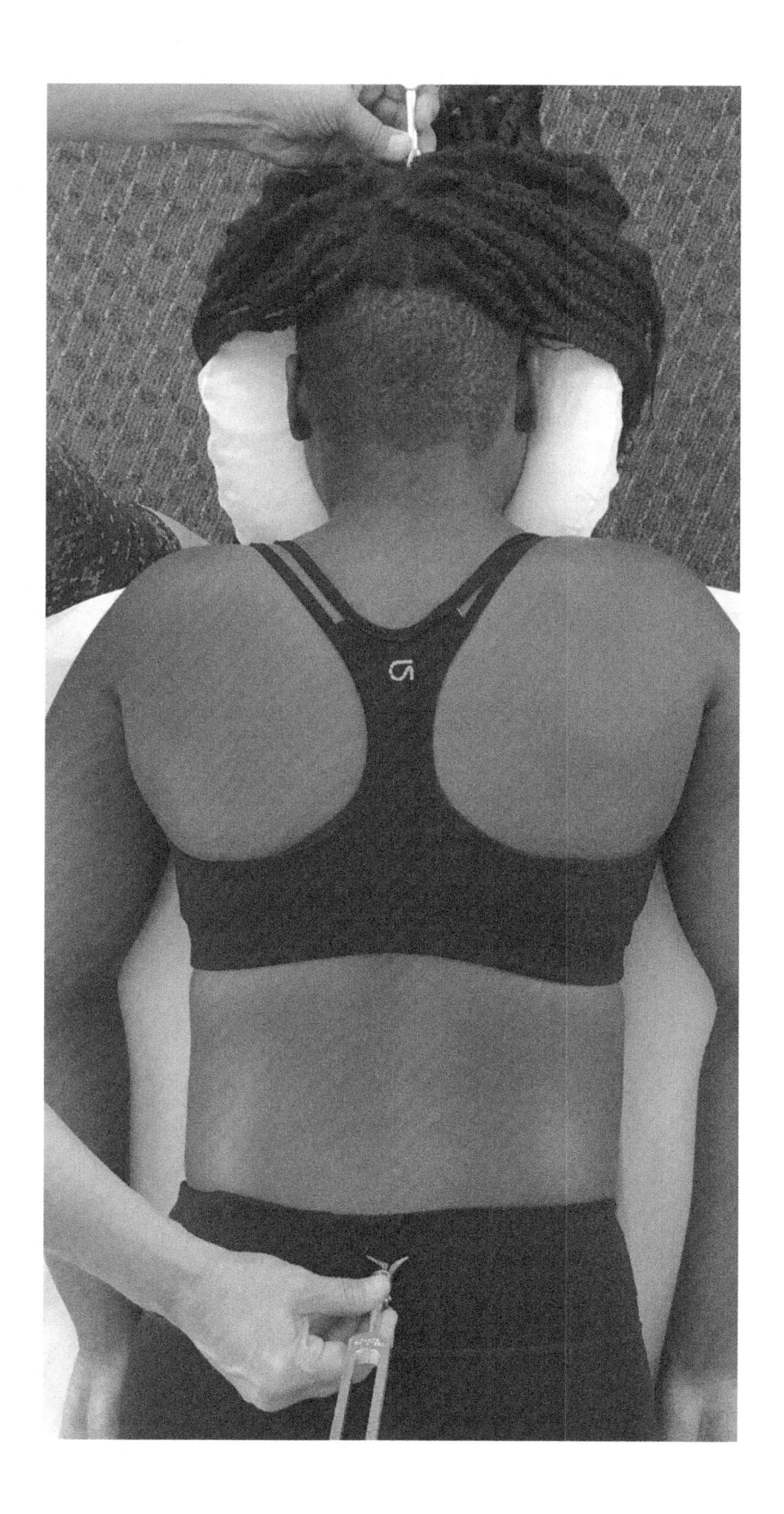

6-6a. Glide the activated tuning forks down the lamina groove of vertebrae from C7 to mid back (or to the sacrum). *(Three pictures: 6-6a, 6-6b and 6-6c)*

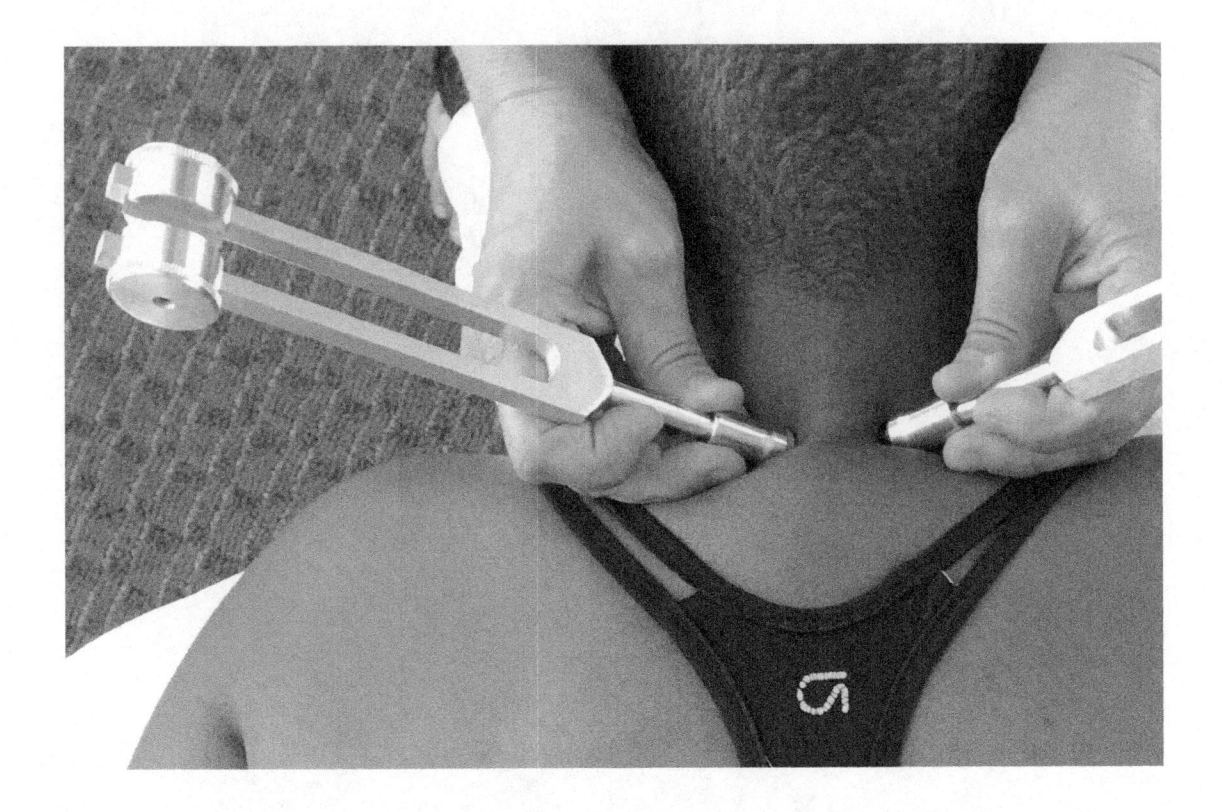

6-6b. Continue down the lamina groove towards the lower back.

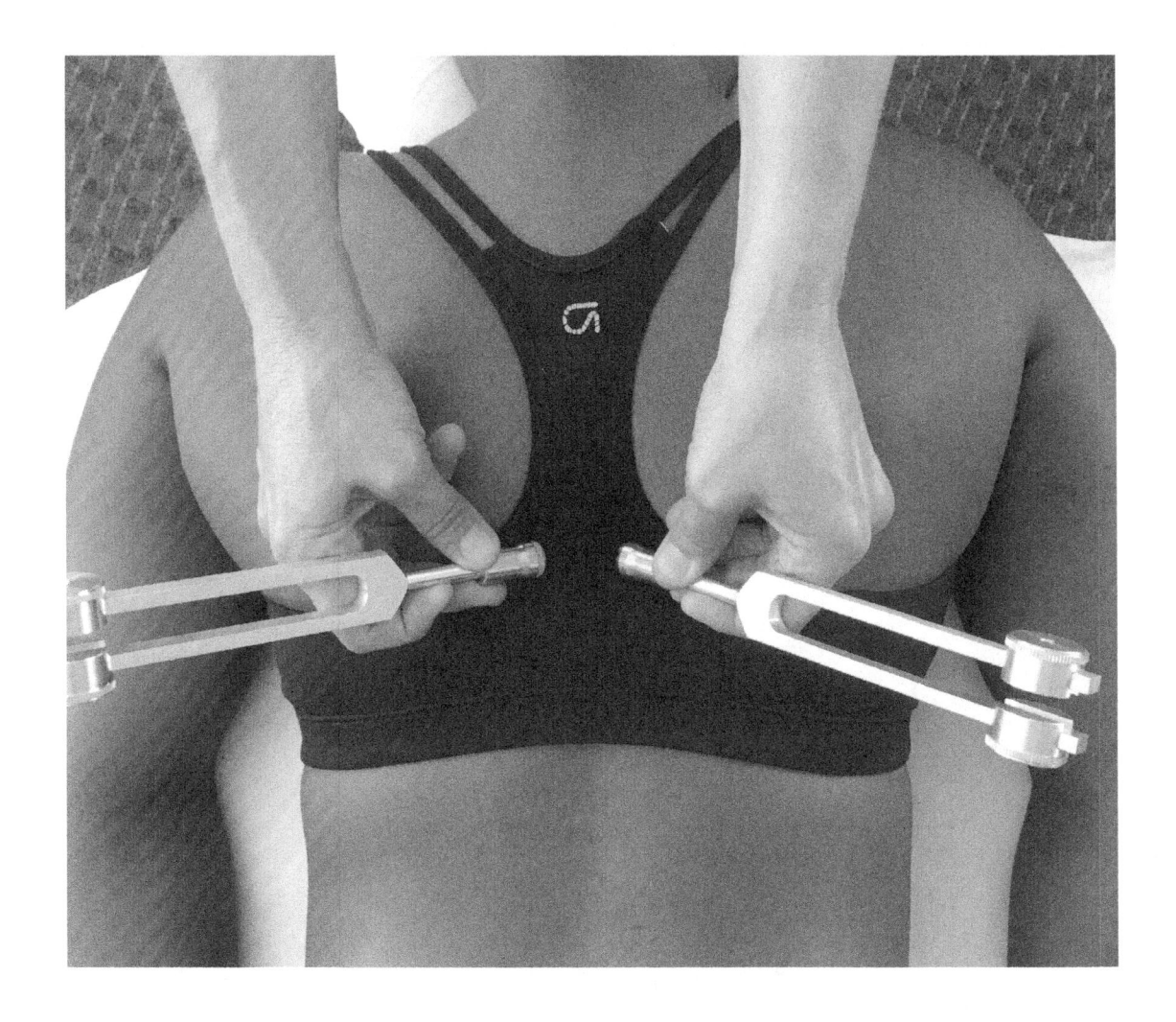

6-6c. Pause at the sacrum or low back for a few beats.

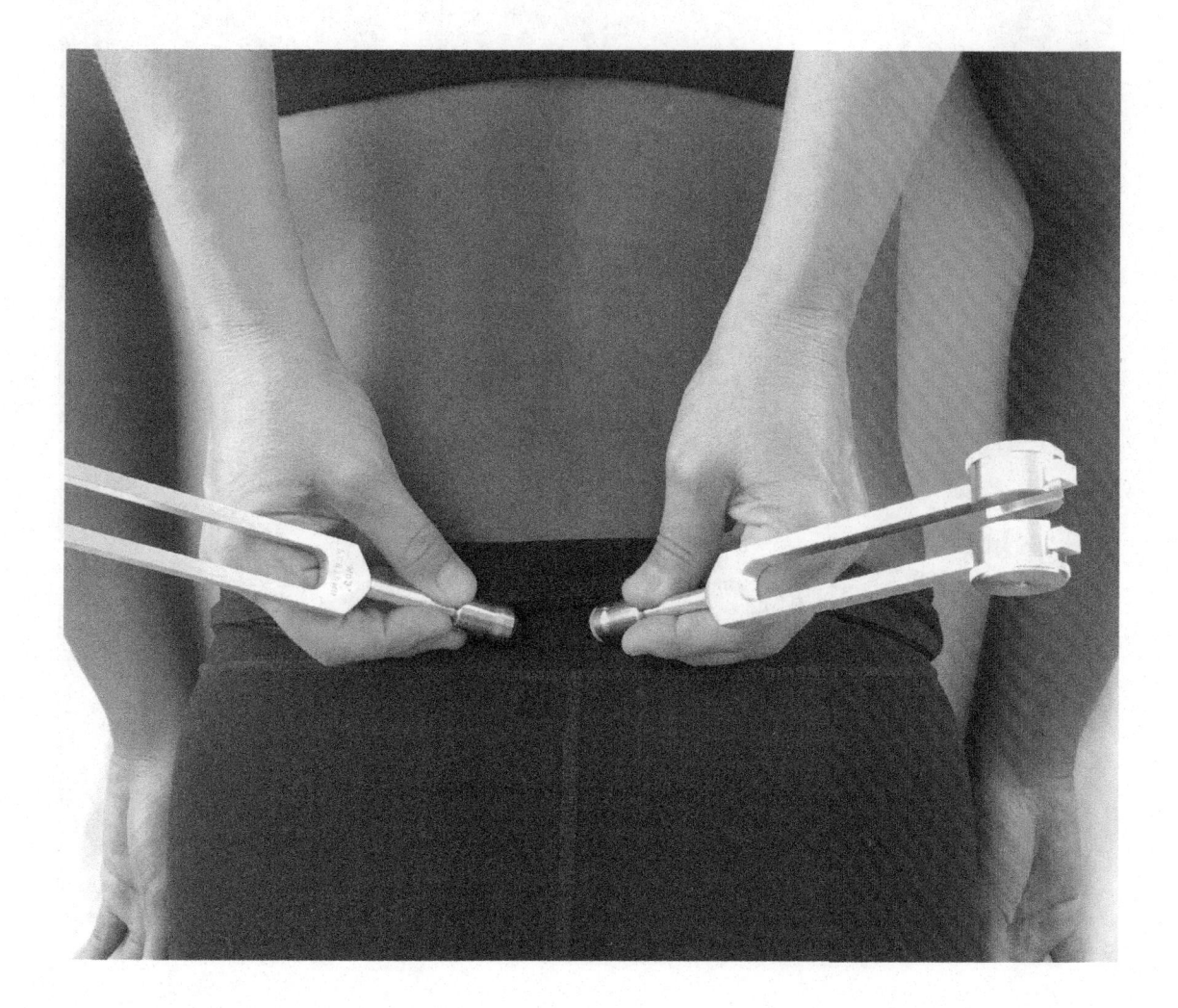

6-7. Glide the activated tuning forks from the midline of the body to the edge of the scapula. use a back and forth motion with some pressure.

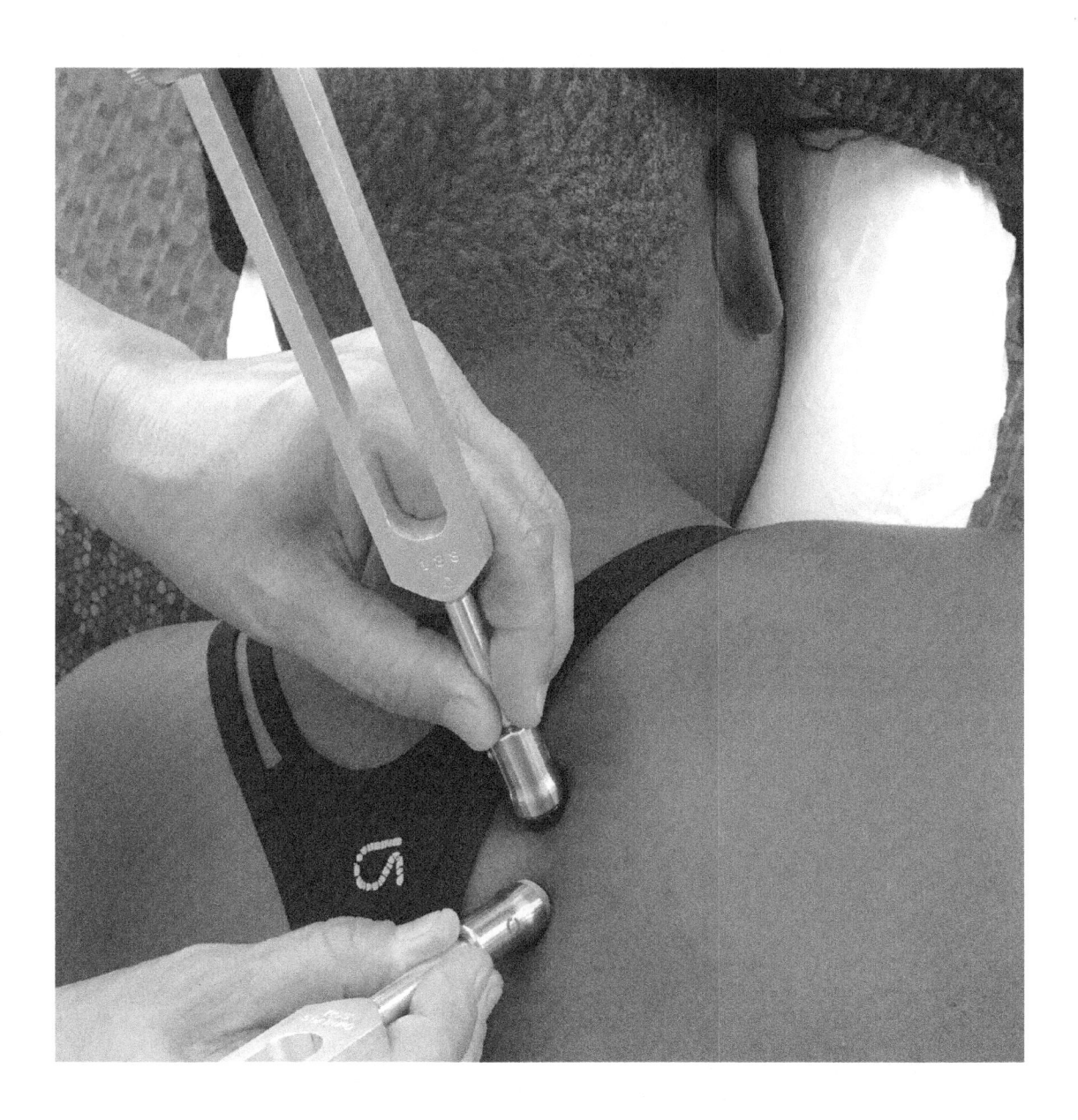

6-8a. Position the activated tuning forks on top of the scapula. *(Two pictures: 6-8a and 6-8b)*

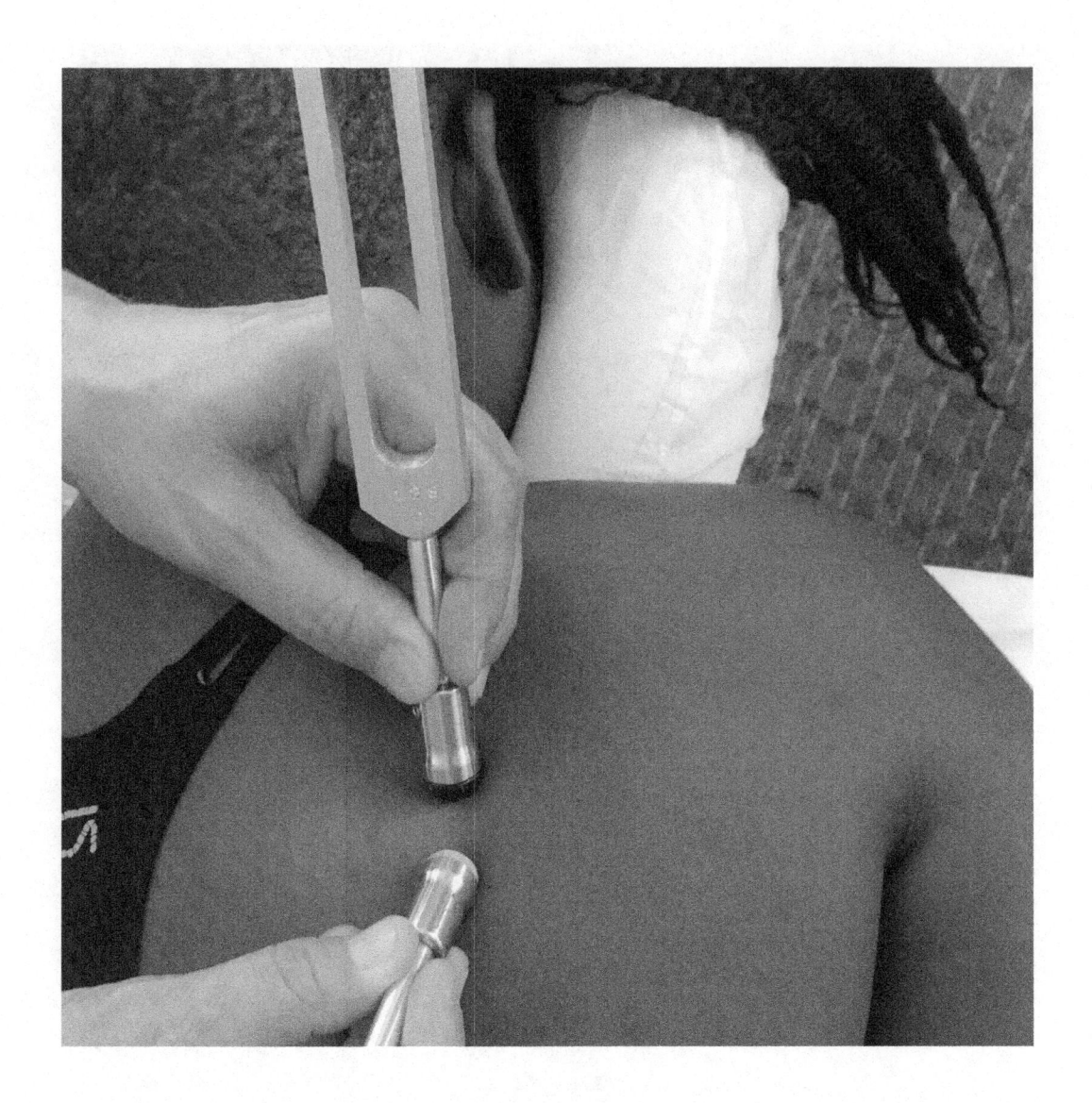

6-8b. Glide both activated tuning forks towards the shoulder joint. This is about three or four passes on the scapula from the midline to the side.

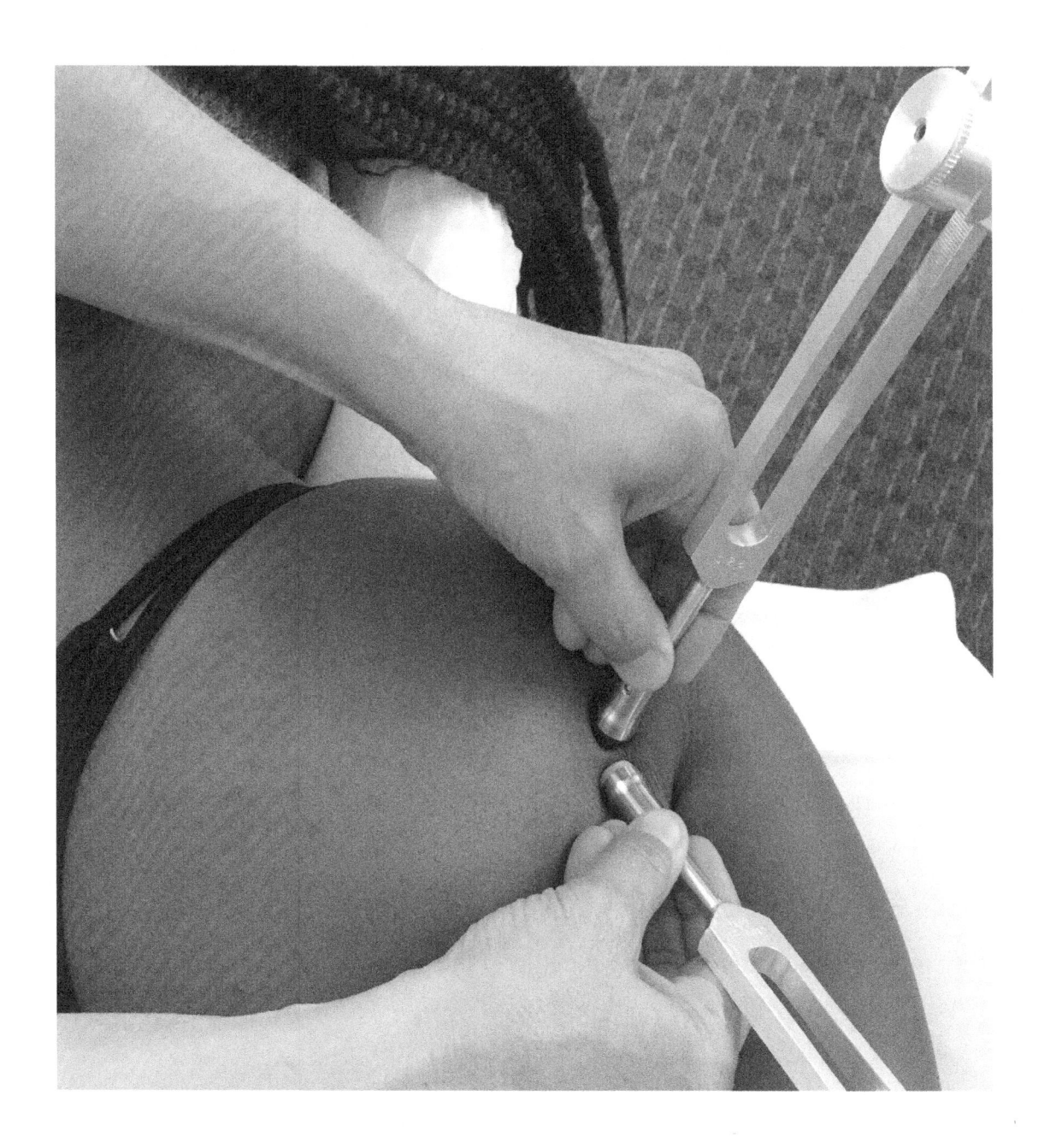

7. Protocol for Shoulders/Arms/Wrists/Hands (supine)

7-1. Position the activated tuning fork ends on the front and back of the shoulder.

7-2. Position one activated tuning fork on the front of the shoulder and the other activated tuning fork onto the fleshy part of the elbow (extensor muscle).

7-3. Position both activated tuning forks on either side of the elbow.

7-4. Glide activated tuning forks down the front and the side of shoulder (anterior and lateral deltoid). Try using a pinching movement as well. *(Two pictures: 7-4a and 7-4b)*

7-5. Glide activated tuning forks down either side of biceps. Can apply a bit of a pinching motion on the second pass.

7-6. Glide/walk/pinch the activated tuning forks down the arm, between the biceps and triceps.

7-7. Glide both activated tuning forks slowly down the forearm. Use a pinching motion with both forks at the fleshy extensor muscle near the elbow.

7-8. Position one activated tuning fork on the elbow, the other activated tuning fork on the wrist.

7-9. Position the activated tuning forks on the front and back of the wrist.

7-10. Position one activated tuning fork on the back of the hand. Glide from the wrist to in between the fingers. Start at the thumb and make one pass between each of the fingers until finishing between the pinkie and ring fingers.

(Two pictures: 7-10a and 7-10b)

7-11. Position the activated tuning fork on the tip of the pinkie finger. Reactivate the tuning fork and move to the tip of the ring finger. Repeat this on each finger until reaching the thumb.

7-1. Position the activated tuning fork ends on the front and back of the shoulder.

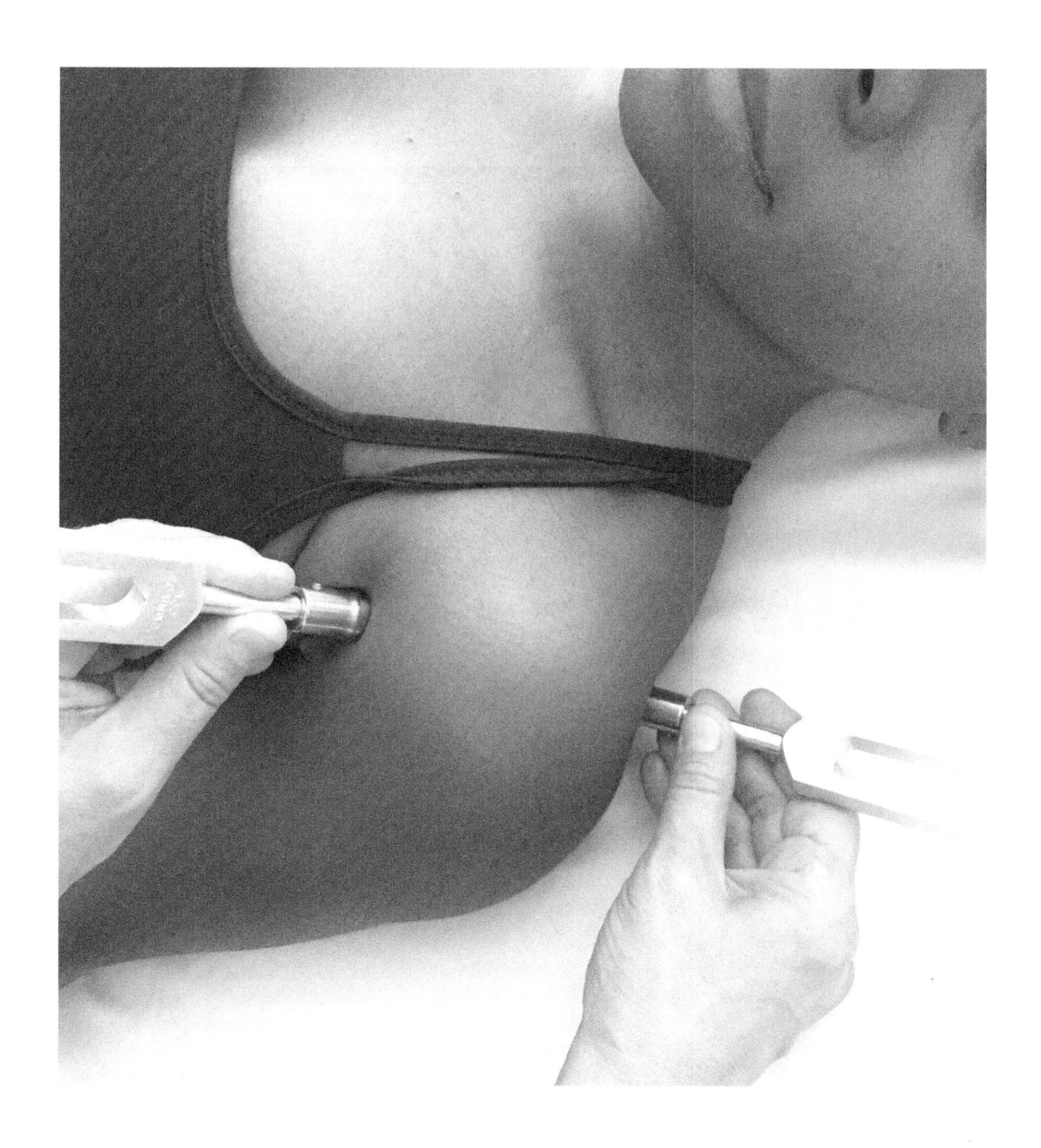

7-2. Position one activated tuning fork on the front of the shoulder and the other activated tuning fork onto the fleshy part of the elbow (extensor muscle).

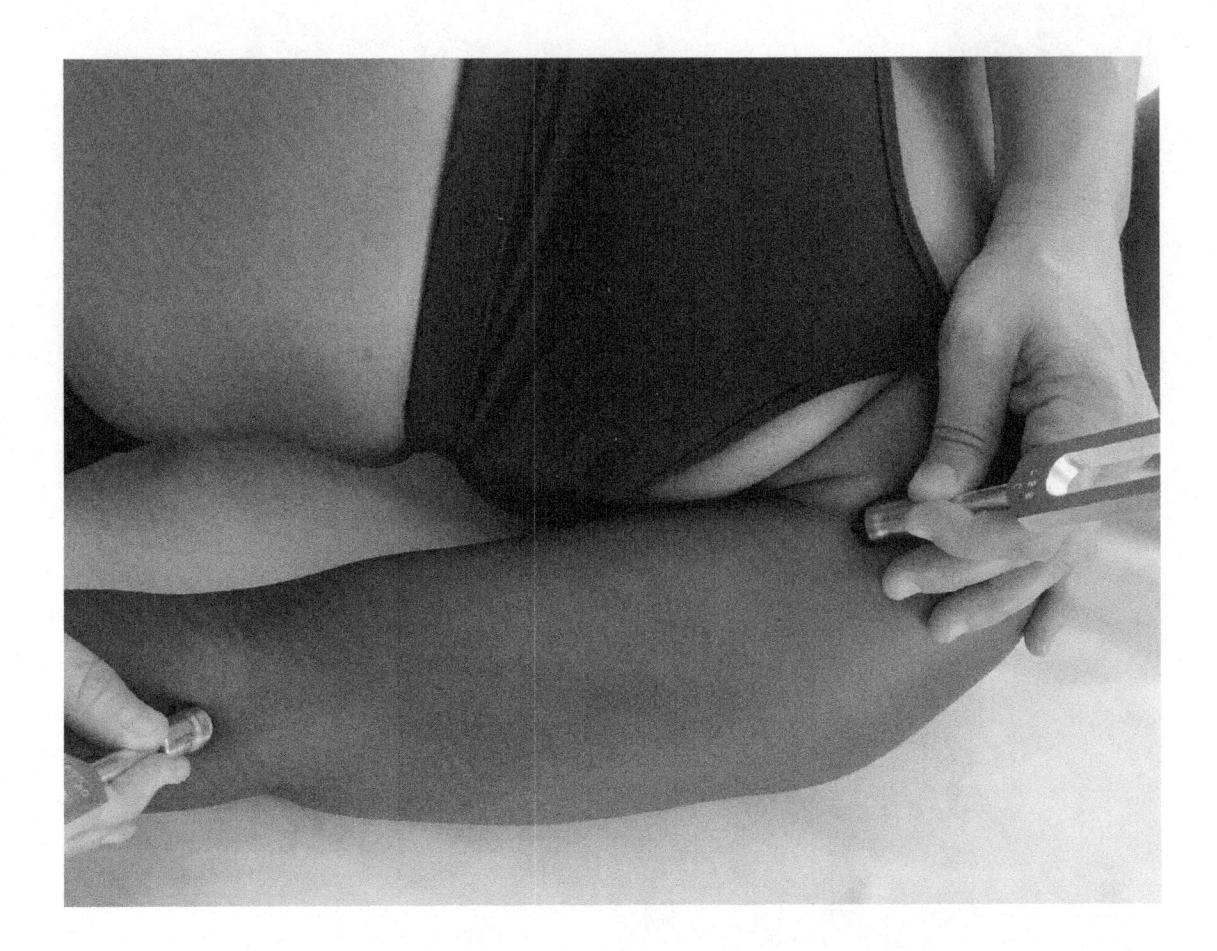

7-3. Position the activated tuning forks on either side of the elbow.

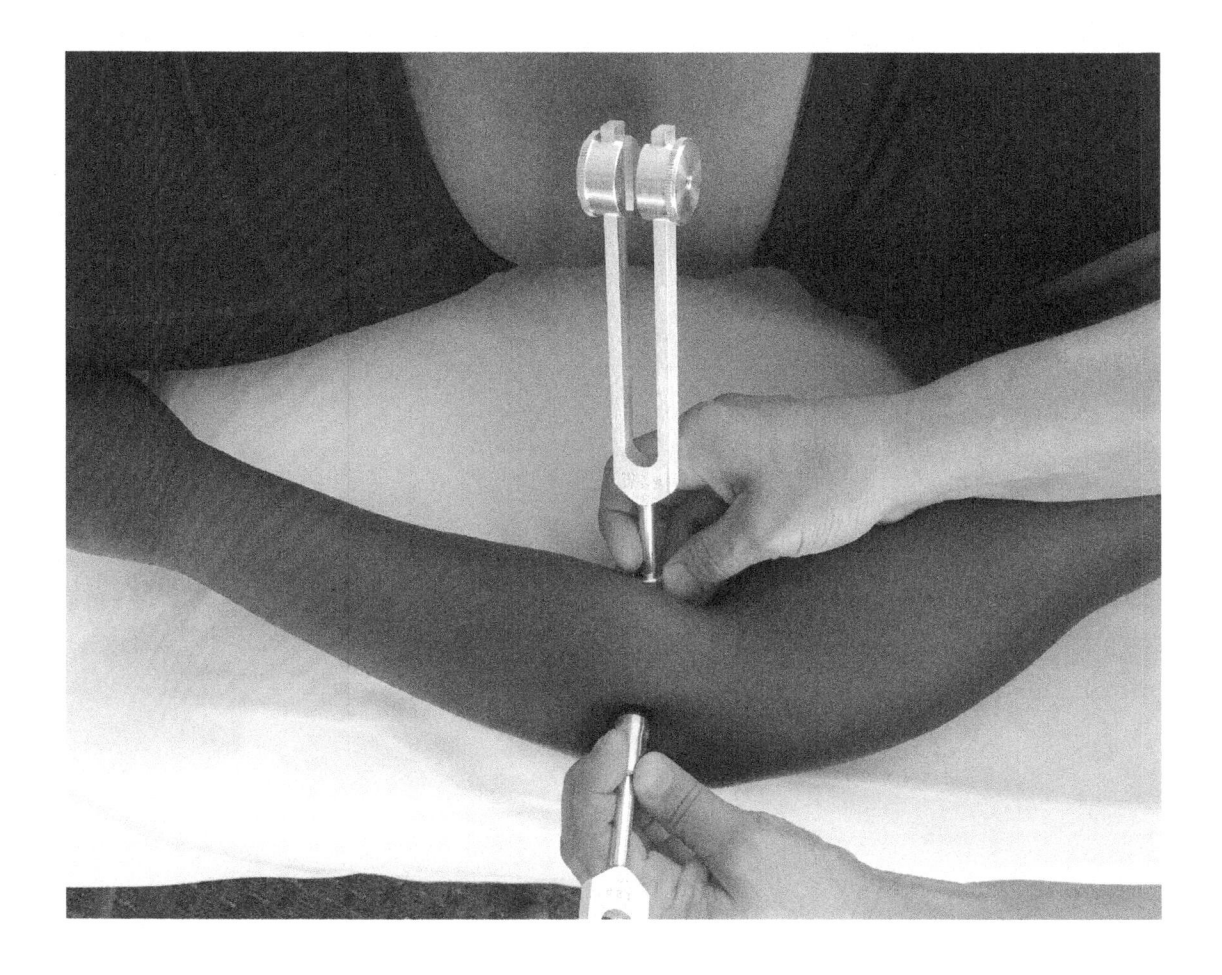

7-4a. Glide the activated tuning forks down the front and the side of shoulder (anterior and lateral deltoid). *(Two pictures: 7-4a and 7-4b)*

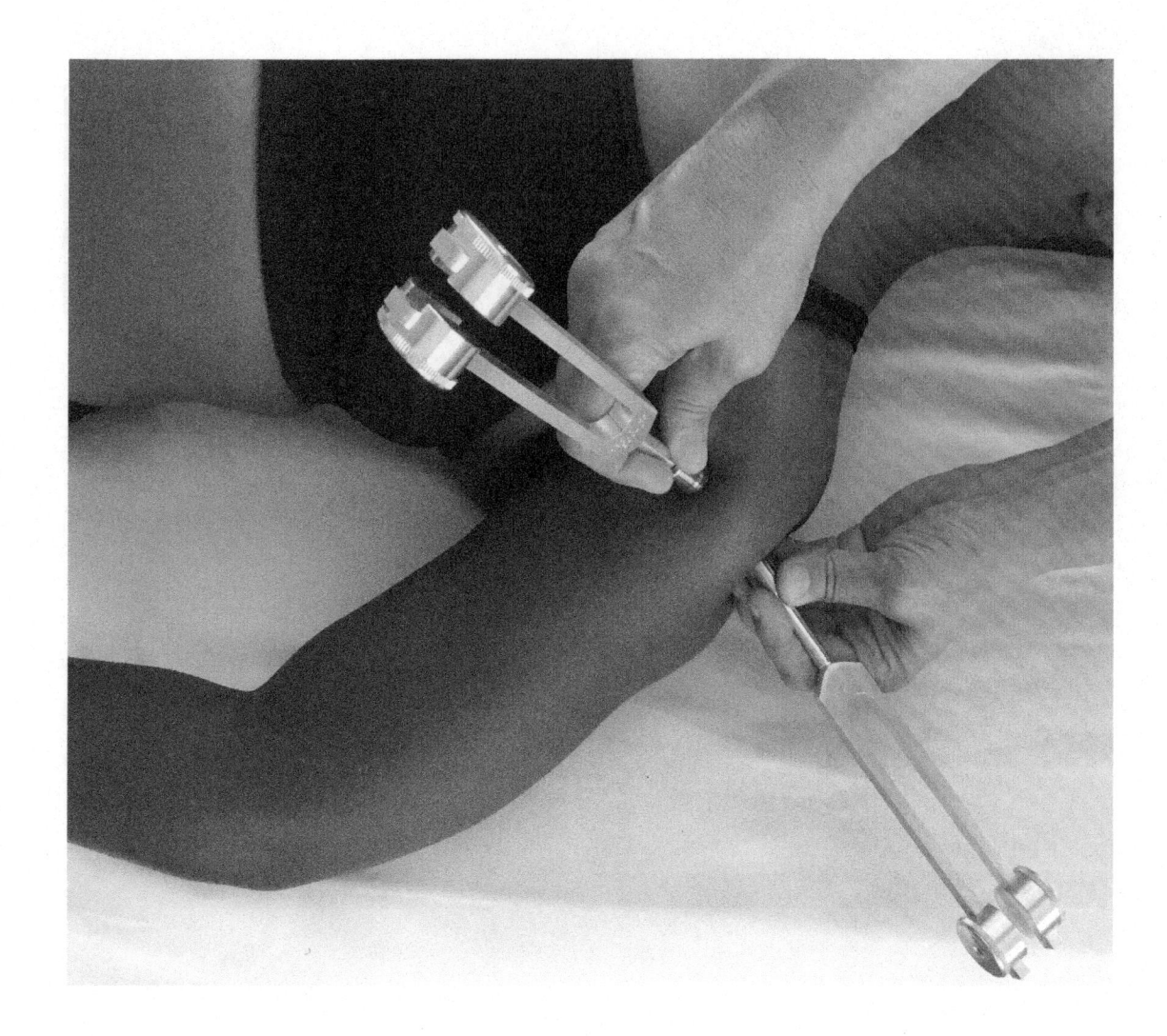

7-4b. Try using a pinching movement as well.

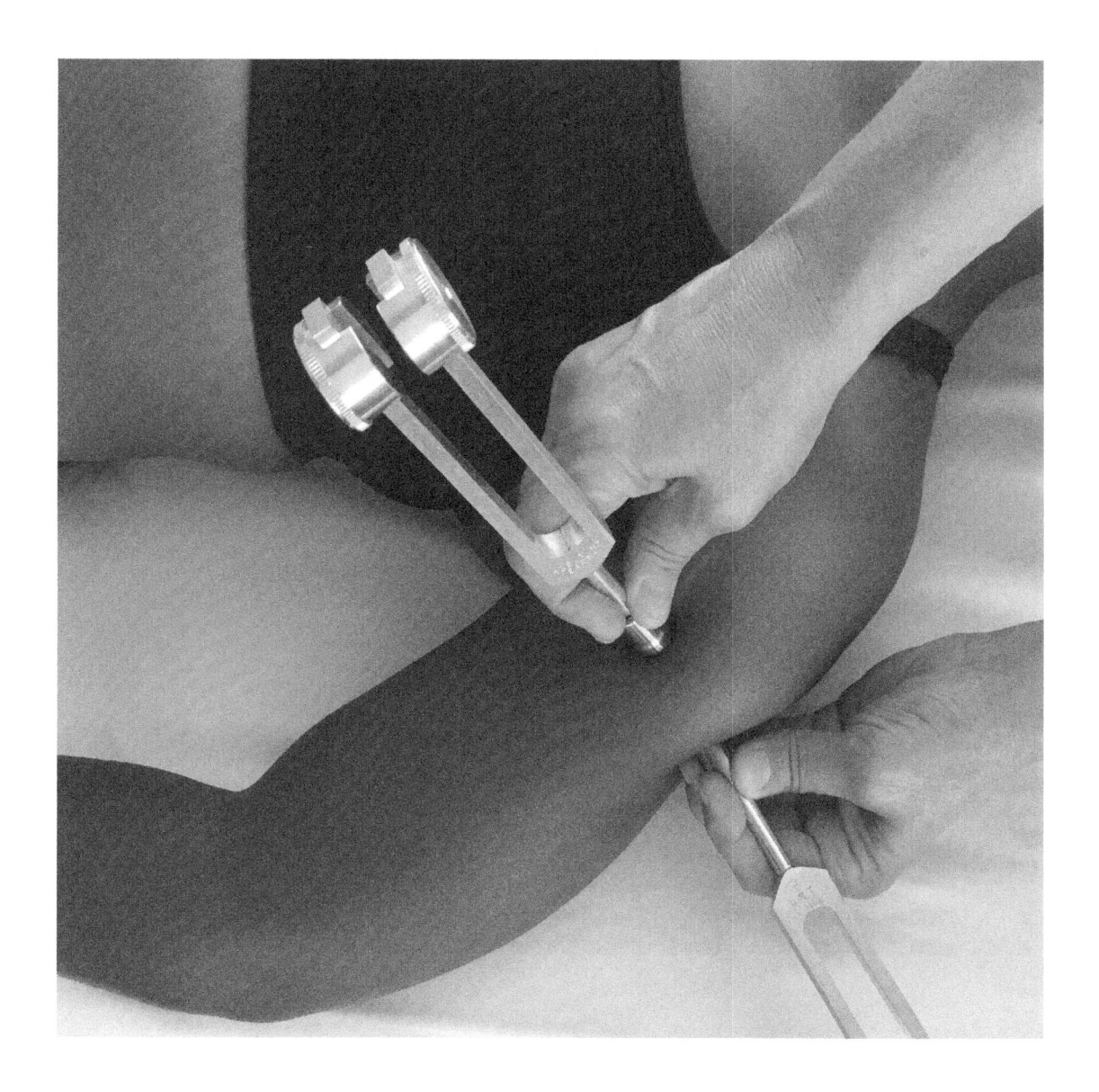

7-5. Glide the activated tuning forks down either side of biceps. Apply a bit of a pinching motion on the second pass.

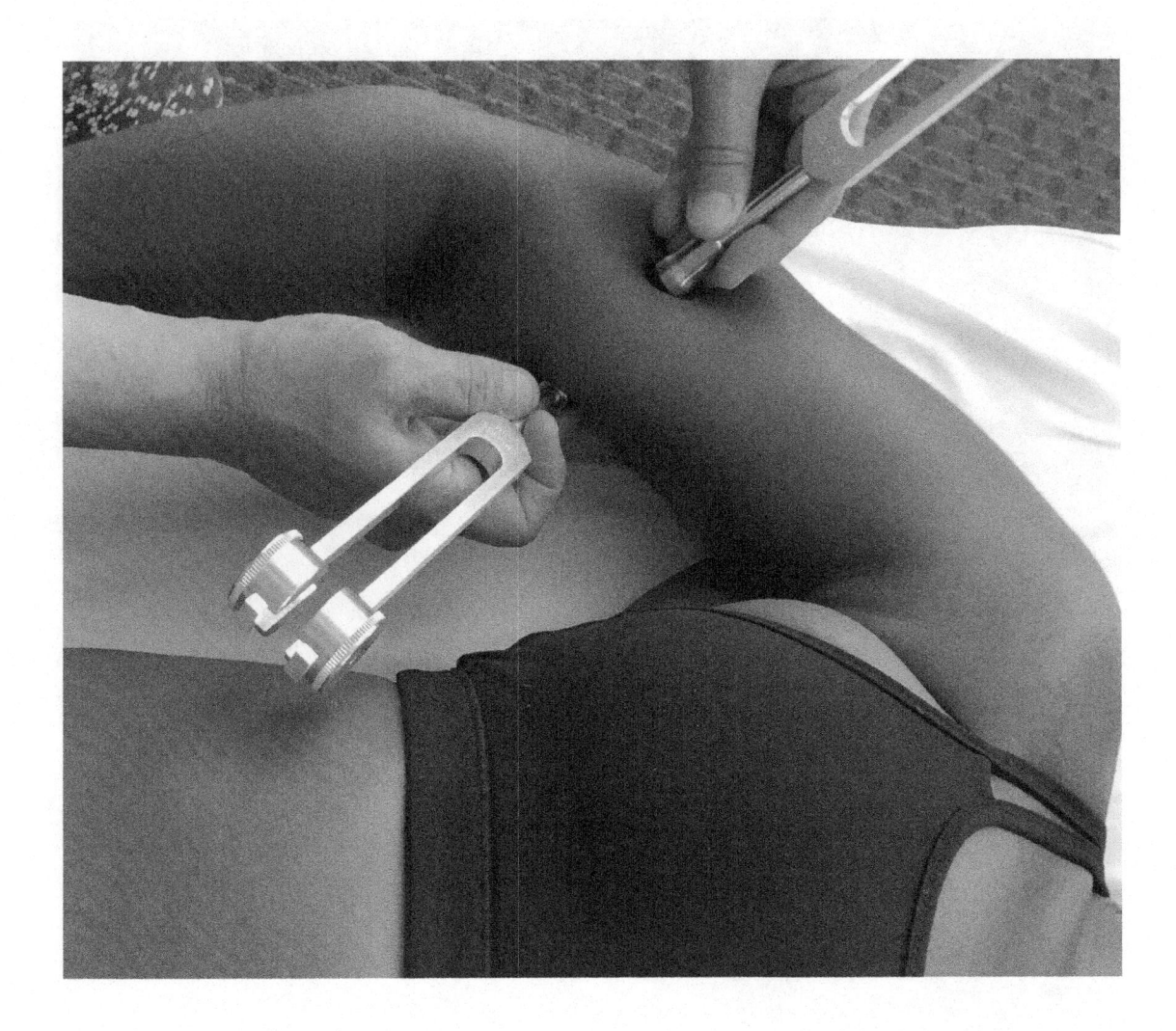

7-6. Glide/walk/pinch the activated tuning forks down the arm, between the biceps and triceps.

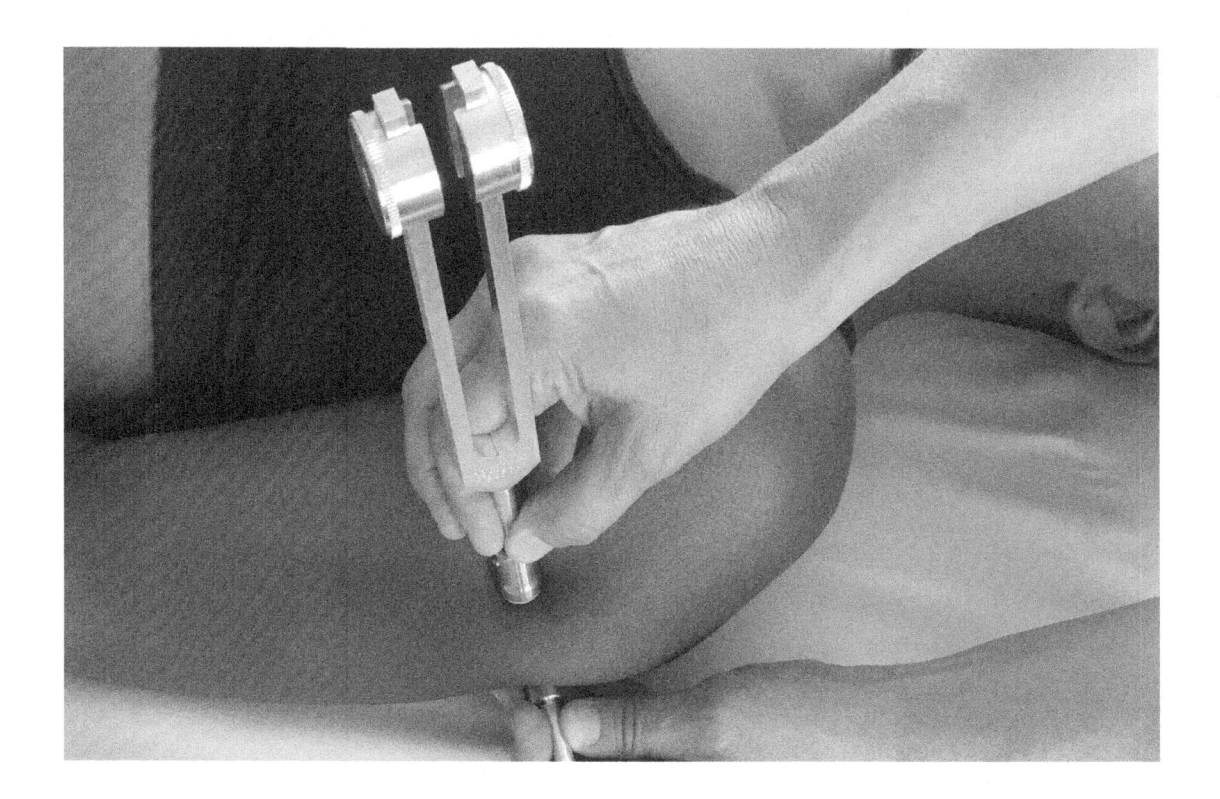

7-7. Glide both activated tuning forks slowly down the forearm. Use a pinching motion with both forks at the fleshy extensor muscle near the elbow.

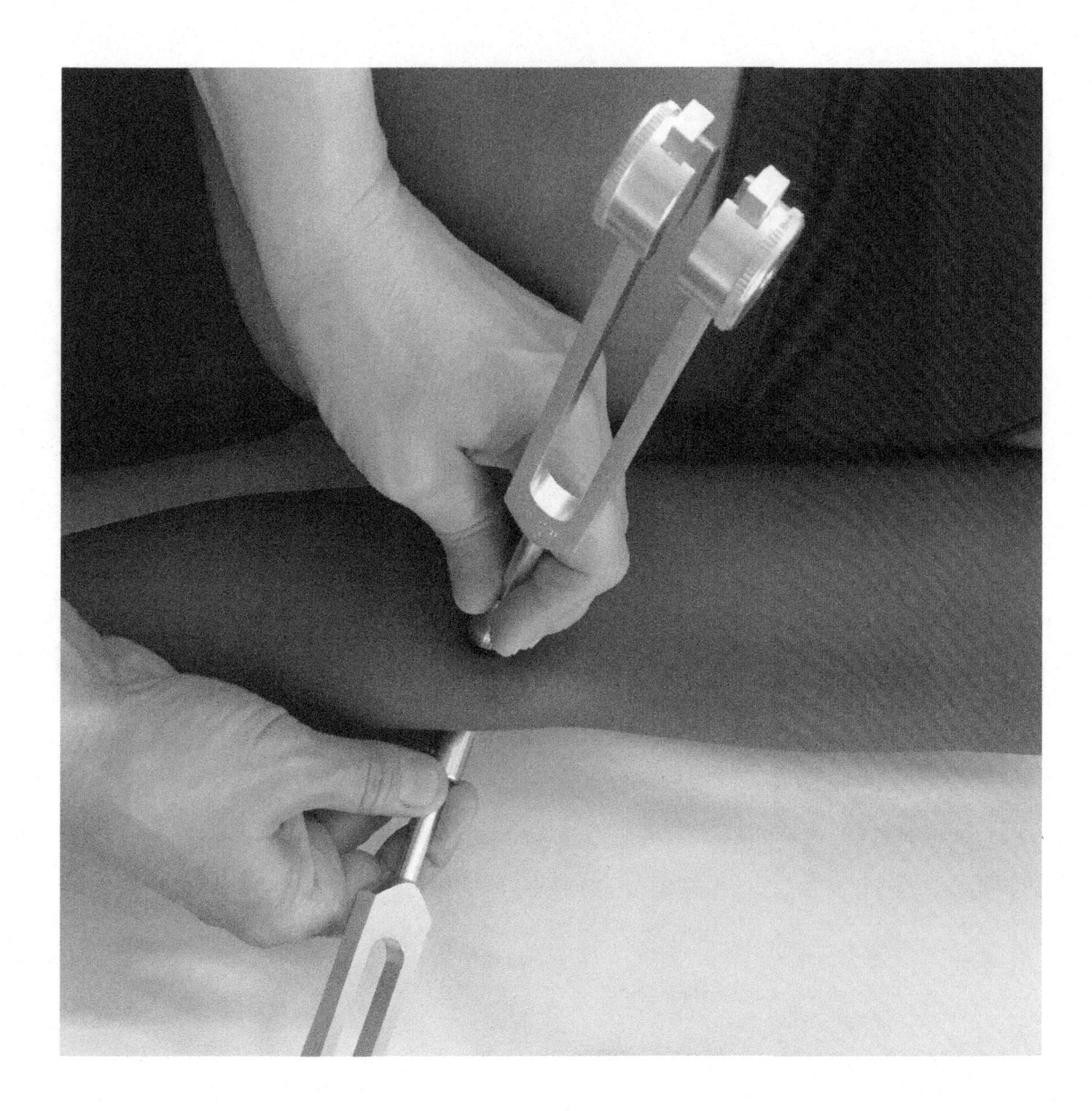

7-8. Position one activated tuning fork on the elbow, one on the wrist.

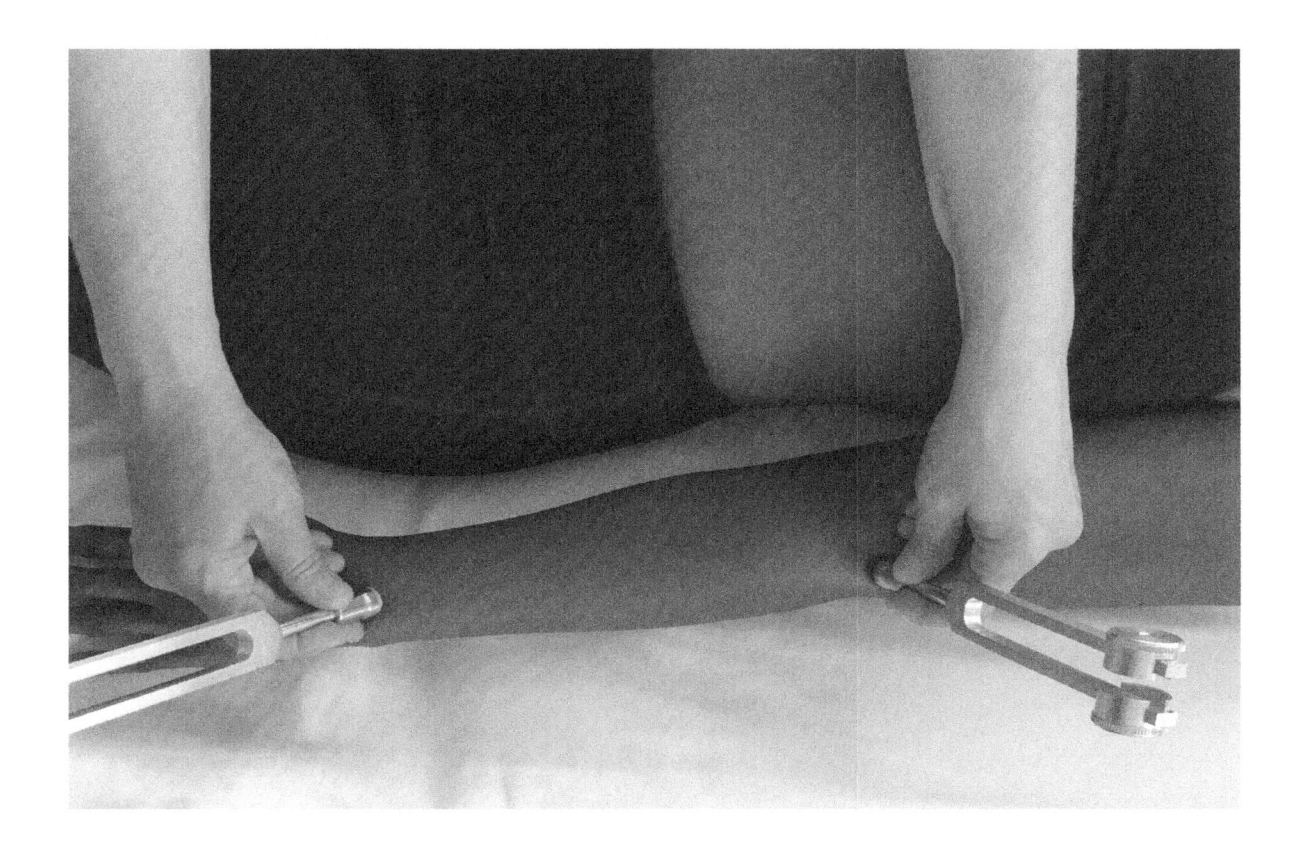

7-9. Position the activated tuning forks on the front and back of the wrist.

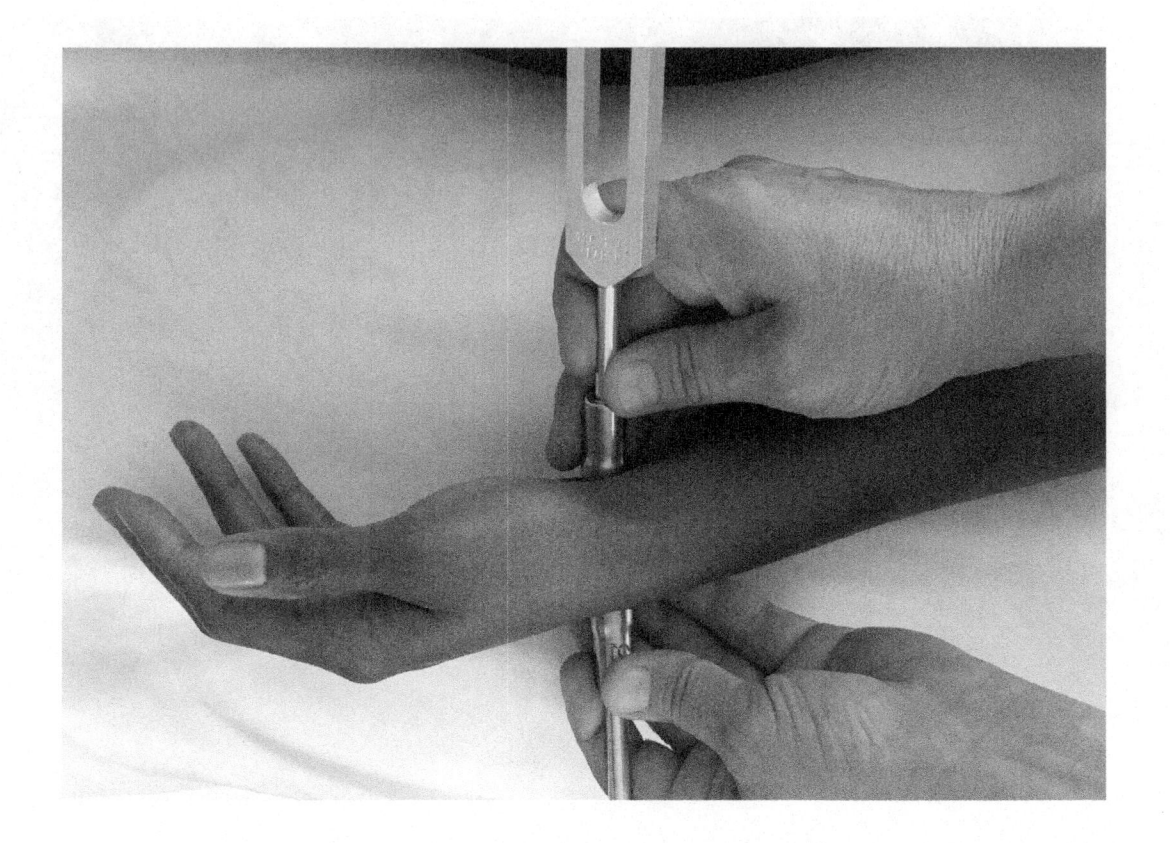

7-10a. Position one activated tuning fork on the back of the hand.

(Two pictures: 7-10a and 7-10b)

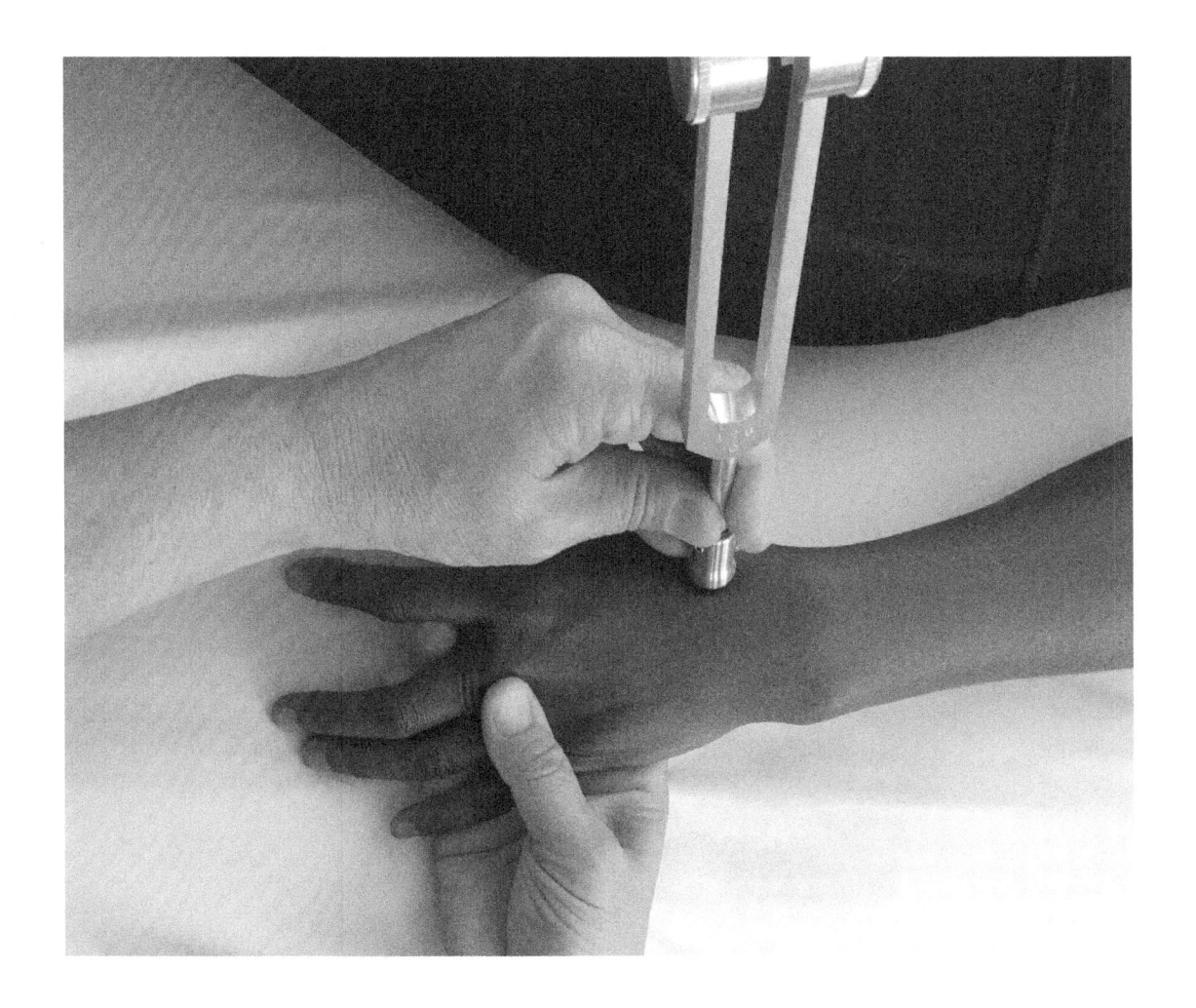

7-10b. Glide one activated tuning fork from the wrist to in between the fingers. Start at the thumb and make one pass between each of the fingers until finishing between the pinkie and ring fingers.

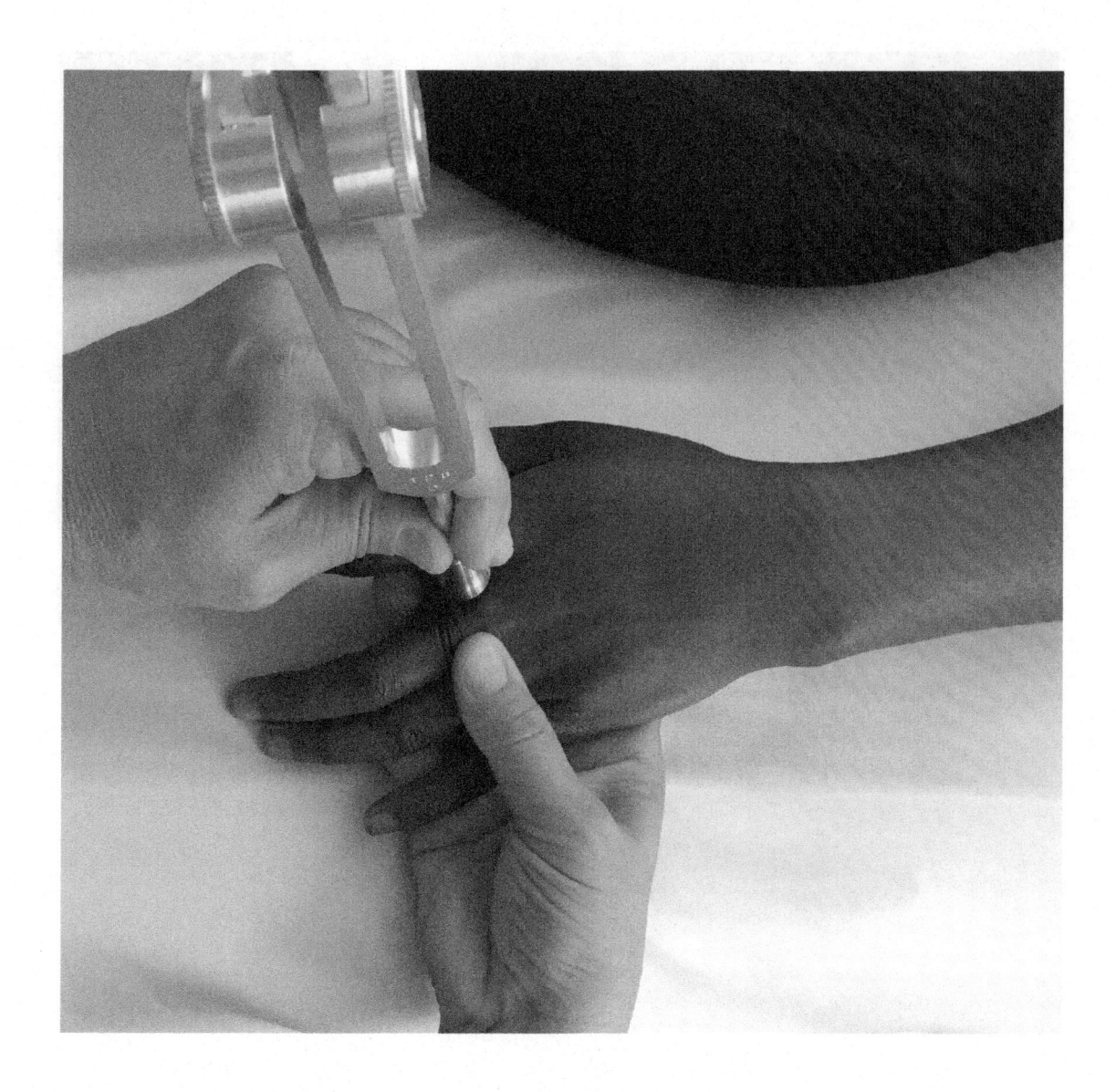

7-11. Position the activated tuning fork on the tip of the pinkie finger. Reactivate the tuning fork and move to the tip of the ring finger. Repeat this with each finger until reaching the thumb.

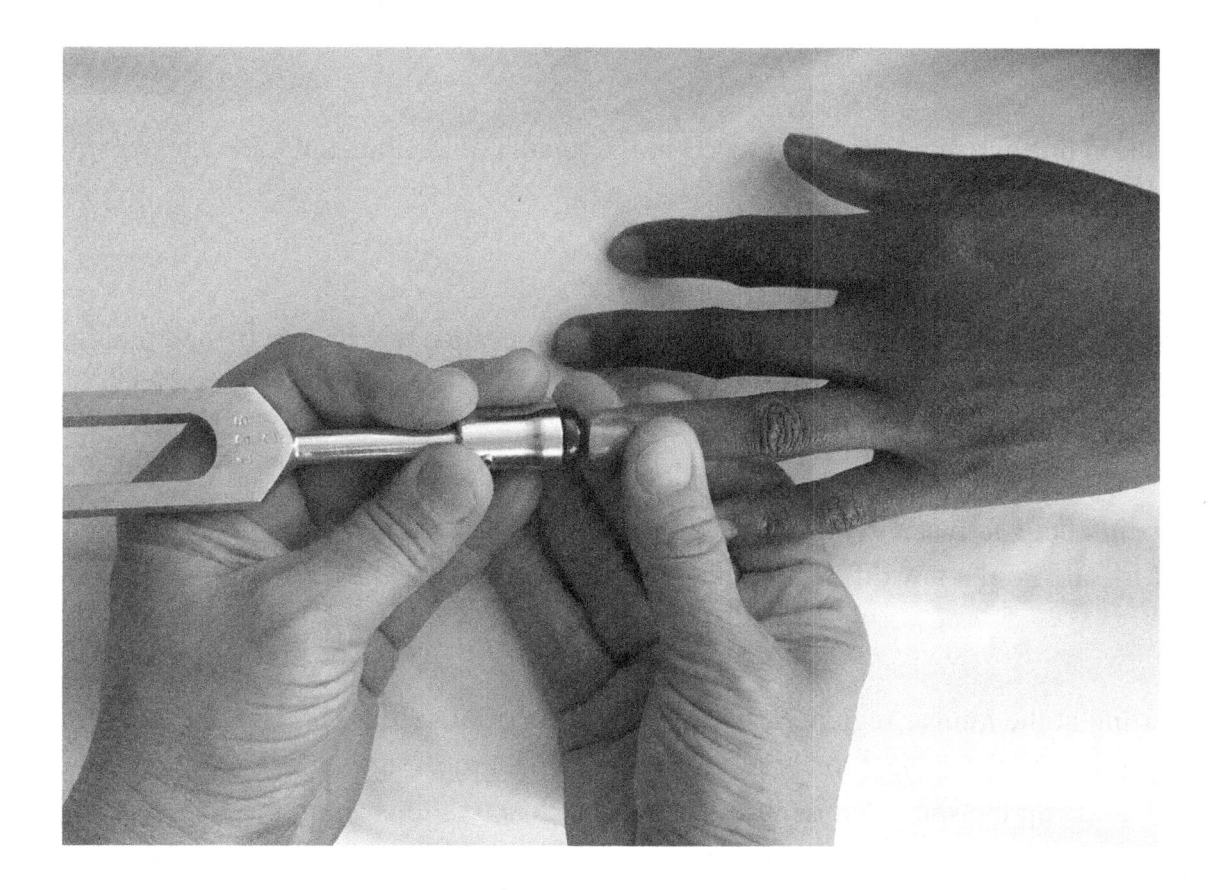

8. Protocol for Spinal Toning (prone)

8-1. Position one activated tuning fork end on the top of the head, the other activated tuning fork on the sacrum.

8-2. Position one activated tuning fork end in the middle of occiput and the other activated tuning fork end on the sacrum.

8-3. Position one activated tuning fork on the upper trapezius, the other activated tuning fork on the side of the sacrum, left then right.

8-4. Position both activated tuning fork ends on the sacrum and just feel into it. Reactivate the tuning fork and hold a few different points before moving on.

8-5. Starting at the lumbar region, position an activated tuning fork end on either side (in the lamina groove) of the spine. Slowly glide up the lamina groove until reaching the occiput. This is a slow glide up the spine that requires multiple fork activations along the way. It feels good to the recipient if the practitioner always leaves one fork on the body while re-activating the second fork. Multiple activations of the tuning forks required.

(Two pictures: 8-5a and 8-5b)

8-6. Now reverse the path and glide down the neck. Reactivate the tuning forks and continue down the sides of the spine, ending at the sacrum. *(Two pictures: 8-6a and 8-6b)*

8-1. Position one activated tuning fork end on the top of the head, position the other activated tuning fork on the sacrum.

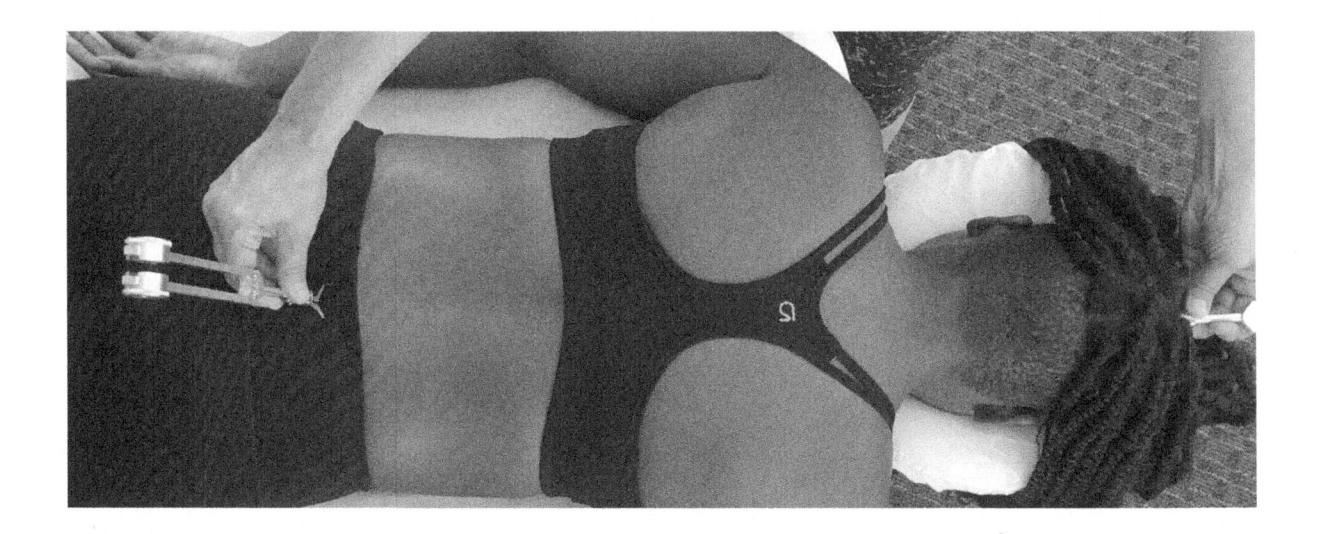

8-2. Position one activated tuning fork end in the middle of the occiput, position the other activated tuning fork end on the sacrum.

8-3. Position one activated tuning fork on upper trapezius, the other activated tuning fork on the side of the sacrum, left then right.

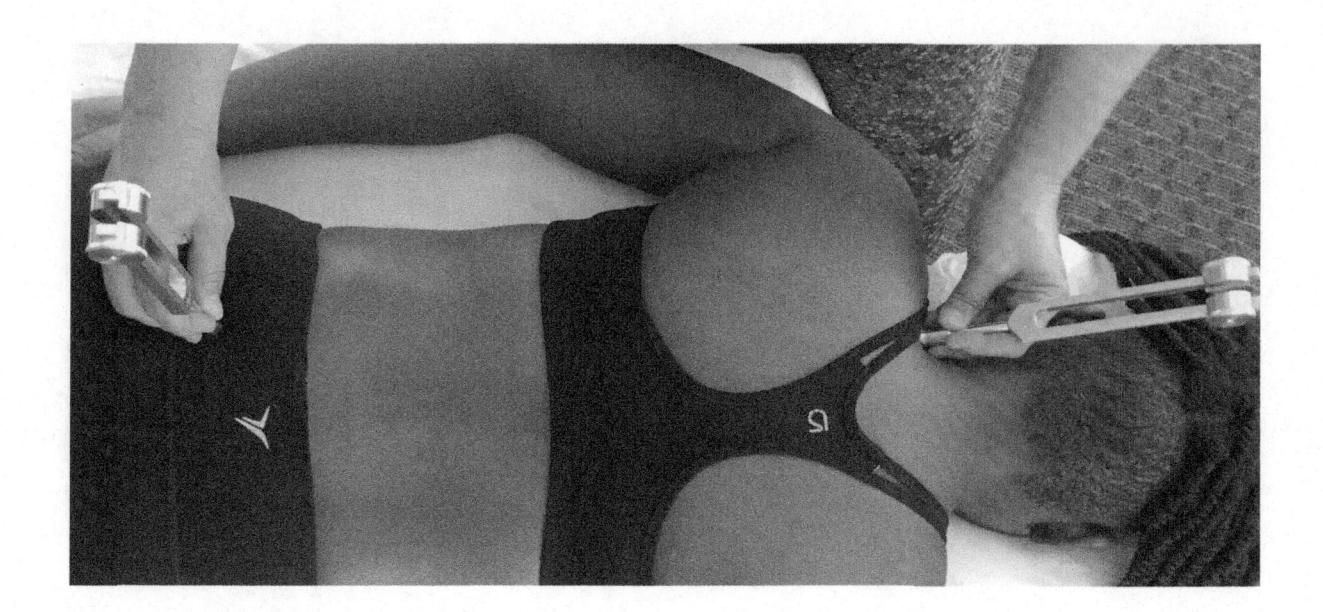

8-4. Position both activated tuning fork ends on the sacrum and just feel into it. Reactivate the fork and hold a few different points before moving on.

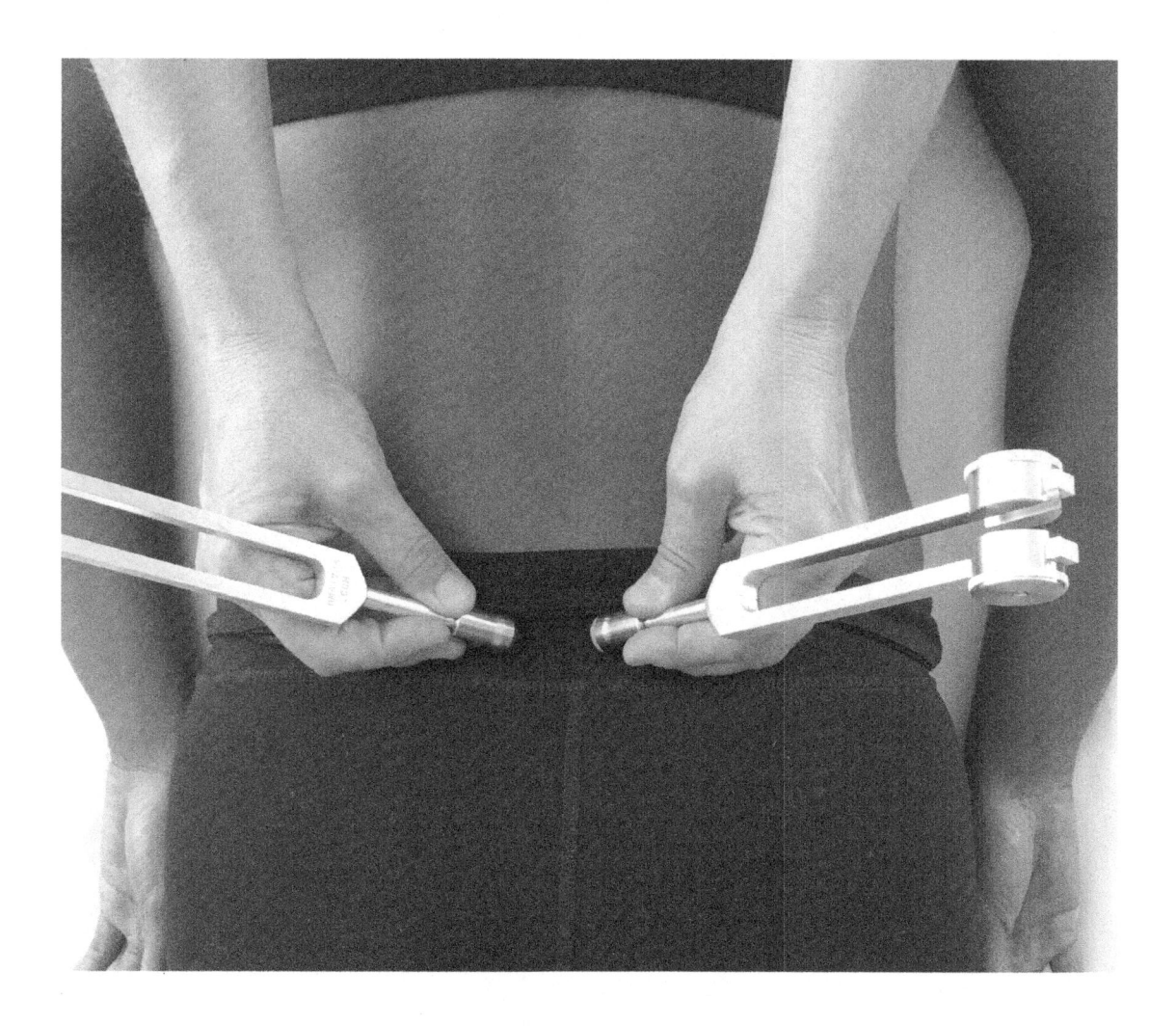

8-5a. Starting a bit lower than in the picture--at the low back region--place an activated tuning fork end on either side of the spine, in the lamina groove. *(Two pictures: 8-5a and 8-5b)*

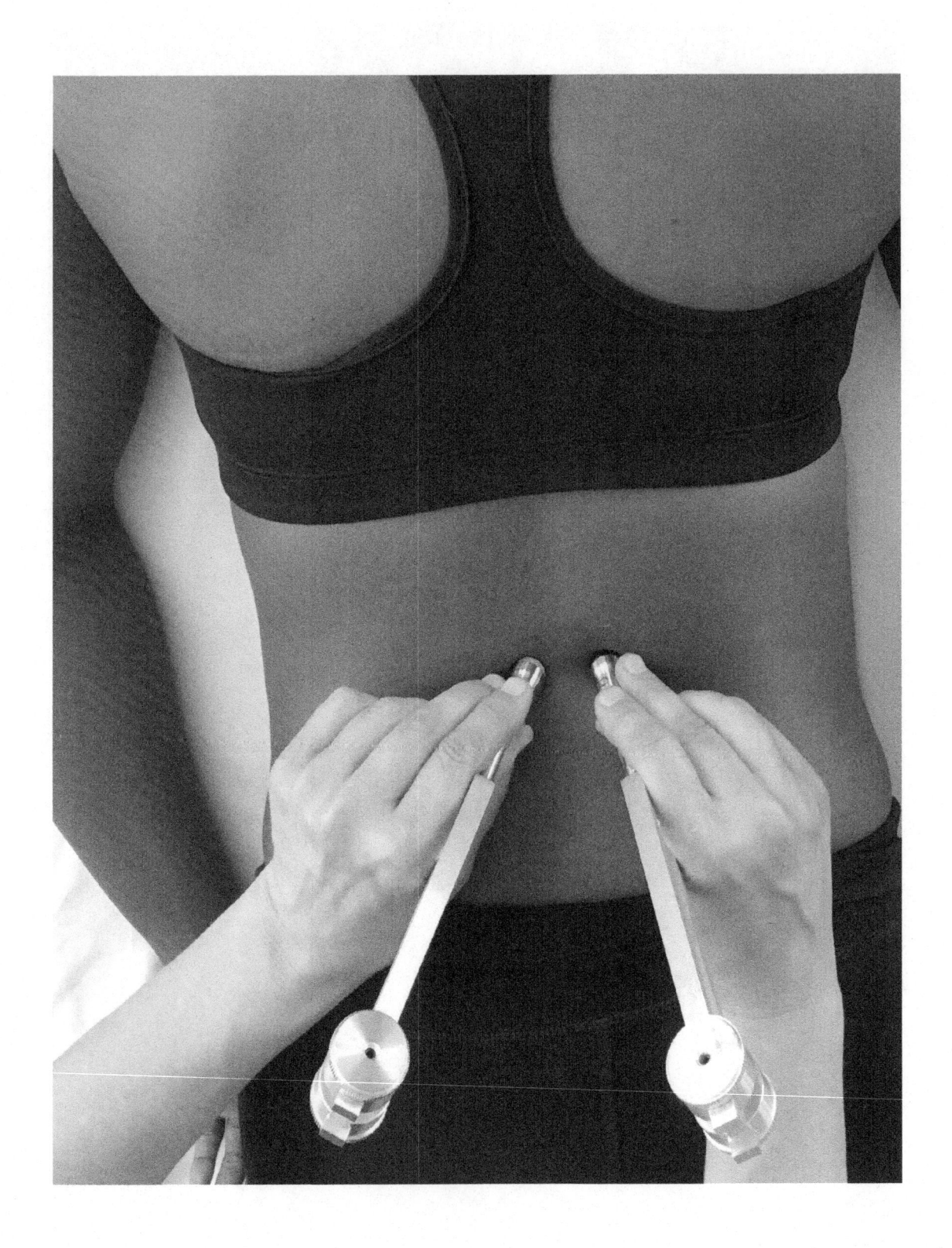

8-5b. Slowly glide up the lamina groove until reaching the occiput. This is a slow glide up the spine that requires multiple fork activations along the way. It feels good to the recipient if the practitioner always leaves one fork on the body while activating the second fork.

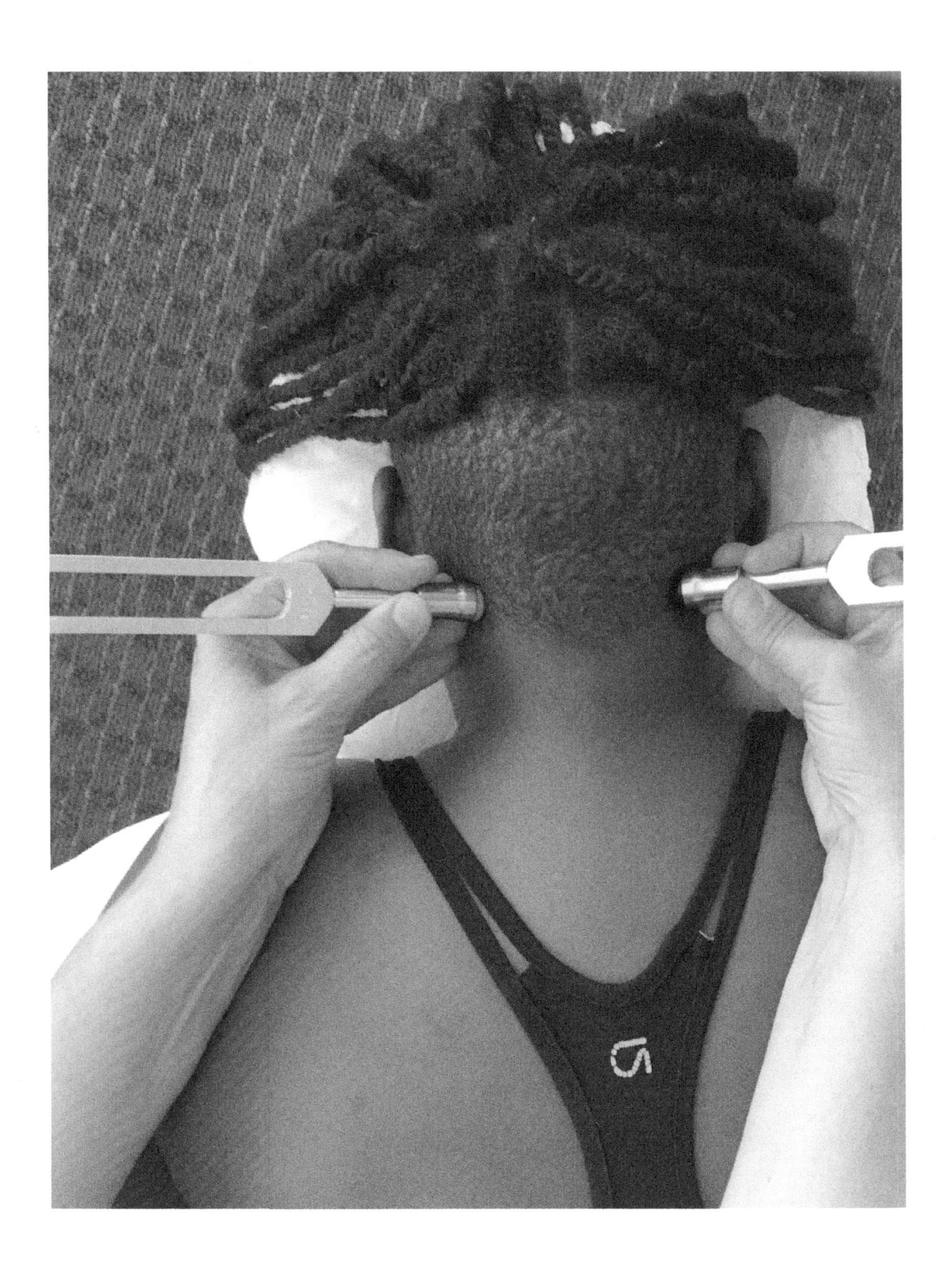

8-6a. Reverse the path and glide down the neck. *(Two pictures: 8-6a and 8-6b)*

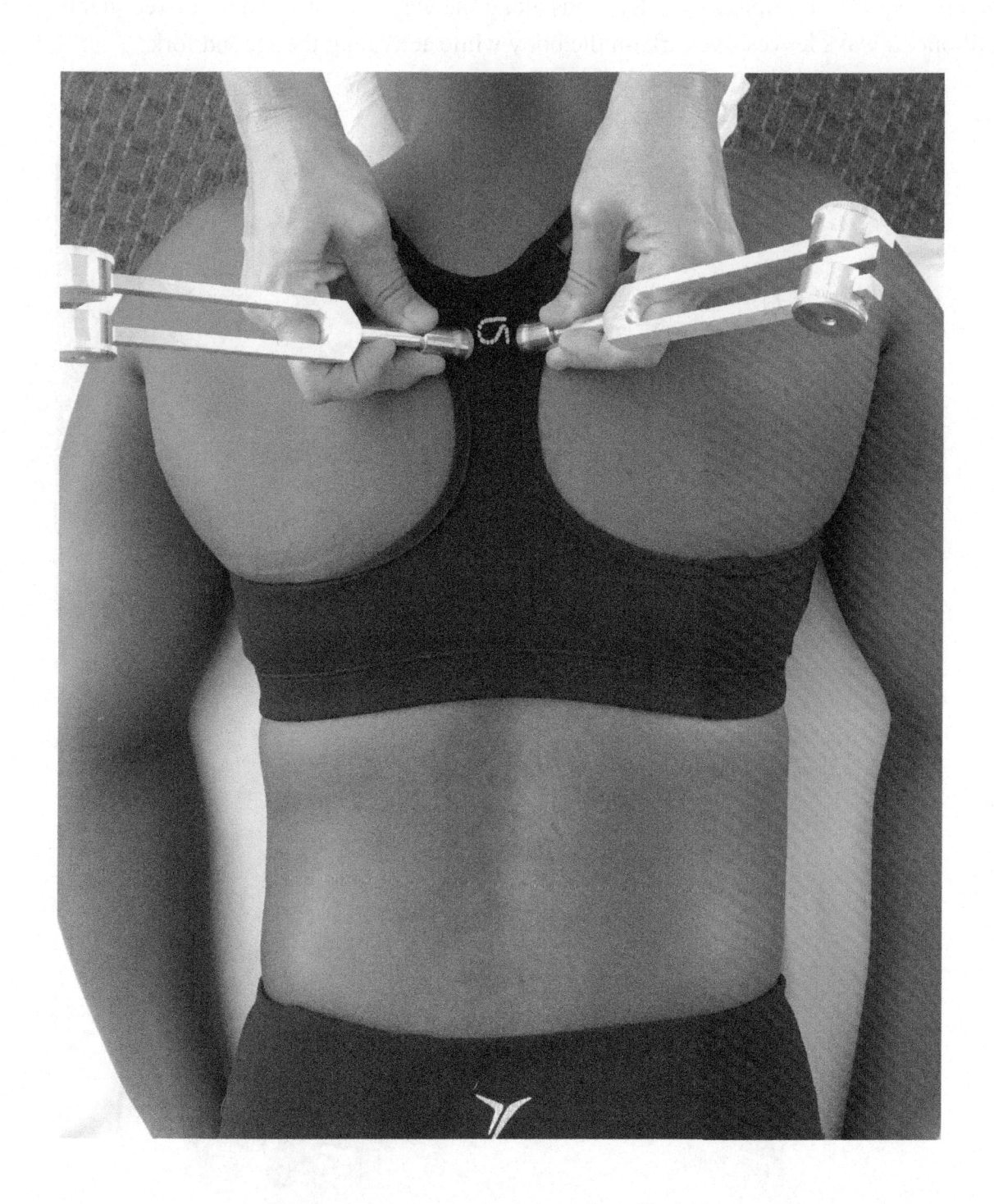

8-6b. Reactivate the tuning forks and continue down the sides of the spine, ending at the sacrum.

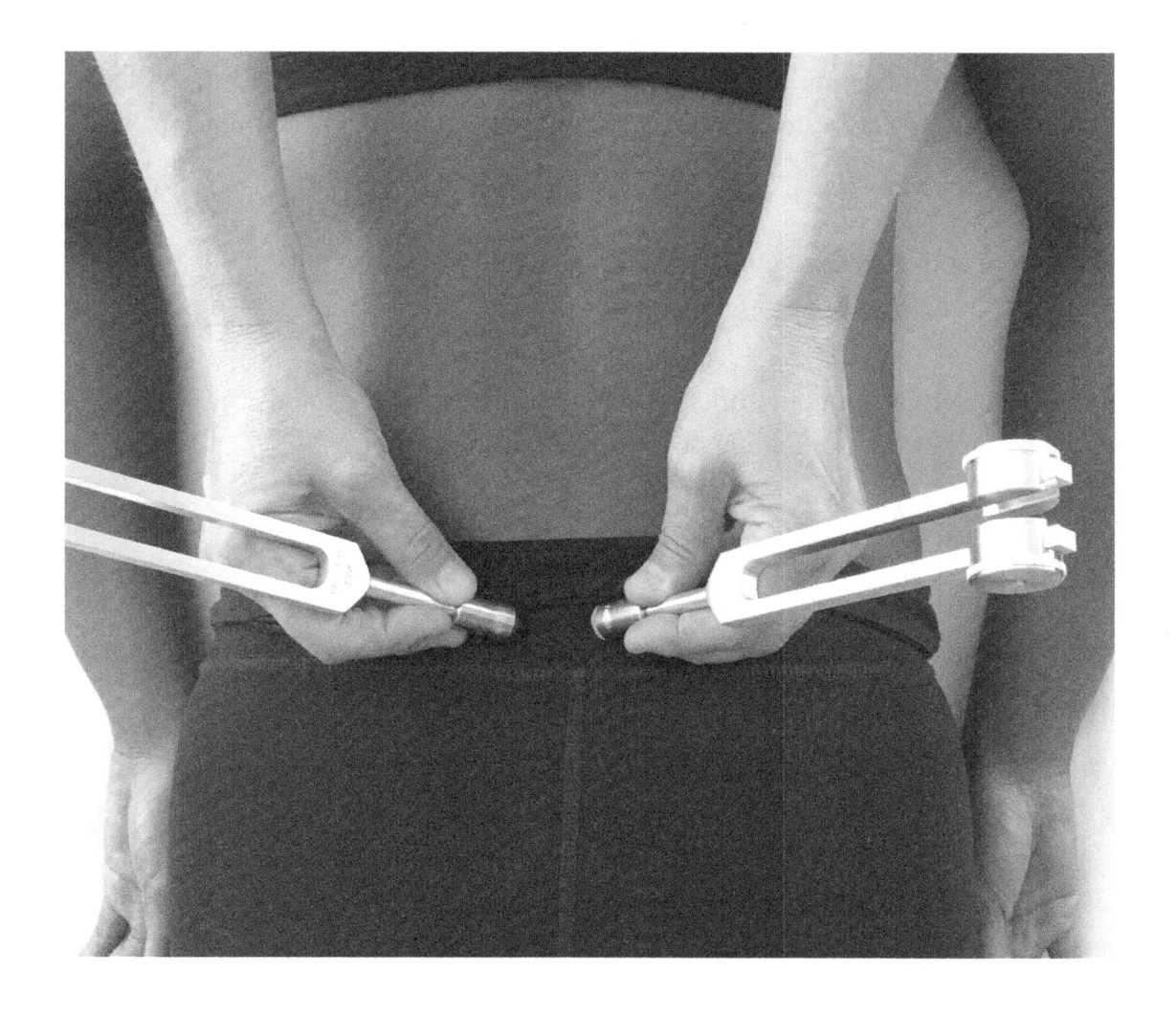

9. **Protocol for Hips/Legs (supine)**

9-1. Position one activated tuning fork end on the hip point (the side of the hip—it feels like a divot). Position the other activated tuning fork on the outside of the knee joint.

9-2. Position both activated tuning forks on either side of the knee joint.

9-3. Position both activated tuning forks at the top of the leg, in the middle of the thigh. Glide slowly down the upper leg, continuing down to the knee insertion.

(Two pictures: 9-3a and 9-3b)

9-4. Position both activated tuning forks on the towards the midline of the leg. Glide slowly down the inside of the upper leg, continuing down to the knee insertion.

(Two pictures: 9-4a and 9-4b)

9-5. Position both activated tuning forks on the outside of the thigh. Glide slowly down the outside of the upper leg, continuing down to the knee insertion on the outside.

(Two pictures: 9-5a and 9-5b)

9-1. Position one activated tuning fork end on the hip point (the side of the hip—it feels like a divot). Position the other activated tuning fork on the outside of the knee joint.

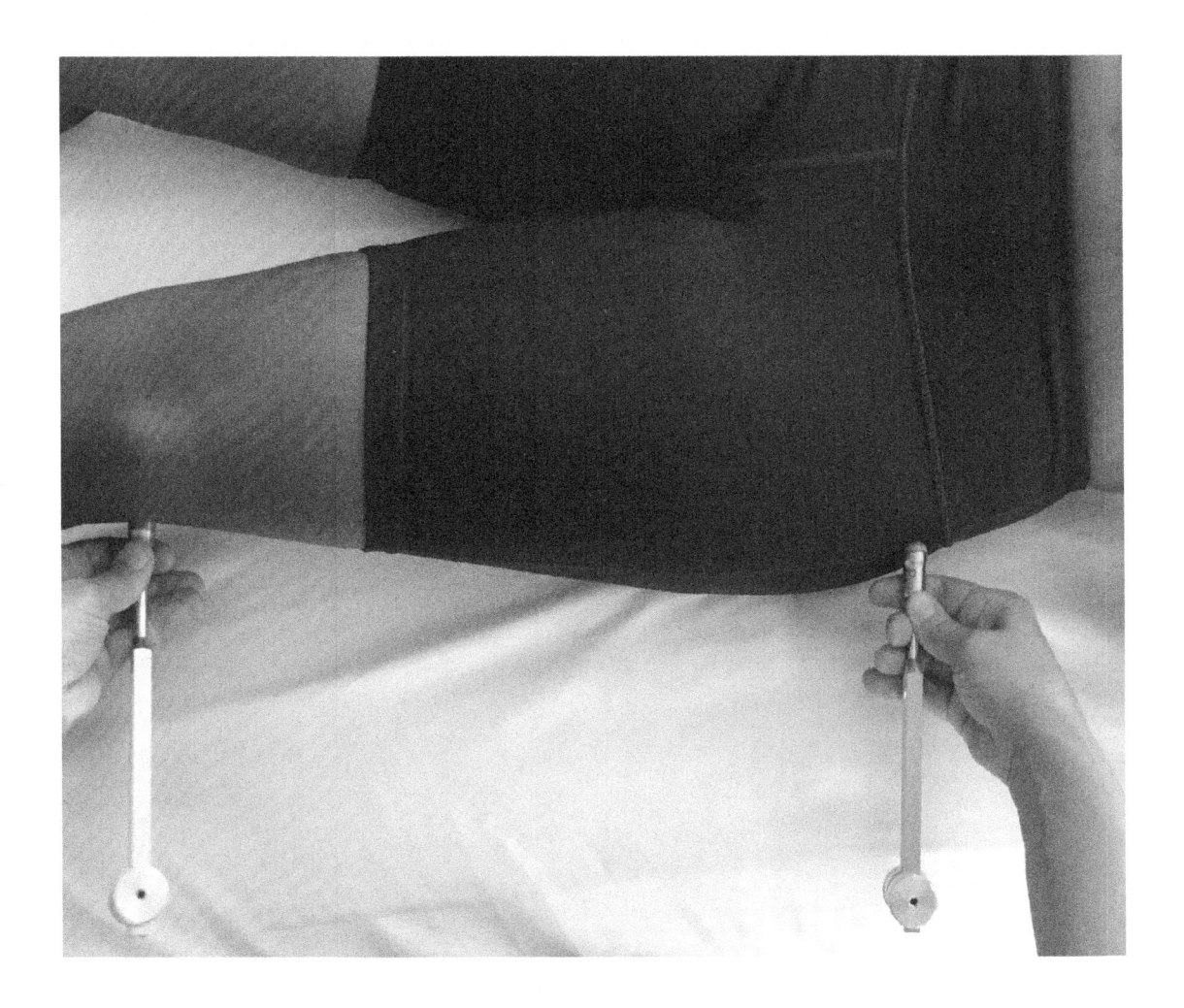

9-2. Position both activated tuning forks on either side of the knee joint.

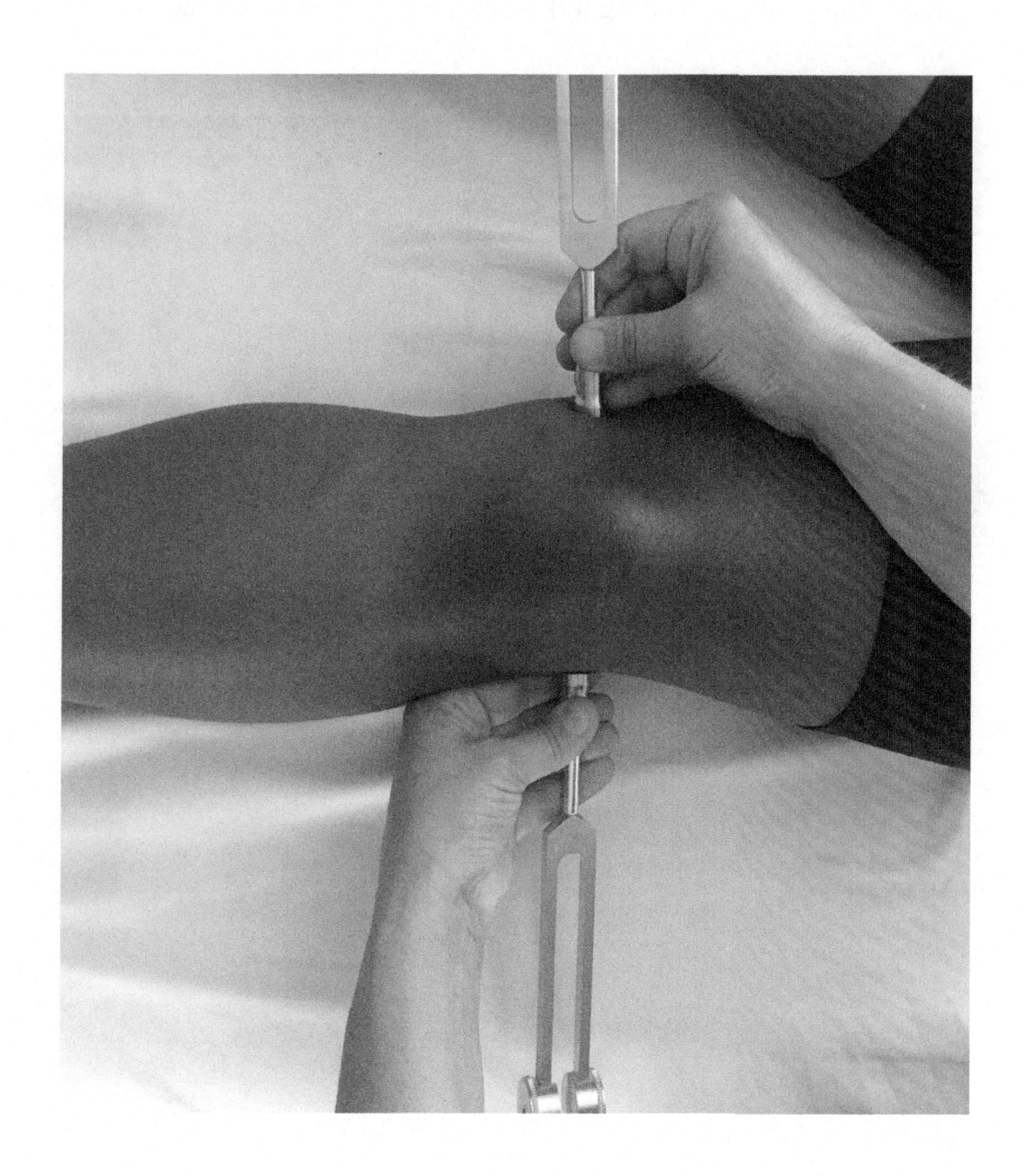

9-3a. Position both activated tuning forks at the top of the leg, in the middle of the thigh.

(Two pictures: 9-3a and 9-3b)

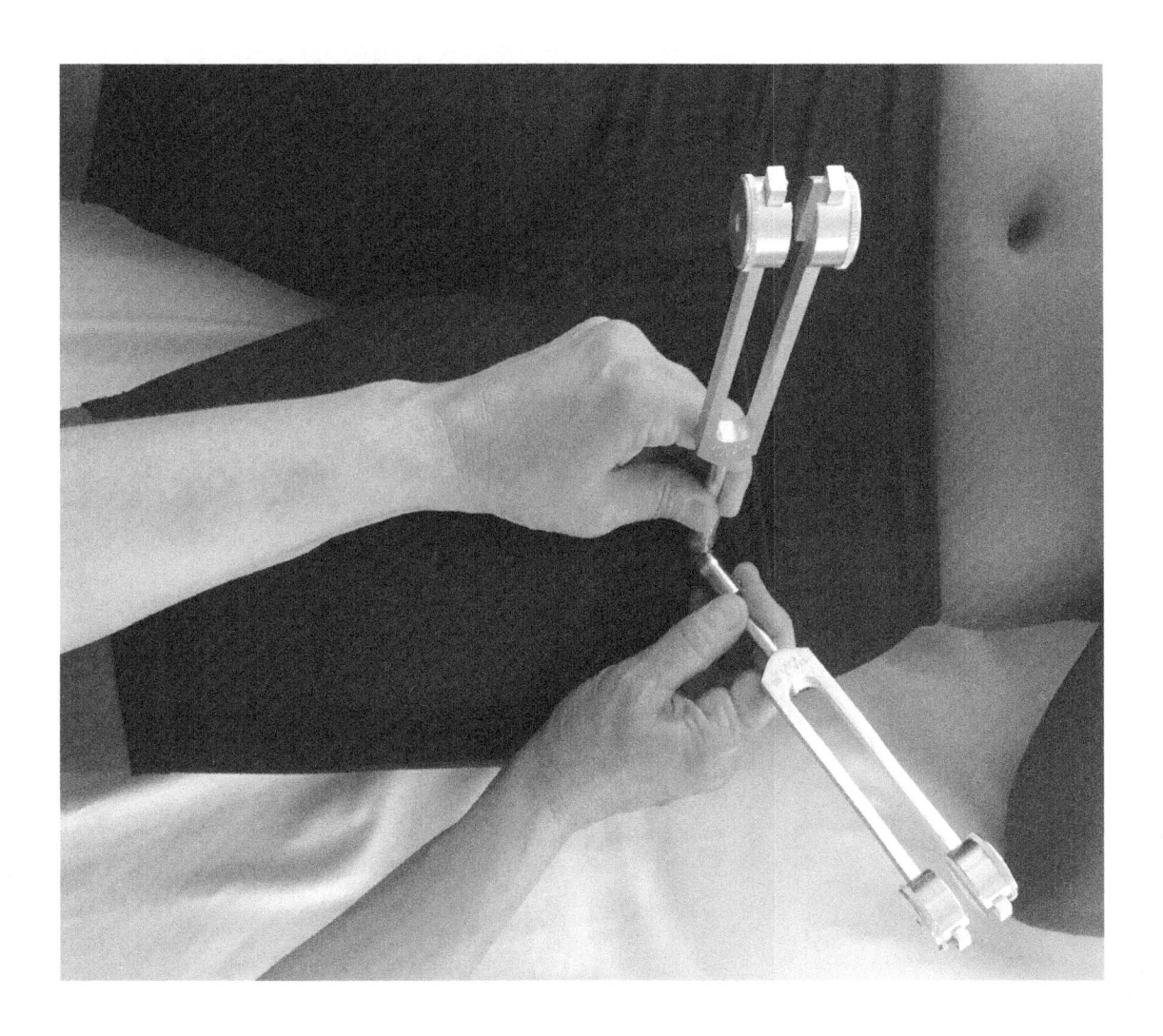

9-3b. Glide both activated tuning forks slowly down the upper leg, continuing down to the knee insertion.

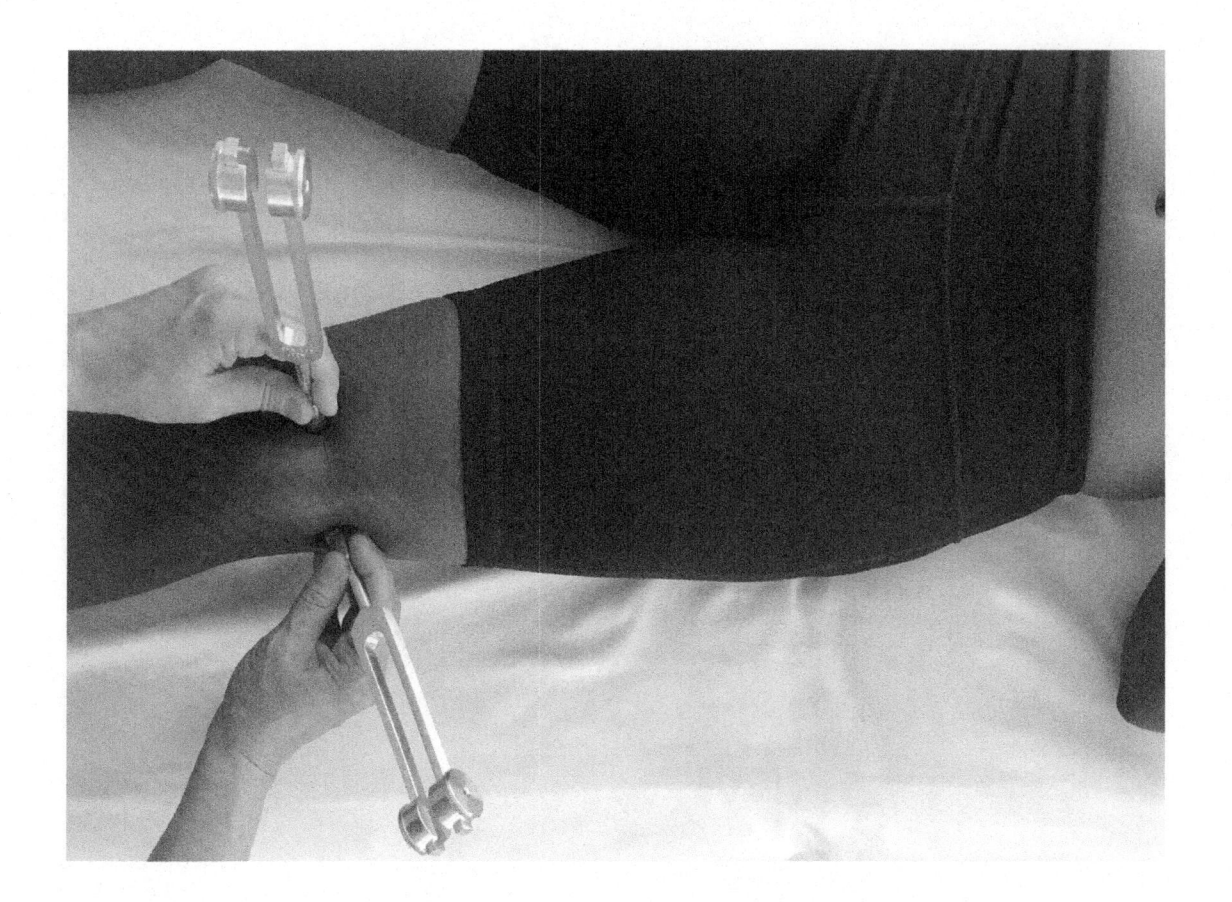

9-4a. Position both activated tuning forks towards the midline of the leg.

(Two pictures: 9-4a and 9-4b)

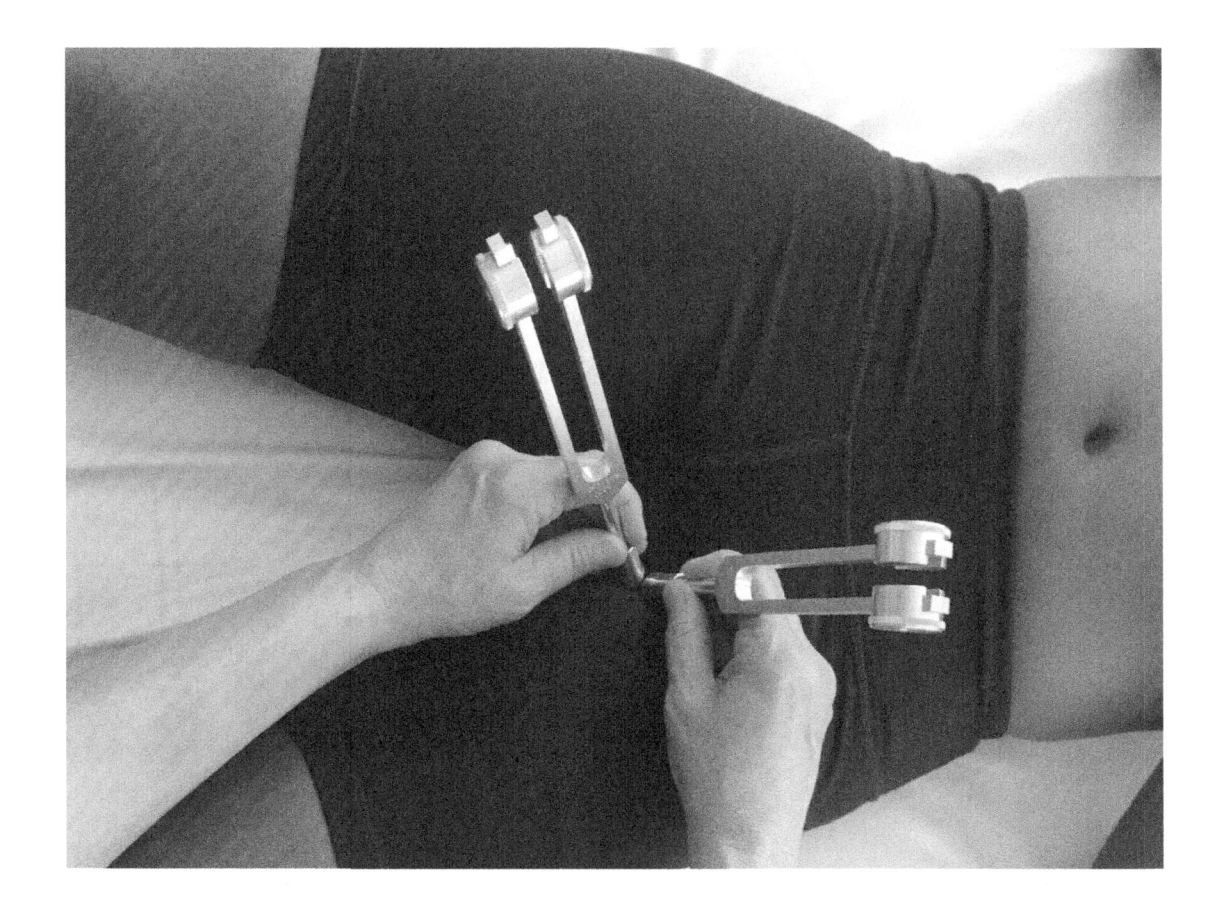

9-4b. Glide both activated tuning forks slowly down the inside of the upper leg, continuing down to the knee insertion.

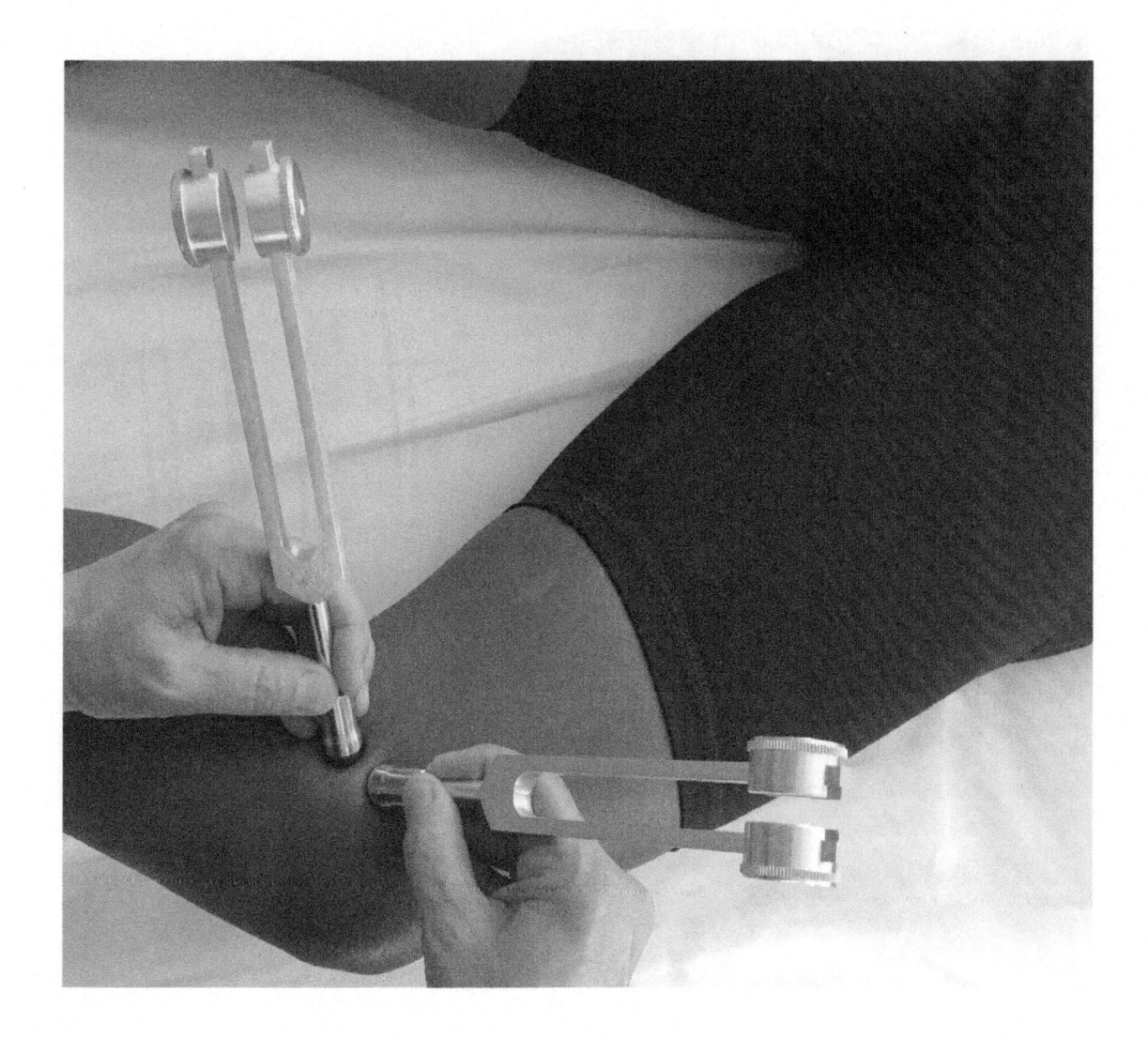

9-5a. Position both activated tuning forks on the outside of the thigh.

(Two pictures: 9-5a and 9-5b)

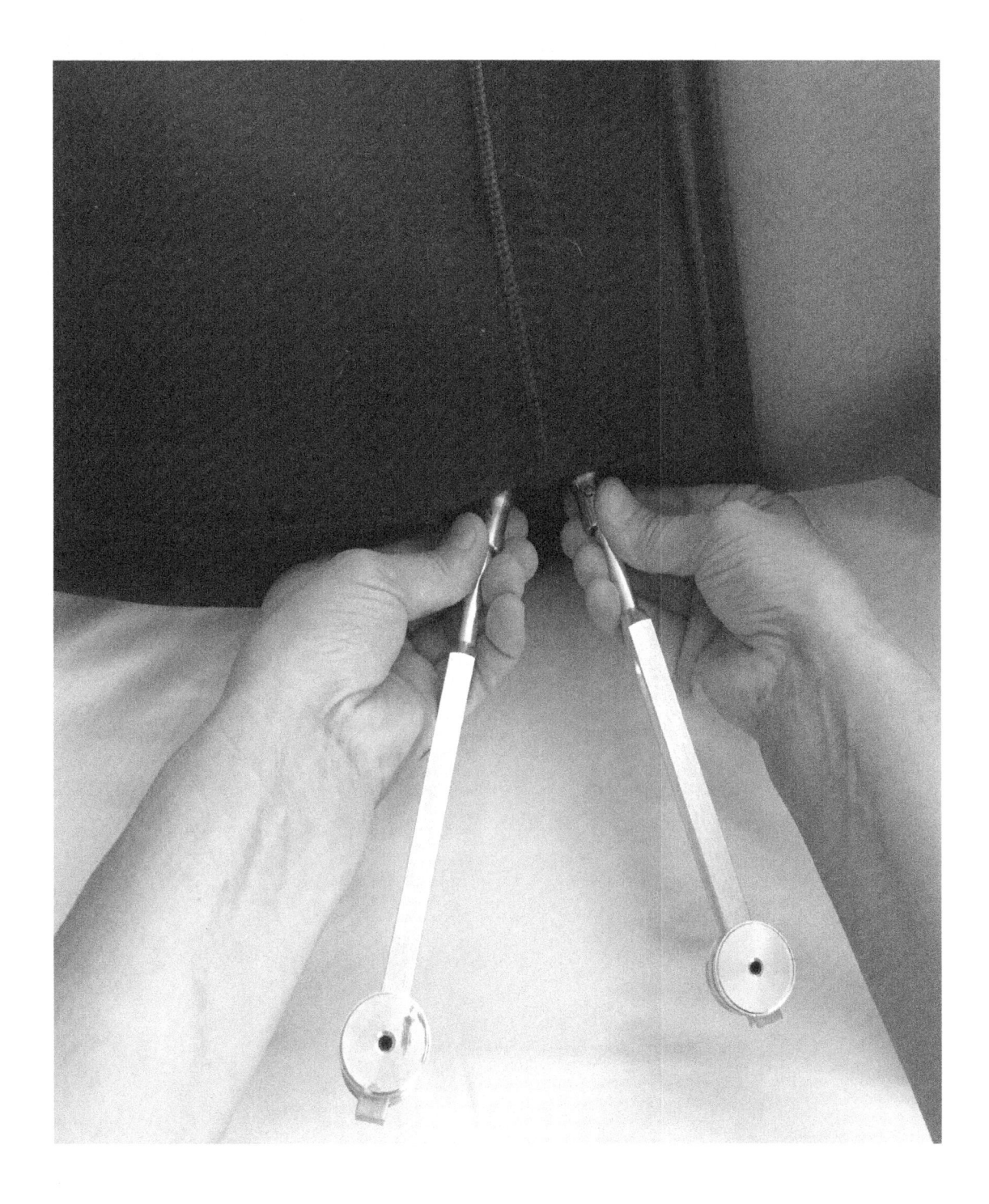

9-5b. Glide both activated tuning forks slowly down the outside of the upper leg, continuing down to the knee insertion on the outside.

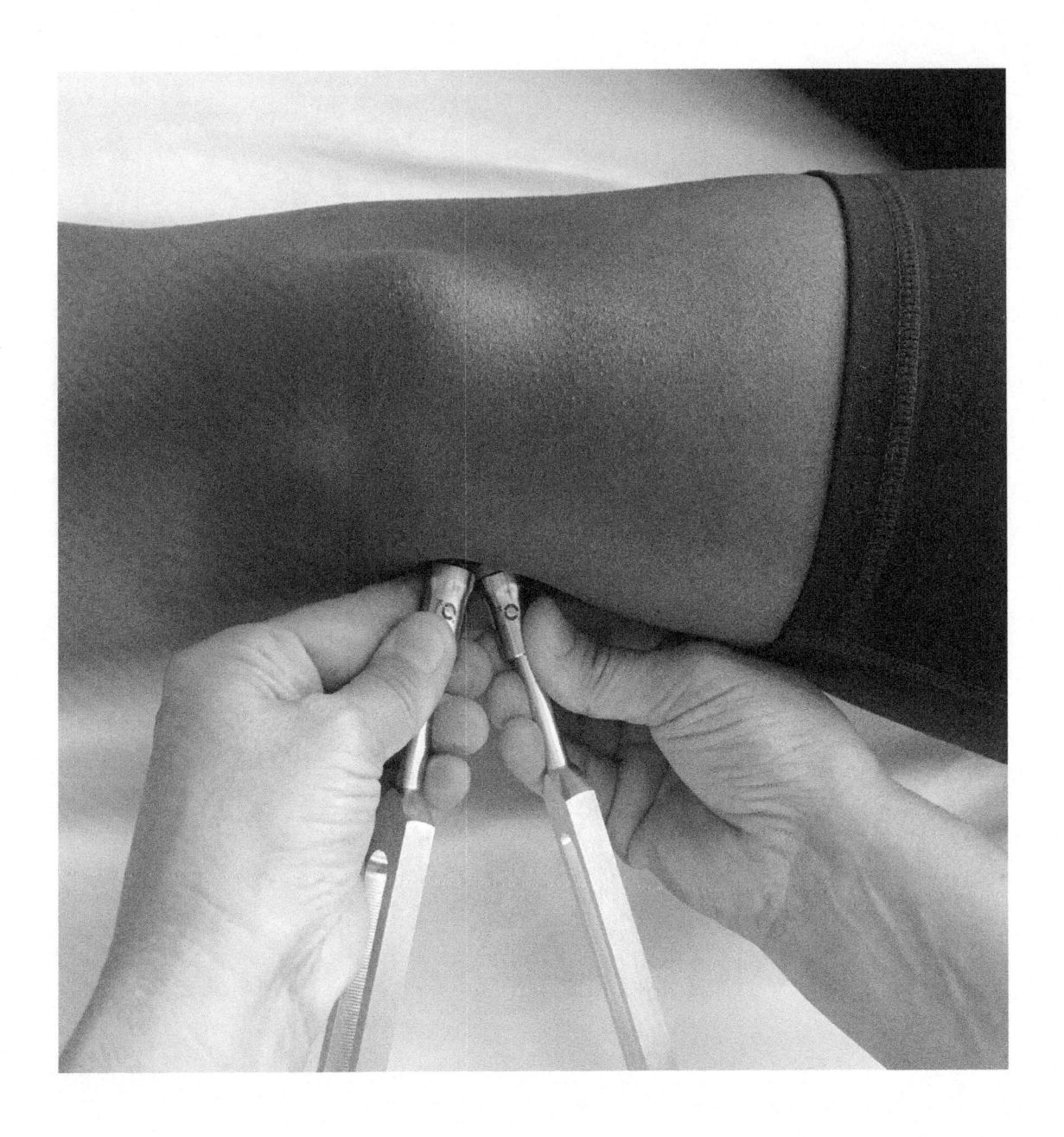

10. Protocol for Hips/Legs (prone)

10-1. Position one activated tuning fork end on the hip point (the side of the hip—it feels like a divot). Position the other activated tuning fork on the outside of the knee joint.

10-2. Position one activated tuning fork on the sit bones (hamstring attachments), position the other activated tuning fork first to the outside of the knee then to the inside of the knee.

10-3. Position both activated tuning forks on the sit bones and slowly glide down the middle of the upper leg, ending just before back of knee. *(Two pictures: 10-3a and 10-3b)*

10-4. Repeat on the inside and outside of the upper leg, always starting at the sit bones.

(No picture)

10-5. Glide both activated tuning forks from upper edge of sacrum, along inner edge of hip bone, out to the greater trochanter of the femur. Move down the sacrum about 1 inch and again glide out to the greater trochanter. Repeat by moving down another inch and gliding out to the greater trochanter. Repeat on the other hip. *(Two pictures: 10-5a and 10-5b)*

10-6. Position both activated tuning forks on either side of the knee. *(No picture)*

10-7. Position one activated tuning fork on the outside knee and the other on the outside ankle.

10-8. Position one activated tuning fork on the hip point and the other on the outside ankle.

10-9. Position both activated tuning forks on either side of the calf muscle and slowly glide down the lower leg, ending on either side of the ankle. Calves can usually take a bit more pressure so experiment with that as well as pinching movements with the two forks.

(Three pictures: 10-9a, 10-9b and 10-9c)

10-1. Position one activated tuning fork end on the hip point (the side of the hip—it feels like a divot). Position the other activated tuning fork on the outside of the knee joint.

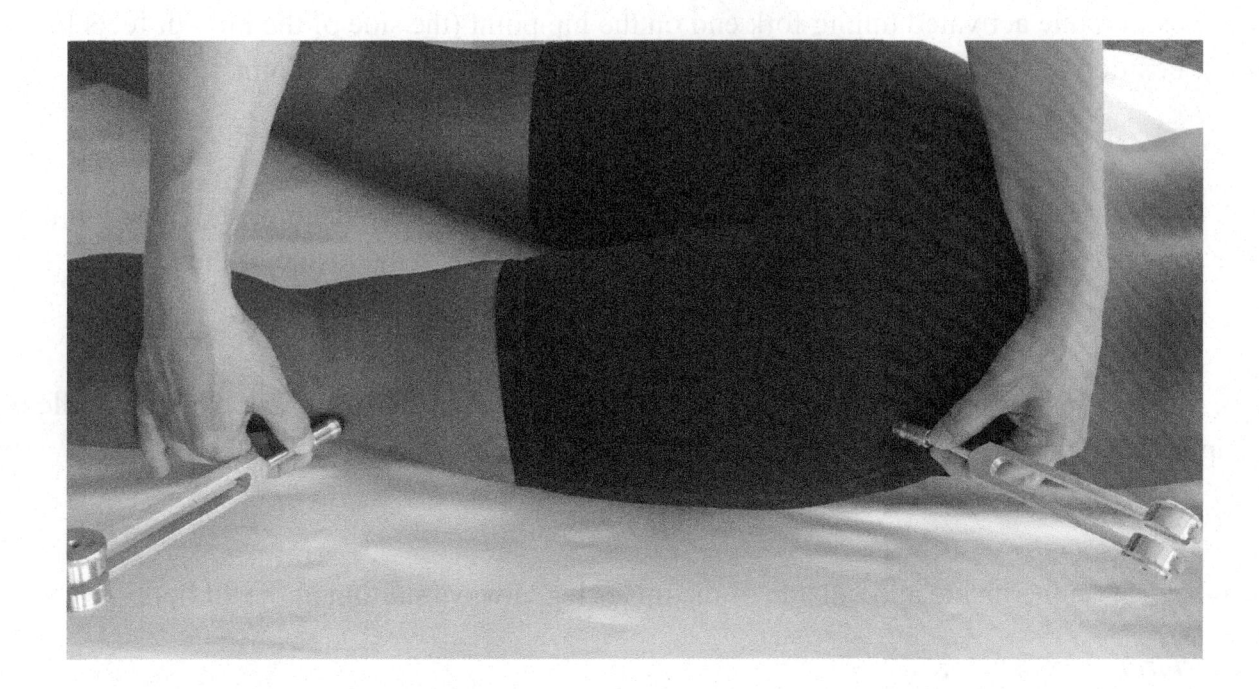

10-2. Position one activated tuning fork on the sit bones (hamstring attachments), position the other activated tuning fork first to the outside of the knee then to the inside of the knee.

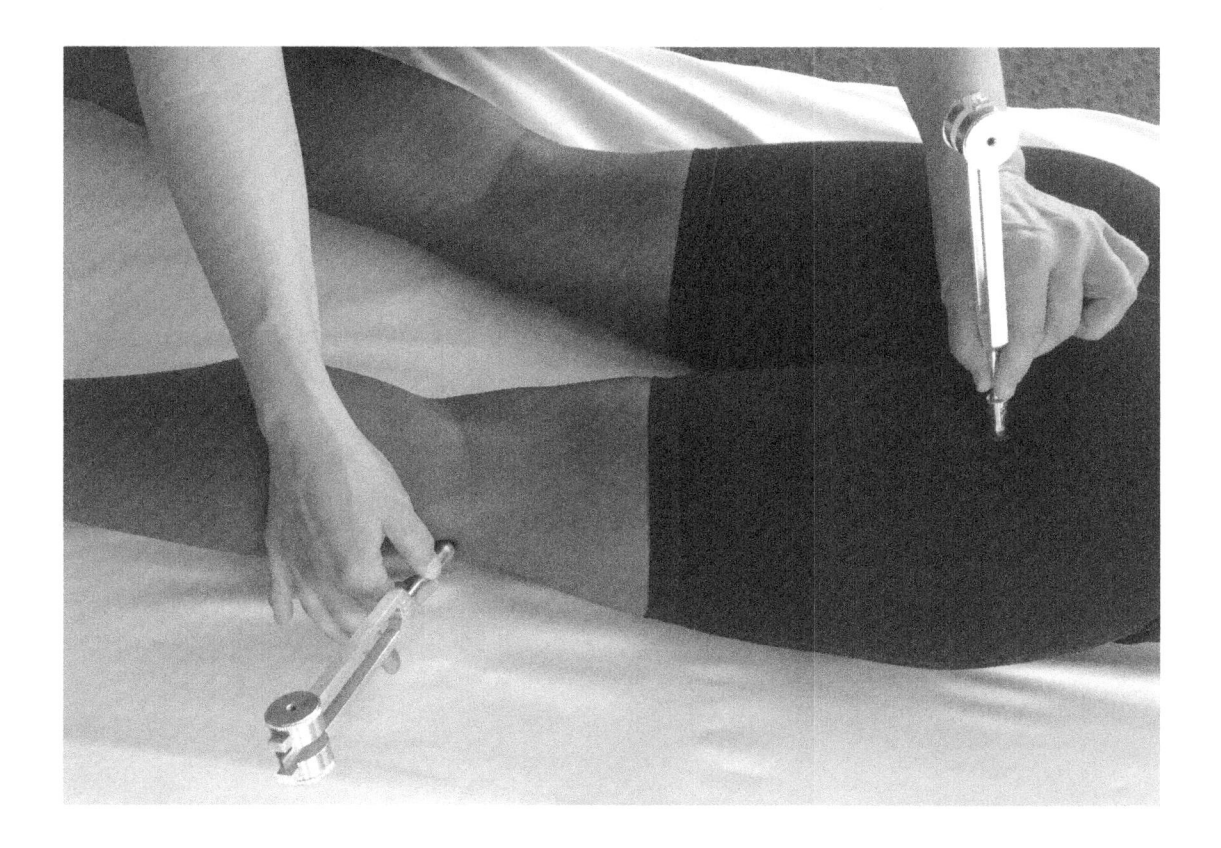

10-3a. Position both activated tuning forks on the sit bones and slowly glide down the middle of the upper leg, ending just before back of knee. *(Three pictures: 10-3a, 10-3b and 10-3c)*

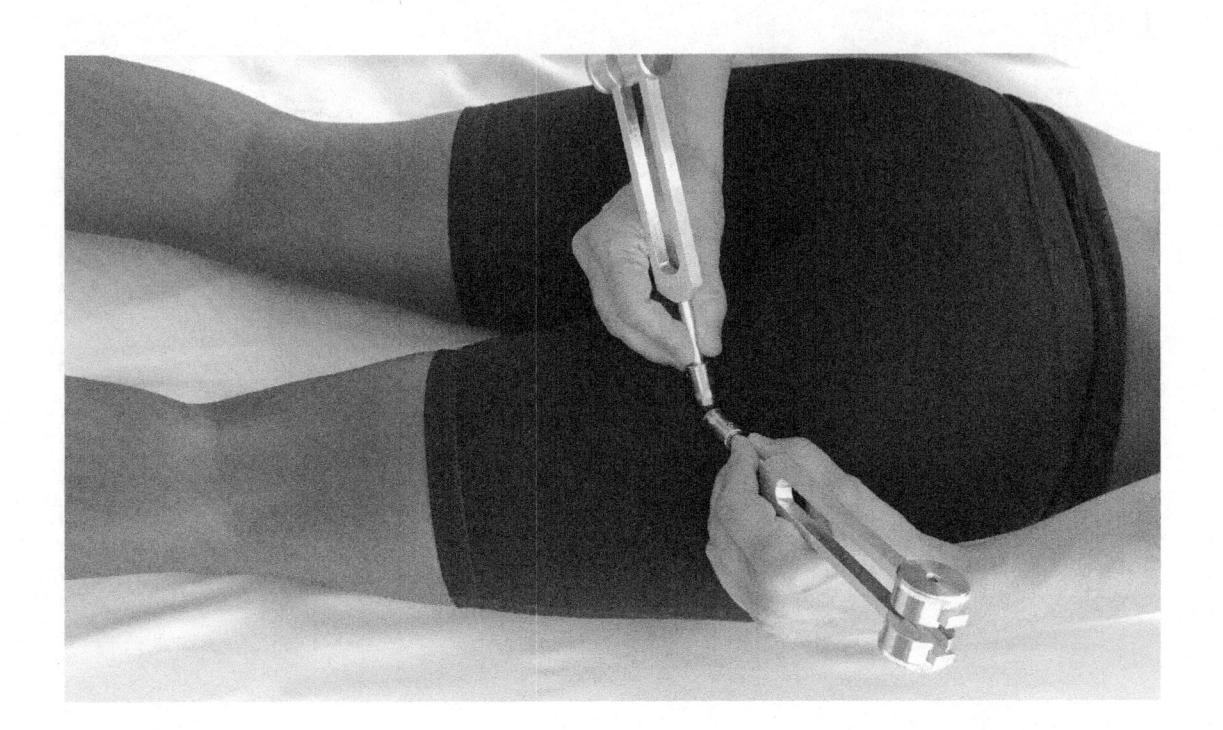

10-3b. Glide both activated tuning forks down the back of the leg.

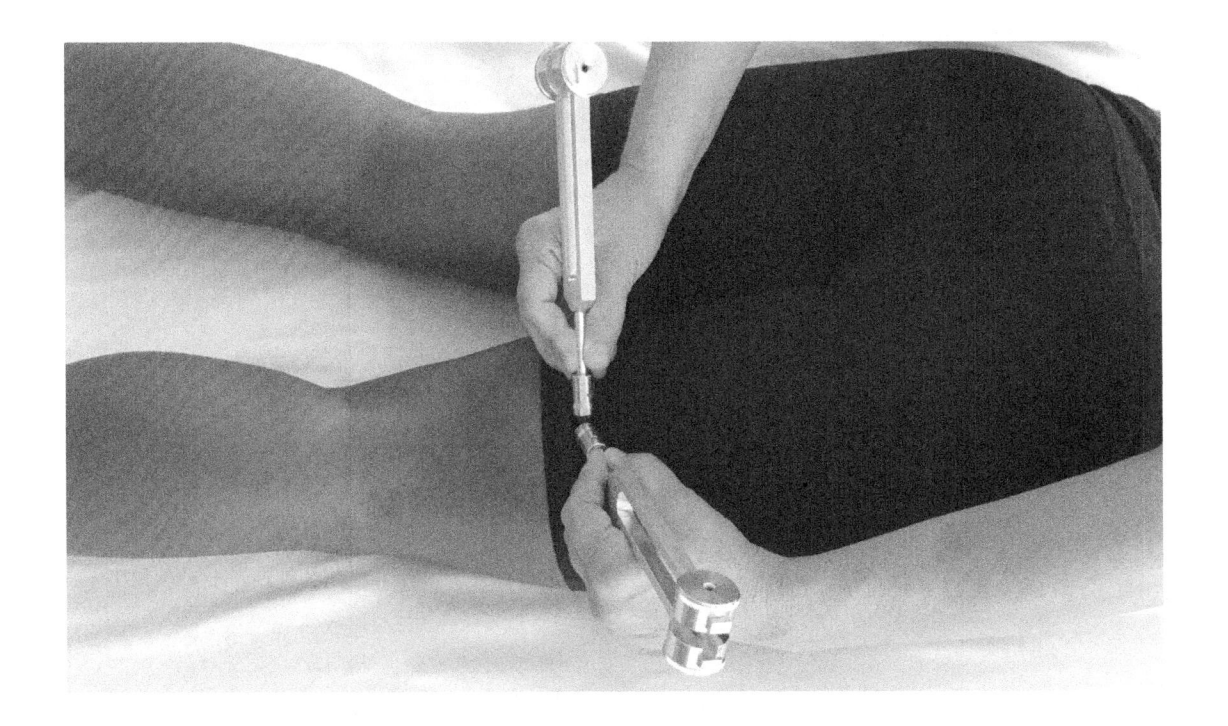

10-3c. End just before the back of the knee.

10-4. Repeat on the inside and outside of the upper leg, always starting at the sit bones.

(*No picture*)

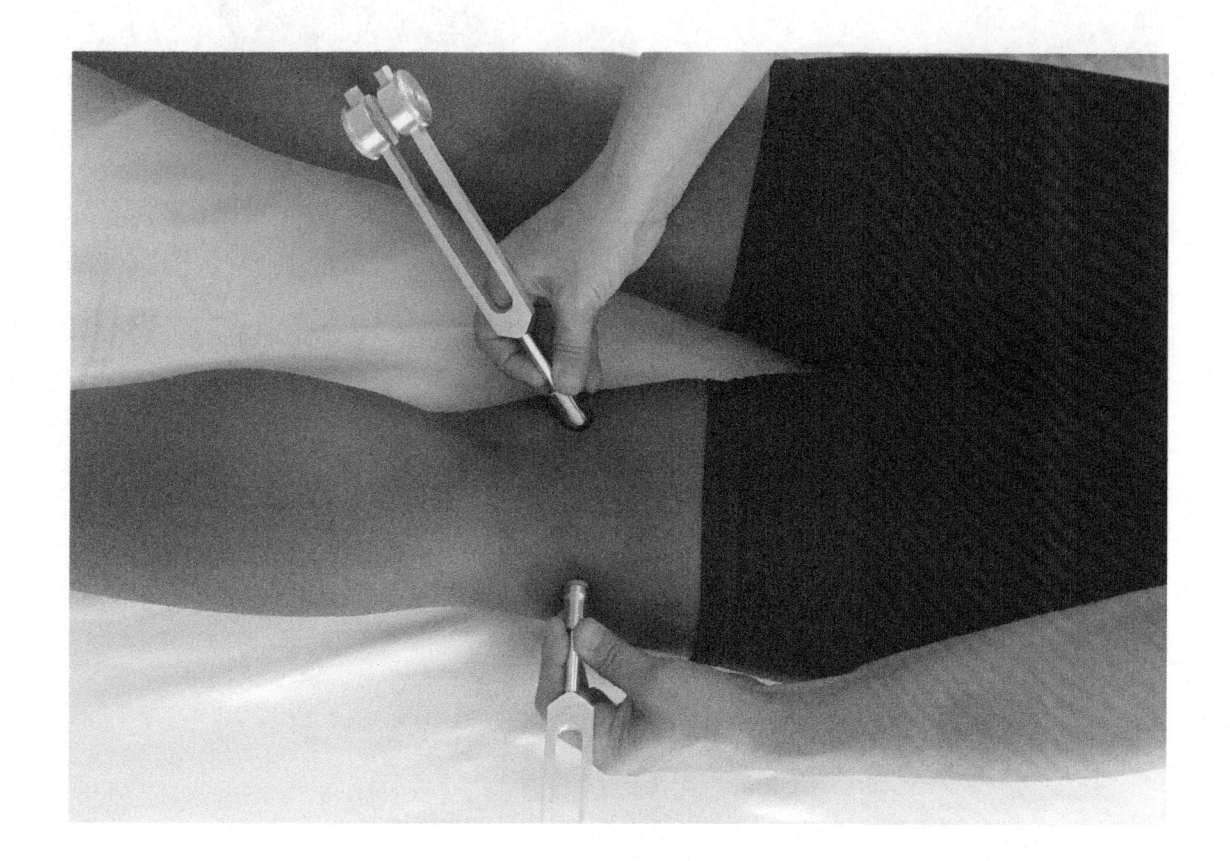

10-5a. Glide both activated tuning forks from upper edge of sacrum, along inner edge of hip bone, out to greater trochanter of the femur. Move down the sacrum about 1 inch and again glide out to the greater trochanter. Repeat by moving down another inch and gliding out to the greater trochanter. Repeat on the other hip. *(Two pictures: 10-5a and 10-5b)*

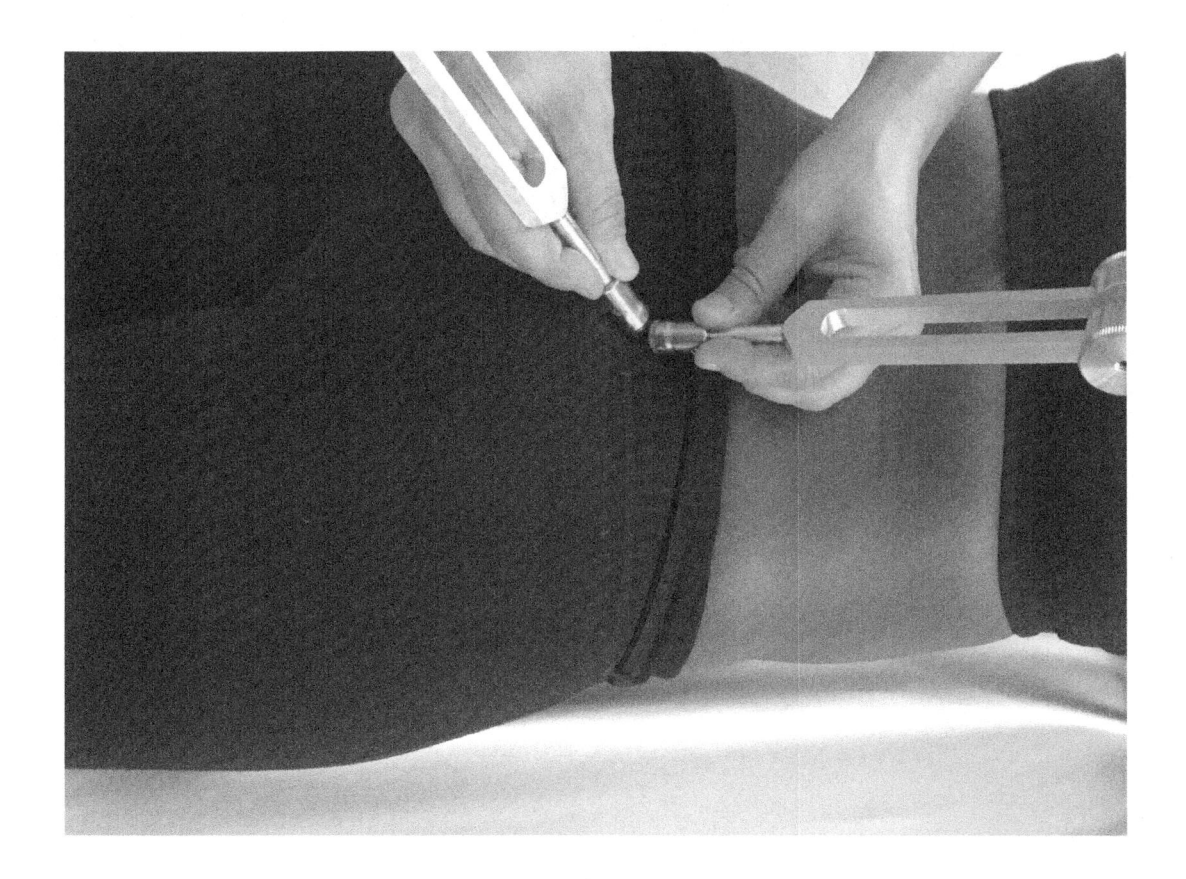

10-5b. Move down the sacrum about 1 inch and again glide out to the greater trochanter. Repeat by moving down another inch and gliding out to the greater trochanter. Repeat on the other hip.

10-6. Position both activated tuning forks on either side of the knee (*NO Picture*)

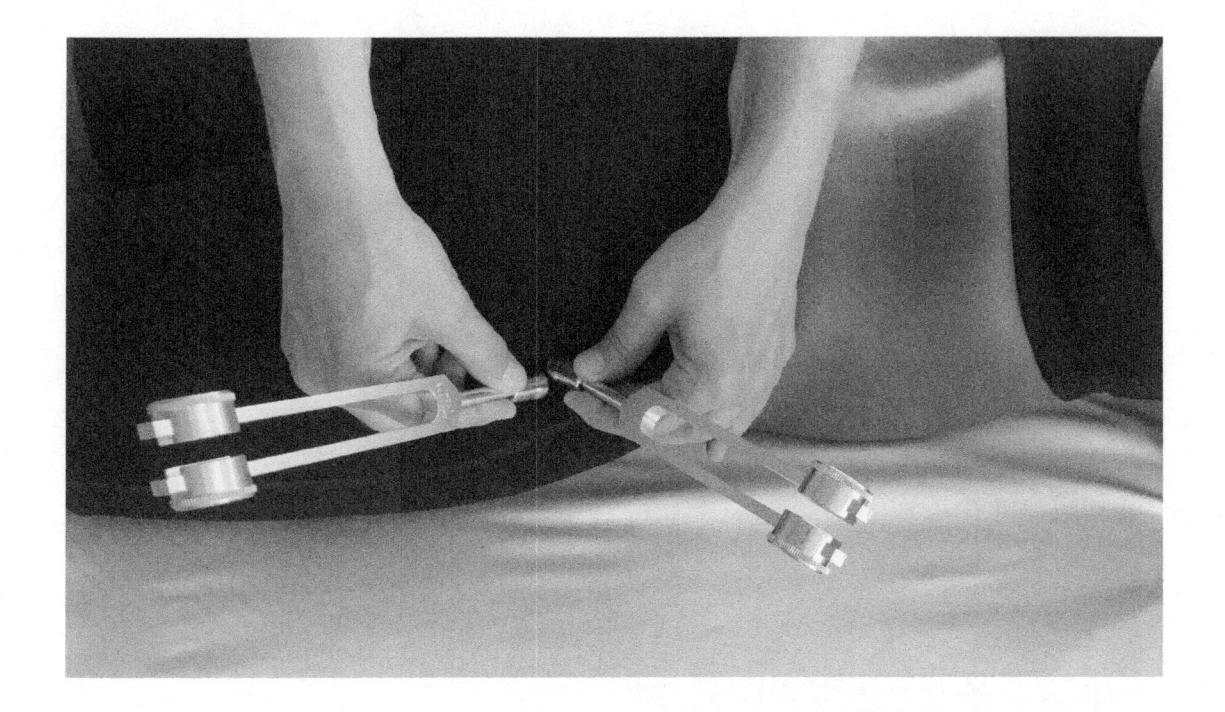

10-7. Position the activated tuning forks on the outside knee and the outside ankle.

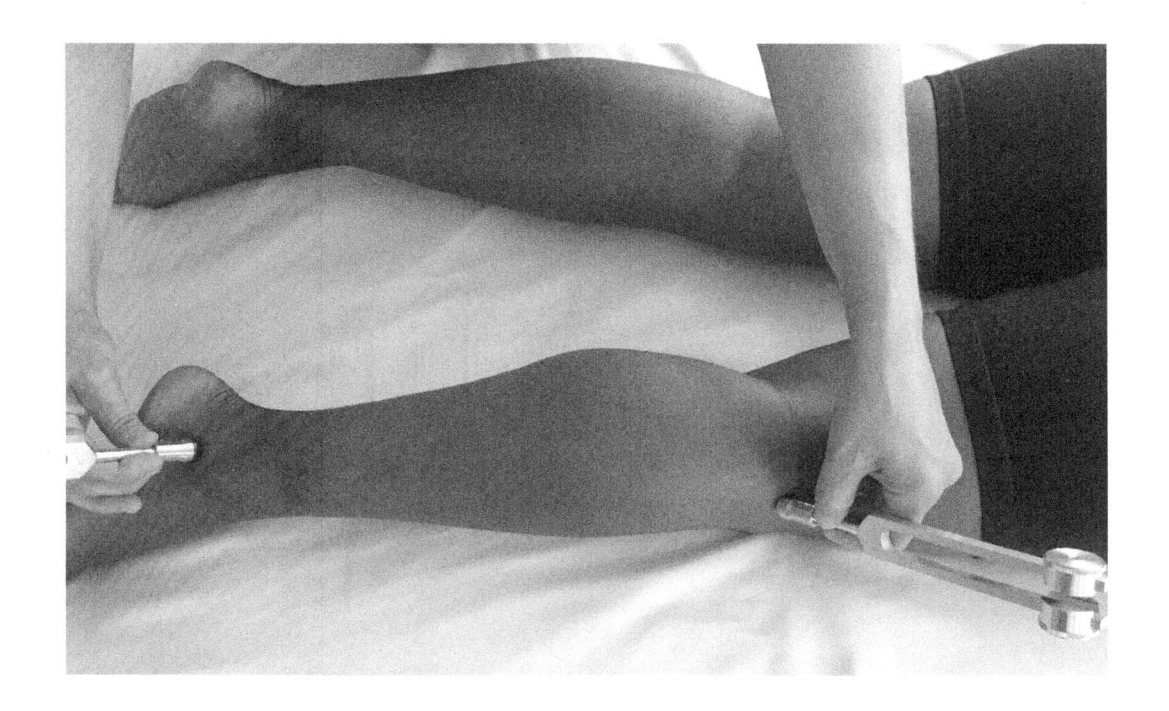

10-8. Position one activated tuning fork on the hip point and the other on the outside ankle.

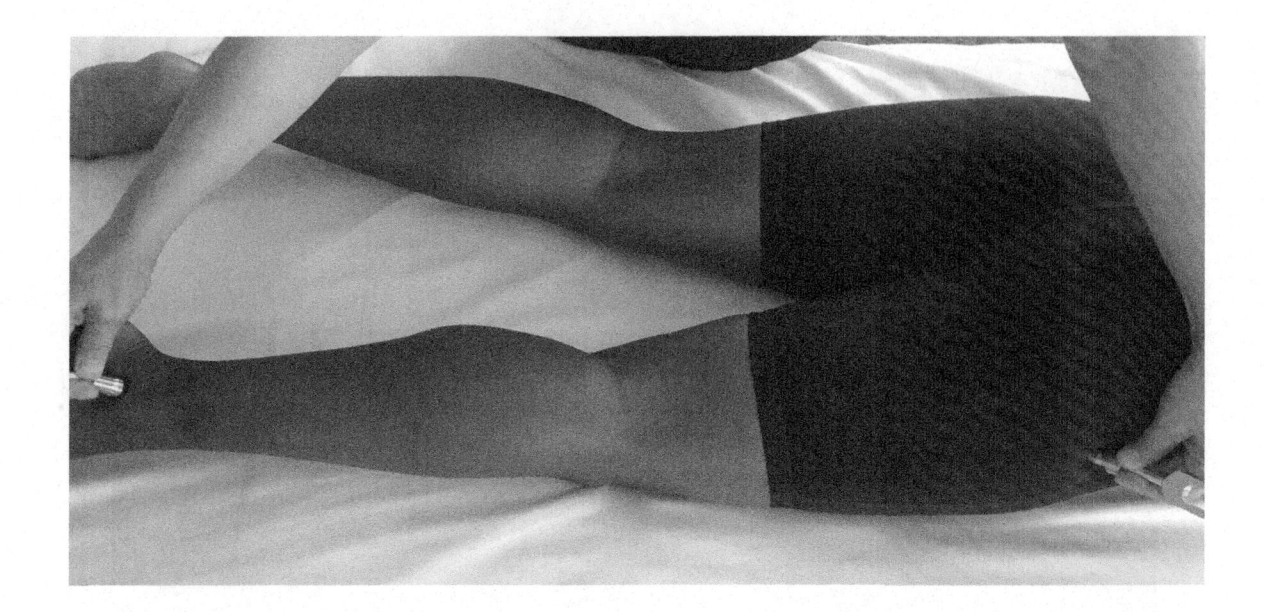

10-9a. Position both activated tuning forks on either side of the calf muscle and slowly glide down the lower leg, ending on either side of the ankle. Calves can usually take a bit more pressure so experiment with that as well as pinching movements with the two forks.

(Three pictures: 10-9a 10-9b and 10-9c)

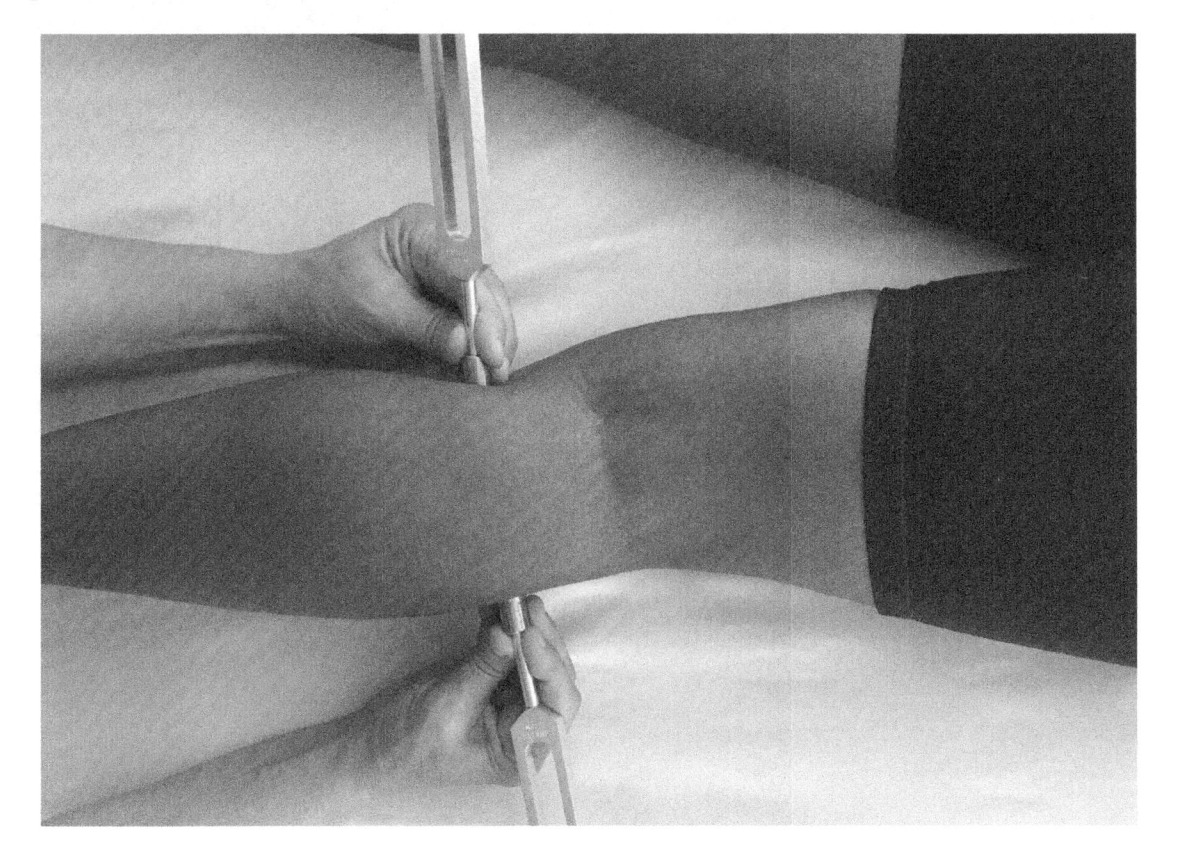

10-9b. Slowly glide down the lower leg.

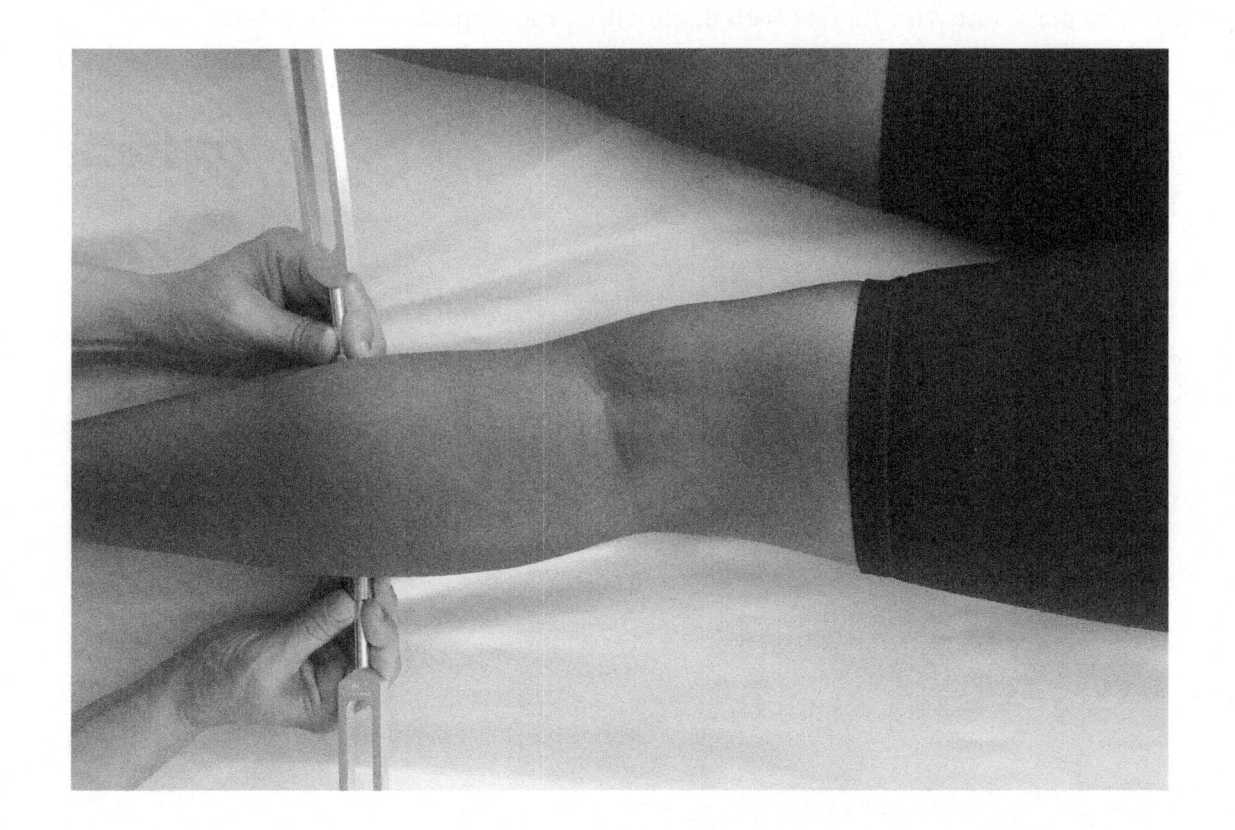

10-9c. End on either side of the ankle and pause here for a beat or two.

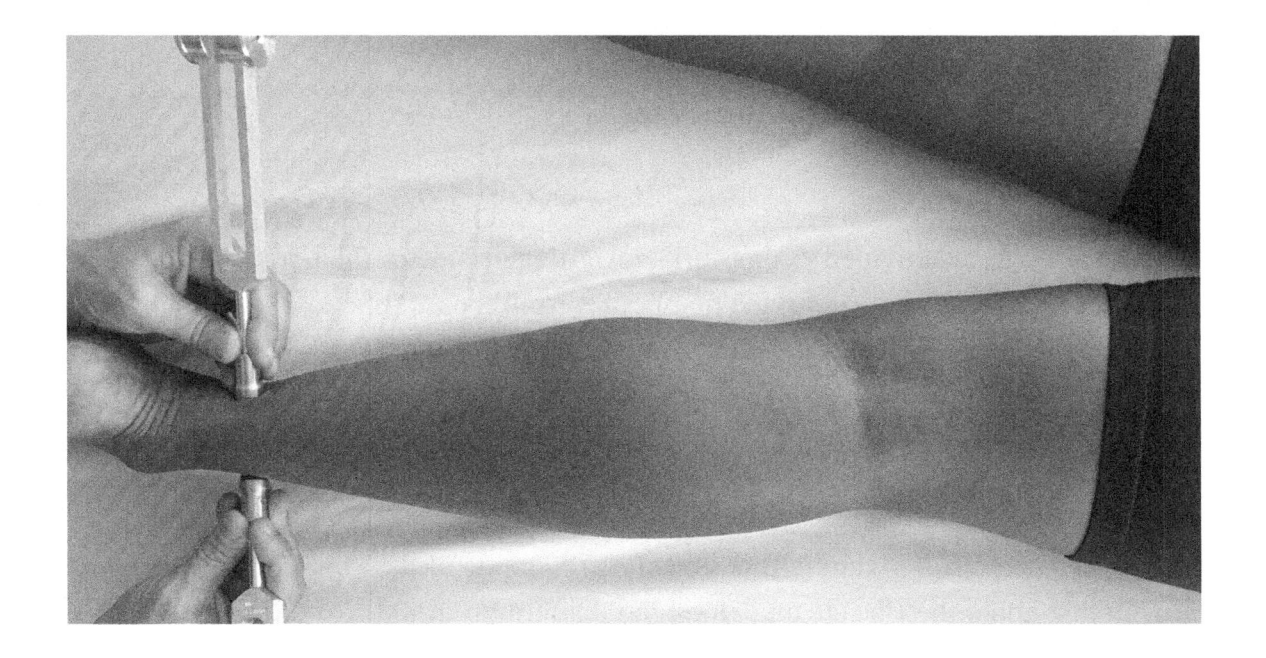

11. Protocol for Diaphragm/Abdominals (supine)

11-1. Position both activated tuning fork ends on either side of the xiphoid process, the rounded tip at the end of the sternum, at the midline of the body.

11-2. Glide or walk both activated tuning forks towards one side of the body. Gently glide or walk just under the ribcage and along the diaphragm from the midline to one side of the body. The tuning forks will have to be reactivated multiple times.

(Three pictures: 11-2a, 11-2b and 11-2c)

11-3. Reposition the activated tuning fork ends on either side of the xiphoid process. Gently glide or walk just under the ribcage and along the diaphragm from the midline to the other side of the body. The tuning forks will have to reactivated multiple times.

(No pictures, see 11-2a-c)

11-4. Position the activated tuning fork ends just inside of the anterior superior iliac spine (ASIS), the bony protrusions at the front hip. Reactivate the tuning fork a few times here.

11-1. Position both activated tuning fork ends on either side of the xiphoid process, the rounded tip at the end of the sternum, at the midline of the body.

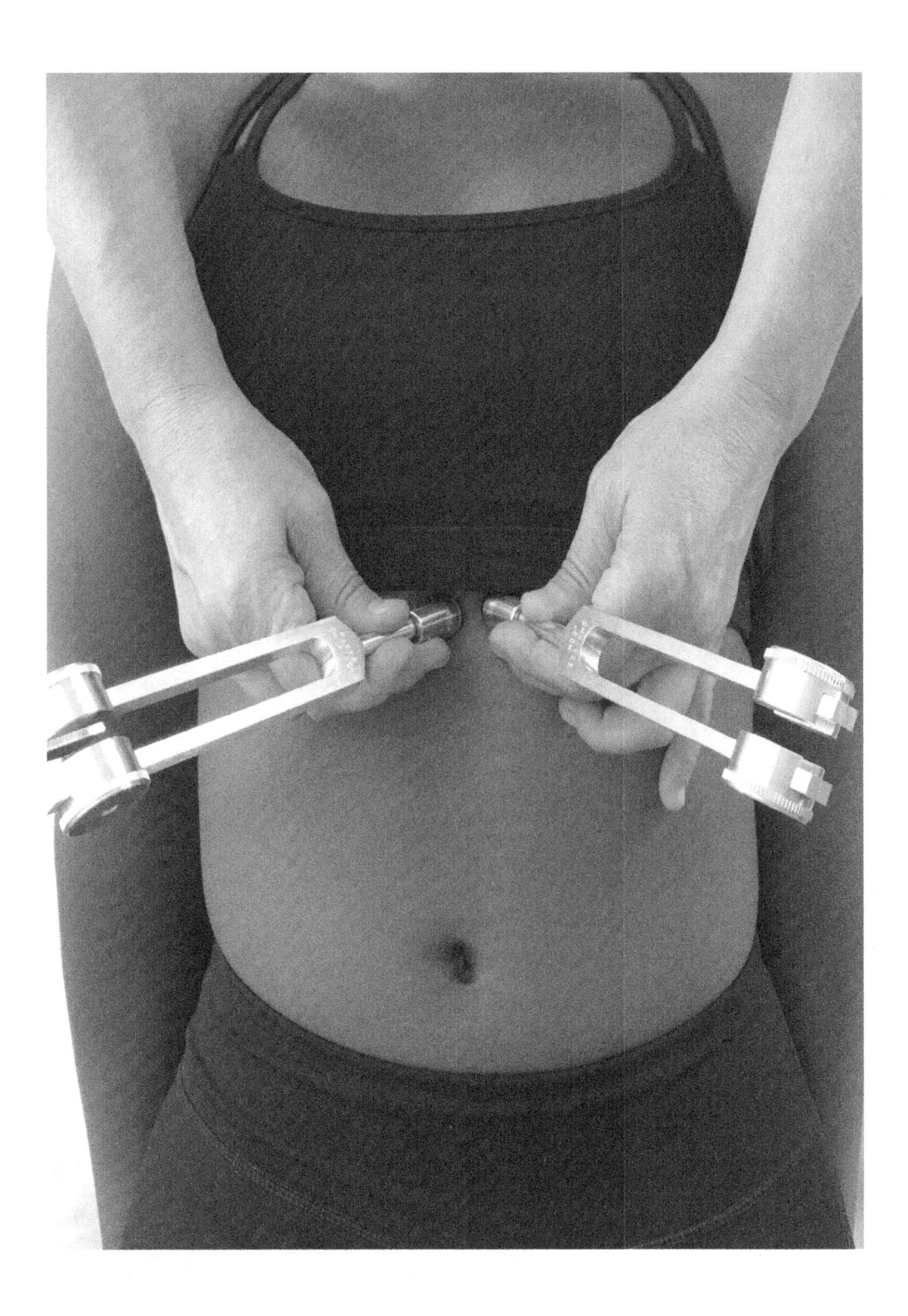

11-2a. Glide or walk both activated tuning forks towards one side of the body.

(Three pictures: 11-2a, 11-2b and 11-2c)

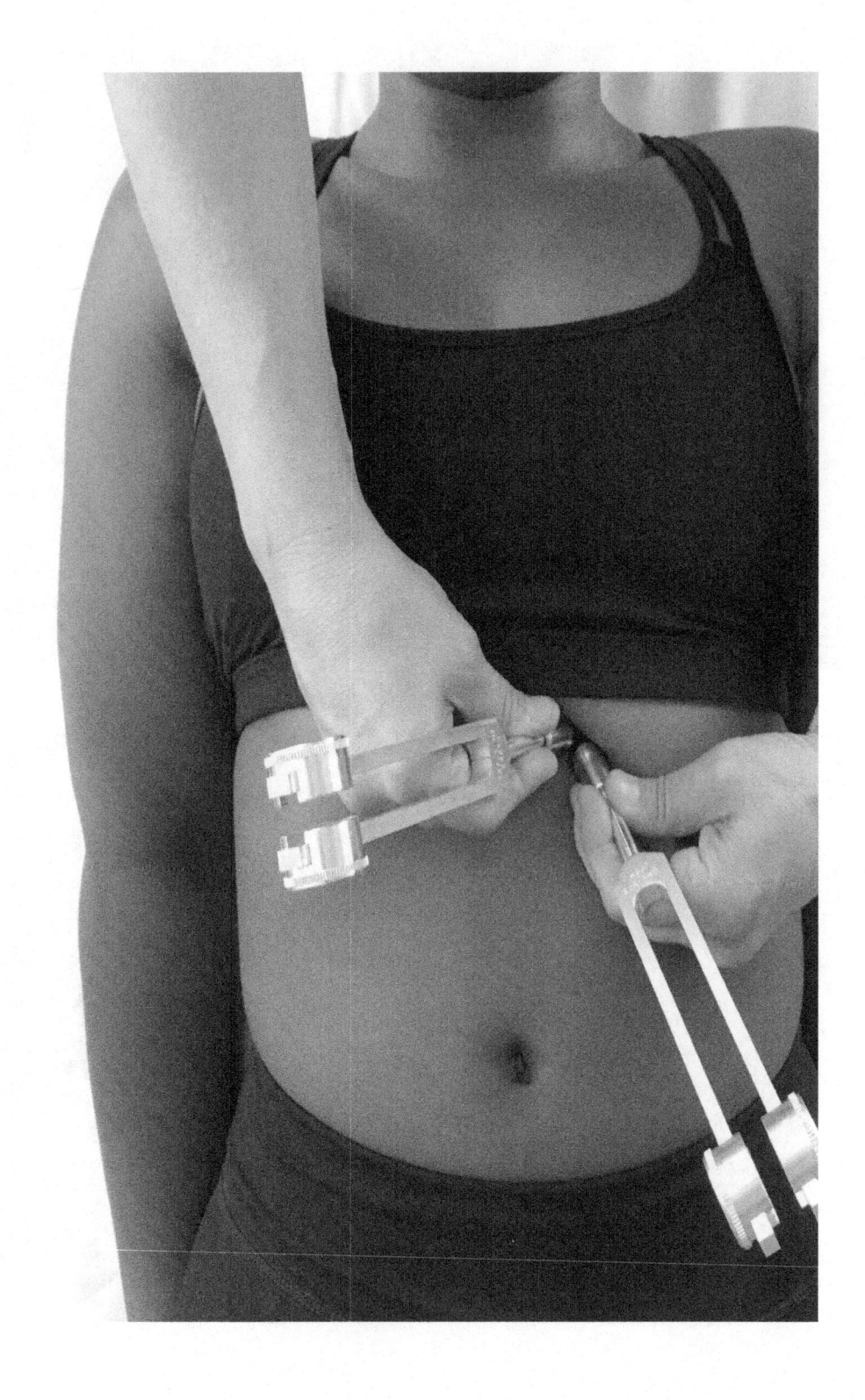

11-2b. Gently glide or walk just under the ribcage and along the diaphragm from the midline to one side of the body. The tuning forks will have to be reactivated multiple times.

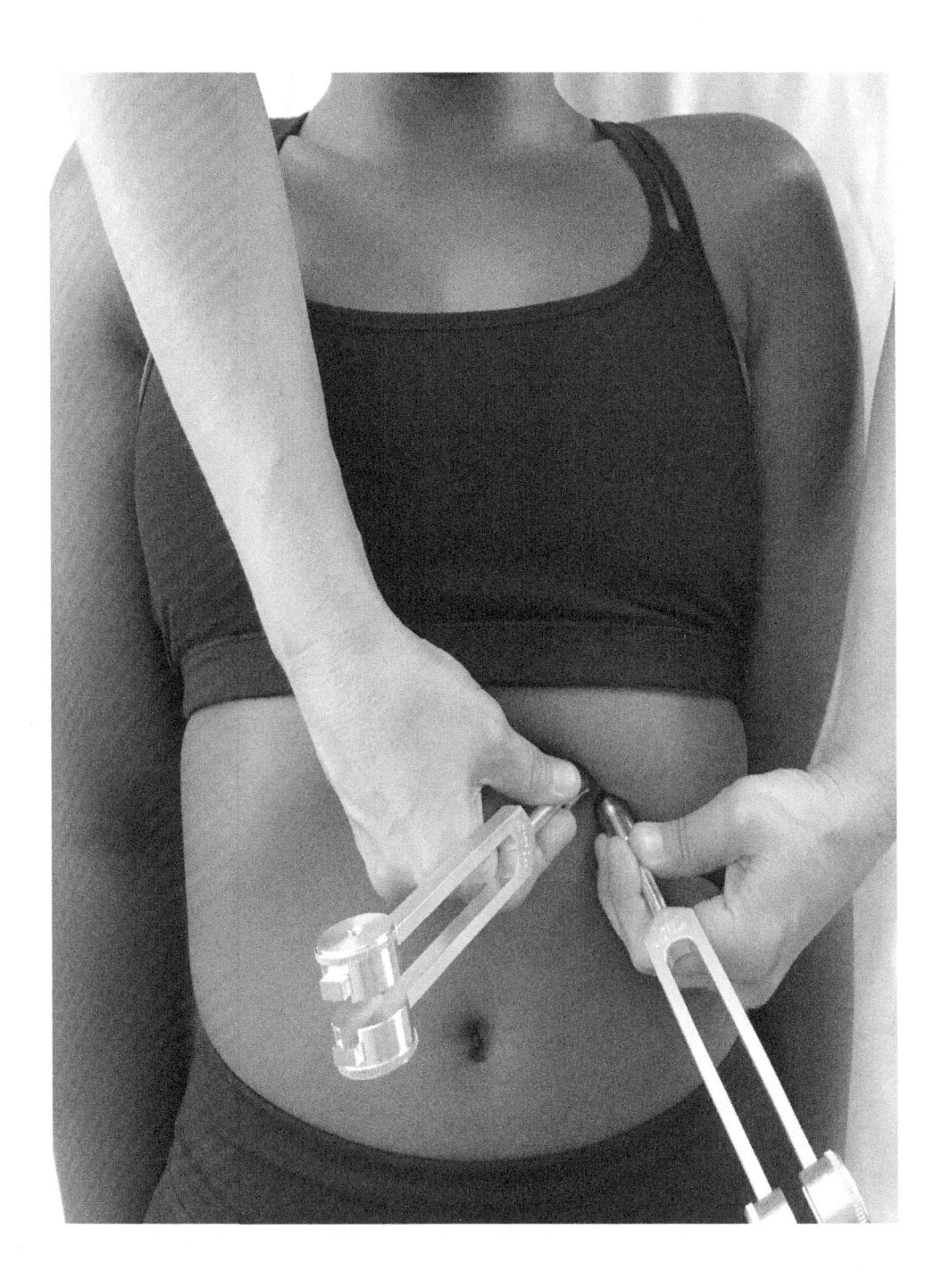

11-2c. Continue walking tuning forks until just before reaching the side of the body.

11-3. Repeat on the other side. (*See pictures 11-2a-c, above*)

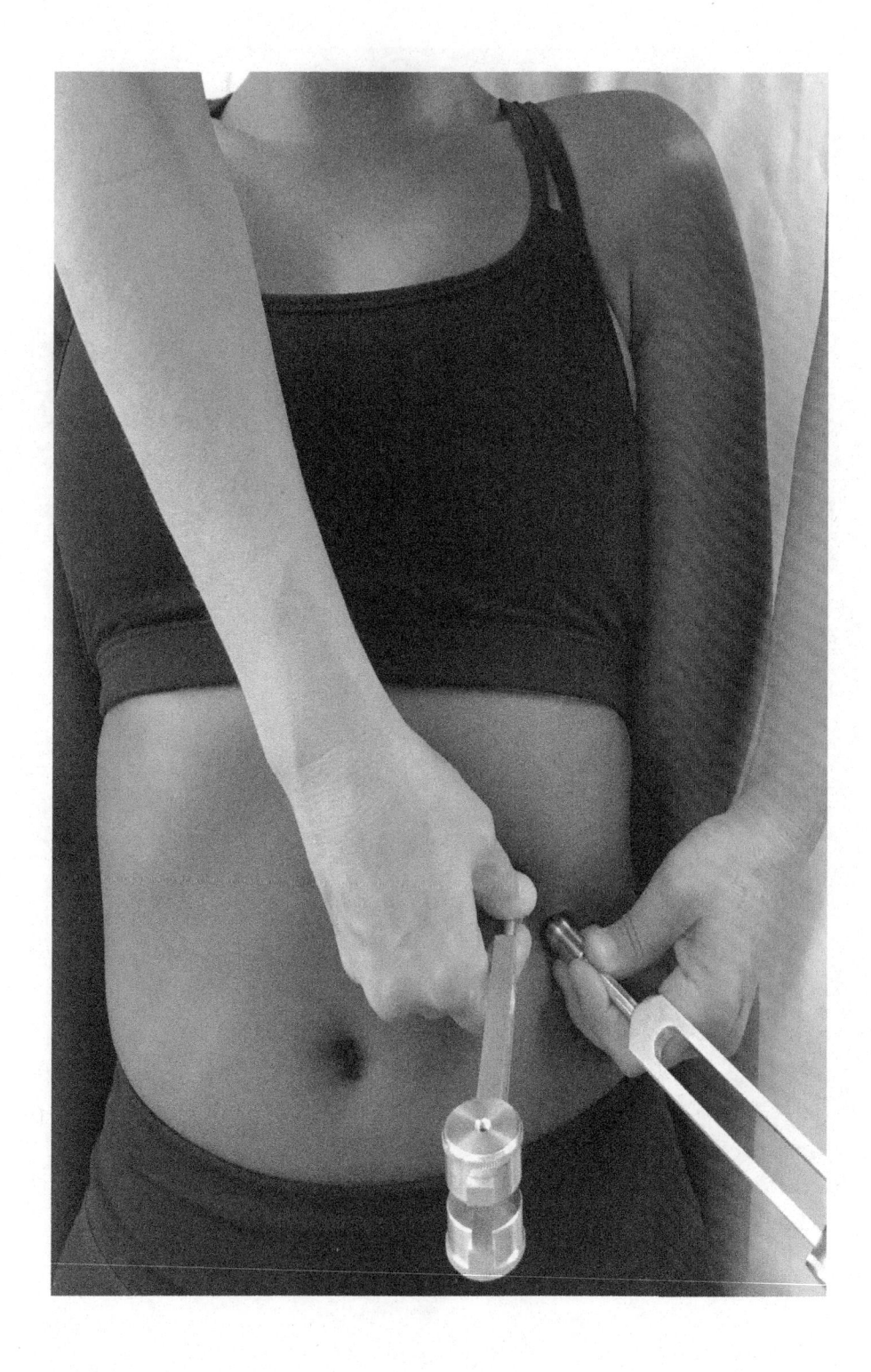

11-4. Position the activated tuning fork ends just inside of the Anterior Superior Iliac Spine (ASIS), the bony protrusions at the front hip. Reactivate the tuning fork a few times here.

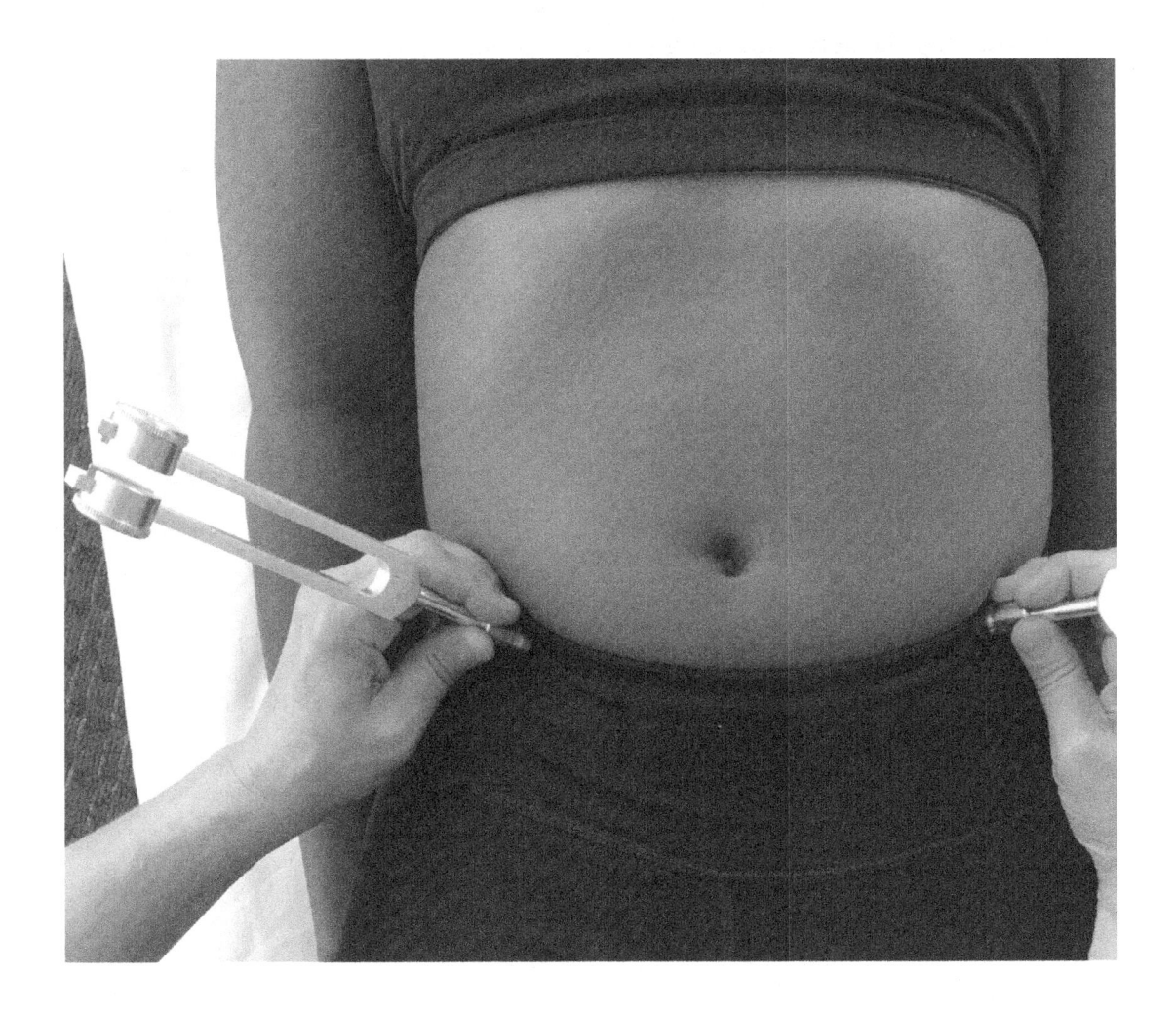

12. Head/Neck/Shoulders/Back Protocol (SEATED, NO Pictures)

1. Begin by positioning the activated tuning fork ends on:
   - The unicorn point at middle of hairline and the middle of the occiput behind the head.
   - The left and right side of the head (just above, and in front of, the ears).
   - The third eye and directly behind the back of the head.
   - The top of the head (seen from above, it's in line with the nose and the middle of ears).

2. Position the activated tuning fork ends on either side of the base of neck/shoulder junction. This is usually a very jammed up area and some people enjoy more pressure. Start with just the pressure of the forks. Build up pressure as needed.

3. Glide the activated tuning forks along the upper trapezius and pause at either side of the shoulders. Glide back in to the midline.

4. Glide the activated tuning forks north to south between the sides of the spine and the medial edge of the scapula (rhomboids)

5. Position the one activated tuning fork in the middle of the occiput and position the other activated tuning fork on the sacrum.

6. Position the activated tuning forks at C1/C2, glide north to south down the neck. Reactivate the tuning forks and continue down the sides of the spine, ending at the sacrum.

Repeat each approach up to three times.

Further Study

Come and spend a dynamic weekend with people from many walks of life and diverse backgrounds. Our weekend classes begin with introductions and move on to lecture, discussion, demonstration and practice via learning pods. There's plenty of space in between to observe, process, learn, stretch and share.

- Be immersed in the practice via direct supervision and interactive participation with immediate feedback to your questions and concerns.

- Learn advanced techniques.

- Practice with colleagues.

- Make new connections.

- Gain a deeper confidence and understanding through personal interaction.

- Share the group experience and have fun.

Reference List

Bentov, Itzhak, *Stalking the Wild Pendulum* (Destiny Books, 1977)

Barnes, John F., *Myofascial Release Perspective: Therapeutic Insight—Fascia, A Liquid-Crystalline Matrix* (2009)

Becker, Robert O., *The Body Electric: Electromagnetism and the Foundation of Life* (William Morrow, 1985)

Beaulieu, John, *Human Tuning* (BioSonic Enterprises, 2010)

Bowman, Katy, *Whole Body Barefoot: Transitioning Well to Minimal Footwear* (Propriometrics Press, 2015)

----------*Move Your DNA: Restore Your Health Through Natural Movement* (Propriometrics Press, 2014)

Cousens, Gabriel, *Spiritual Nutrition Book: Six Foundations for Spiritual Life and the Awakening of Kundalini* (North Atlantic Books, 2005)

Cowan, Thomas, *Human Heart, Cosmic Heart: A Doctor's Quest to Understand, Treat, and Prevent Cardiovascular Disease* (Chelsea Green Publishing, 2016)

Goldman, Jonathan and Andi, *The Humming Effect: Sound Healing for Health and Happiness* (Healing Arts Press, 2017)

Gordon, Richard, *Your Healing Hands: The Polarity Experience* (North Atlantic Books, 2004)

Haner, Jean, *Clear Home, Clear Heart* (Hay House, 2017)

HeartMath.Org

Jenny, Hans *Cymatics: A Study of Wave Phenomena & Vibration* (MACROmedia Publishing, 2001)

LeCorre, Erwan, *The Practice of Natural Movement: Reclaim Power, Health and Freedom* (Victory Belt Publishing, 2019)

Lipton, Bruce, *The Biology of Belief 10th Anniversary Edition: Unleashing the Power of Consciousness, Matter & Miracles* (Hay House, 2016)

McTaggart, Lynn, *The Field Updated Edition: The Quest for the Secret Force of the Universe* (Harper Perennial, 2008)

Myers, Thomas, *Anatomy Trains: Myofascial Meridians for Manual and Movement Therapists* (Churchill Livingstone, 2014)

Northrup, Christiane, DrNorthrup.com/muscle-fascia/

Ober, Clinton, S. Sinatra, M. Zucker, *Earthing: The Most Important Health Discovery Ever!* (Basic Health Publications, 2014)

Oschman, James L., *Energy Medicine in Therapeutics and Human Performance* (Butterworth-Heinemann, 2003)

Pollack, Gerald H., *The Fourth Phase of Water: Beyond Solid, Liquid and Vapor* (Ebner & Sons, 2013)

Schumacher, E.F., *Small is Beautiful: Economics as if People Mattered* (Harper Perennial, 2010)

Selye, Hans, *Stress in Health and Disease* (Butterworth, 1976)

Tennant, Jerry, *Healing is Voltage: Acupuncture Muscle Batteries* (CreateSpace Independent Publishing, 2015)

Thornhill, Wallace and David Talbott, *The Electric Universe* (Mikamar Publishing, 2007)

Villoldo, Alberto, *One Spirit Medicine: Ancient Ways to Ultimate Wellness* (Hay House UK, 2015)

Wikipedia, *Piezoelectricity*

About the Author

Trained as a Massage Therapist and educator, with almost four decades in the health and wellness world, Kiki Quest leads wellness-based workshops with an emphasis on boosting the body's voltage and raising its everyday resilience. She is also a lifelong visual artist, raw-food chef and was the founder of Kiki's Raw, a grab-and-go, raw-food product line in San Francisco, California. Hooked on tuning forks since ordering her first set from Sheffield, England in the 1990s, Kiki is delighted to connect, learn and share with people everywhere. To co-sponsor a class in your area, please email Kiki at KikiQuest33@gmail.com

vibrattuning.com

Made in the USA
Coppell, TX
04 July 2025